The Crowood Press

Reinhold Messner

THE CRYSTAL HORIZON

Everest—The First Solo Ascent

Translated by Jill Neate and Audrey Salkeld

First published in Great Britain 1989 by
The Crowood Press
Ramsbury, Marlborough
Wiltshire, SN8 2HR

This impression 2001

Paperback edition 1998

Title of the original German edition:

Der Glaserne Horizont
© 1982 BLV Verlagsgesellschaft mbH, Munchen

English translation © The Crowood Press 1989

British Library Cataloguing in Publication Data

Messner, Reinhold
    The crystal horizon : the solo ascent of Everest.
    1. Asia. Everest, Mountaineering expeditions
    I. Title I. Glaserne Horizont, English
    915.49′6

    ISBN 186126 176 4

Maps: Helmut Hoffman and Anina Westphalen

Typeset by Chippendale Type, Otley, West Yorkshire
Printed and bound in Spain by Graficas Estella, S.A. (Navarra)

Contents

Mount Everest from the 6,000 metre camp of the British 1921 expedition.

Everest–
South–North–Solo

'The idea of climbing Mount Everest has been vaguely in men's minds for thirty or forty years past,' wrote Sir Francis Younghusband in 1921. He went on: 'It stands to reason that men with any zest for mountaineering could not possibly allow Mount Everest to remain untouched. The time, the opportunity, the money, the ability to make the necessary preliminary preparation might be lacking, but the wish and the will to stand on the summit of the world's highest mountain must have been in the heart of many a mountaineer . . .'

But what urges a person to climb Mount Everest after it has been frequently ascended? And to do so during the unfavourable weather conditions of the monsoon? I had already been to the top once. Why a second time? 'Because it is there', Mallory said in 1924. That alone is not it. My motivations are many.

In 1978, during my first ascent of Everest with Peter Habeler, what the mountain meant to me was a compound of days, metres to be climbed, and stresses to be endured. With the passing of time, it regained its mystery for me, until one day I had a clear aim similar to that of the first Everest explorers:

'Men simply cannot resist exercising and stretching to their fullest extent the faculties and aptitudes with which they each happen to be specially endowed. One born with an aptitude

Col. Sir George Everest, after whom the mountain is named.

for painting is dull and morose and fidgety until he can get colours and a brush into his hand and start painting. Another is itching to make things – to use his hands and fashion wood or stone or metal into forms which he is continually creating in his mind. Another is restless until he can sing. Another is ever pining to be on a public platform, swaying the audience with his oratory and playing on their feelings as on a musical instrument. Each has his own inner aptitude which he aches to give vent to and bring into play. And more than this, he secretly owns within himself an exceedingly high standard – the highest standard – of what he wants to attain along his own particular line, and he is never really content in his mind and at peace with himself when he is not stretching himself out to the full towards this high pinnacle which he has set before him.'

The notion of climbing the mountain again, and this time alone, was for a long time mere fantasy. Only when the day-dreams – stirred up by all that I had read about Maurice Wilson, George Mallory and the monks of Rongbuk – outgrew fancy, did there begin an exciting year in my life.

In this book I intend to describe how the resolve matured, to tell of Tibet as I experienced it; Nena's diary and descriptions of the adventures of the Everest pioneers come into it, as well as the ever-recurring question: why?

7

Through Tibet to Mount Everest – in the pioneer period

The British expedition to Lhasa under Sir Francis E. Younghusband (1903–1904) and the Chinese revolution of 1911 rid Tibet almost completely of Chinese influence. Until 1949 it was under the leadership of the Dalai Lama, a constitutionally controversial but de facto autonomous state under theocratic-lamaistic rule. Between 1921 and 1949 seven British expeditions attempted to climb Mount Everest. Additionally, there were two illegal attempts

made by solo climbers. In October 1950 the army of the People's Republic of China invaded Tibet. In a treaty Communist China guaranteed the self-government of Tibet, but at the same time pursued the military occupation of the country.

The economics of the country were based on the growing of barley, wheat, millet, peas and beans as well as summer grazing on the high steppes. There were some sawmills, tanneries, foundries and papermills. Crafts (gold and silversmiths and armourers, saddlemakers, carpet weaving, ceramics, wood carving) flourished especially in the towns. In the monasteries, which were at the same time centres of science and learning, painting, mask painting and carving of printing blocks were cultivated. In 1980 I found a very different Tibet!

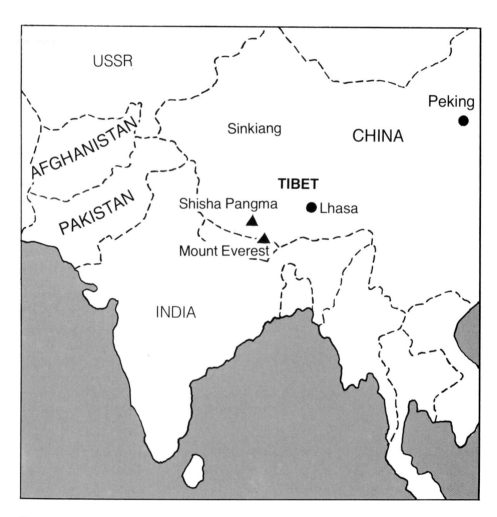

The oxygen apparatus of the 1920s: a light duralumin frame on the back carried four oxygen cylinders of a total weight of about 20 kilos. The oxygen, bottled at 120 atmospheres, was released through valves, and the air supply was controlled by way of flow-meters which were in front of the climber. Four oxygen cylinders supplied enough gas for approximately five hours. Empty cylinders could be replaced by reserve cylinders.

Mallory and Irvine, as well as their comrades on the first British Mount Everest expedition, experienced the then independent Tibet as a free, cheerful country.

In 1921 on the first reconnaissance Mallory missed the possibility of reaching the north-east side of Mount Everest from Rongbuk. Only in 1922 did the ascent up the East Rongbuk Glacier establish itself as the ideal approach to the North Ridge. This route is today still the most frequently used from the north.

Over
In the shelter of a moraine just under the end of the Rongbuk Glacier the British set up their base camp in 1922 and 1924. Although this spot – there is water here – is ideal for a main camp, it was shunned by the Chinese and Japanese expeditions in the post-war period. I was the first after World War II to camp there again. During the monsoon Mount Everest is a snow peak, but during the pre-and post-monsoon periods it shows itself as a rock peak.

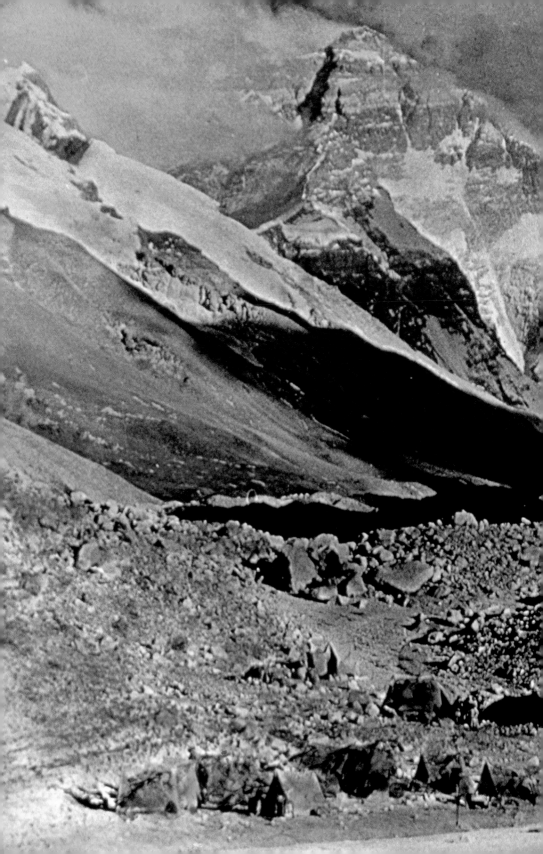

The entire North-East Ridge, not climbed to this day, was recognized by the British in the 1920s and 1930s as too difficult a route. It was Mallory who discovered the North Ridge (right of picture) as the ideal approach to the North-East Shoulder.

Opposite
'The North Col Camp IV (7,000m) was sited on a flat platform of firm ice and snow at the edge of a huge steep slope. However, the tents there were not visible from Camp III – the advanced base camp on the glacier under this great ice cliff.' (Noel)

In 1924 Norton, photographed here by Somervell, climbed as far as the Great Couloir which runs down the North Face of Mount Everest left of the summit. In contrast to Mallory, Norton thought nothing of the route on the North-East Ridge; instead he traversed across downward-sloping slabs beneath the ridge, thereby establishing a height record without oxygen which stood until 1978.

The almost 500 metre-high ice wall leading to the North Col, also called the Chang La face, is one of the keys to the north side of Mount Everest. It is without doubt the most dangerous passage on the route used by the British and Chinese. I knew that this face held great risks for a solo climber.

Captain John Noel, photographer on the 1922 and 1924 expeditions, used this special camera made of duralumin. The telephoto lens, which had a high magnification, had a telescopic view-finder, equipped with a parallax compensation, with six-times magnification. The camera had hand-drive as well as motor-drive from a 6 volt battery. The batteries were very light and with their nickel-alkali filling they maintained their full strength even when in long use. All moving parts ran on bearings like a clock and thus needed no oil which could freeze. This apparatus was a hand-made precision job. The camera is today in London's Science Museum.

'The unusual building of Shekar Monastery, which has reputedly stood for 500 years on the rocky edge of this elevated conical peak on the Tibetan plateau. The local people are very skilled at laying stone slabs cemented only with clay. Further up the mountain is the dzong; this is Tibetan for fort. There lives the governor of the province with his soldiers. From the tower which is built on the tip of the peak one has a good view of Mount Everest at a distance of 150 kilometres.' (Noel)

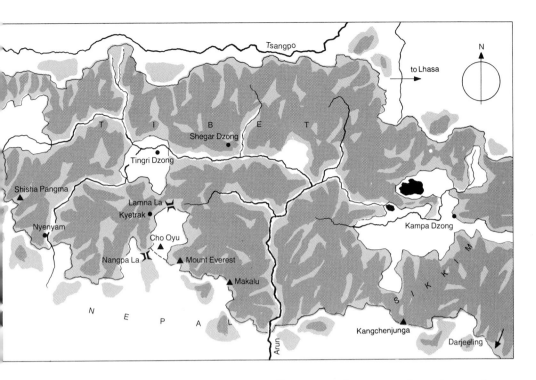

Formerly communications followed for the most part the caravan routes. On these tracks the first British Everest expeditions explored the country to the north between Kangchenjunga and Shisha Pangma. The road network has been built since the assumption of power by China. Between Lhasa and Chengdu there is an air link. By the building of strategically important main roads to the neighbouring Chinese regions and provinces the Red Chinese government was able to gain ever greater influence in Tibet. Tibetan opposition to the growing Chinese presence exploded in March 1959 in an uprising. After the crushing of this the Dalai Lama and some 20,000 Tibetans fled to India, Nepal, Bhutan and Sikkim. The Tibetan Government was finally removed. With over 1.2 million square kilometres – approximately an eighth of China – the autonomous region of Tibet is divided into five prefectures. As Tibet lies on average more than 4,000 metres above sealevel it is called now, as before, the 'roof of the world'. After the distribution of land to the poor, peasants' co-operatives and producers' co-operatives were founded and the youth subjected to a harsh indoctrination. With the proclamation of the 'Autonomous Region of Tibet' in 1965 the formal affiliation of Tibet to the People's Republic of China was effected. At the time of the Cultural Revolution renewed unrest broke out in 1967. Since 1979 the Chinese central government has endeavoured, by means of concessions of small liberties to the Tibetans (free trade, free religious practice) to bind the disaffected Tibetan people closer to itself. Only a peaceful Tibet is a bulwark against aggression from the south and west.

Gyangtse Dzong, destroyed during the Cultural Revolution.

Mount Everest –
Fairytale and Reality

The forces of mountains are sublime and far-reaching;
the ability to ride on the clouds is permeated by the mountains;
and the ability to follow the wind
is inevitably liberated by the mountains.

From Dōgen's The Mountains and Rivers Sutra

Mount Everest – Fairytale and Reality

Homewards

As first light enters the tiny windows of the Sherpa hut, Oswald Oelz, who we all call Bulle, opens his eyes. Around him everyone is getting up and dressing. Men are pulling on their coats. A fire crackles in the mud hearth. Morning already! Bulle had begun to snore almost as soon as he had stretched himself out on the narrow plank bed by the window last night, and although it is true he woke once briefly, fairly soon afterwards, for the rest of the night, he has slept deeply. Now, his watch tells him it is 7 a.m. We look across at each other and sit up. It is as if a new life were beginning. In an hour we must be in Syangpoche; we don't want to miss the aeroplane back to Kathmandu. Bulle yawns, his mouth wide open, then fetches his socks from the window recess and peers outside. It is a cold, clear autumn day. Hoar-frost lies on the meadows and there is snow on the mountains to the south. The feeling of being at home here vanishes with the packing of rucksacks. Yaks are being driven westwards, down to Namche Bazar; for a long time we can still hear the tinkling of their bells. Bulle says nothing, but I seem to sense what he murmurs in his heart. Towards the end of a trip, we often find ourselves communicating in this way. This time, however, having abandoned our Ama Dablam attempt, Bulle seems depressed. Faced with the prospect of going home, he feels unhappy at the way the expedition went: not because we failed to reach the summit of Ama Dablam, but perhaps because he feels his own performance could have been better. When will he get another opportunity? Bulle enjoys his work as a hospital doctor, but he has no new adventure planned for the foreseeable future. That makes him feel lonely. At home in Zurich, he lives alone.

The region of Solo Khumbu is another world. One should be able to stay up here, build a hut, live for years. The land of the Sherpas radiates peace and calm. Many say that Ama Dablam is the most beautiful mountain in the world. Like a giant it rises behind our lodgings against the light; it looks like a woman with outstretched arms.

The little aeroplane standing on the stony landing ground in Syangpoche is full to bursting. It has brought some tourists and is waiting on other guests of the 'Everest View' Hotel who must be flown back to the capital as speedily as possible. There is no room for us.

The 'Everest View' Hotel.

Everest and Nuptse from the west.

Here they come: following the suitcase-laden yaks, there comes a spindly old woman with garish green-coloured hair, supported on two ski sticks. Behind her Sherpas are carrying someone suffering from altitude sickness on a stretcher. We are at an altitude of close to 4,000 metres here.

See Mount Everest and die, I think grimly. Among the new arrivals is another green-haired woman, opulently beringed, in her middle-sixties and evidently hell-bent on spending all the money that her late husband has amassed on travelling. 'Isn't it beautiful', she cries, staring incessantly through her camera. She landed ten minutes ago. She photographs non-stop. I am amazed at her stamina. Yet her shrill cries of enthusiasm are not for the mountains, the

scenery or the people around her. They are for the hotel, the aeroplane, the unloaded oxygen equipment. What, I ask myself, are people like this doing in Nepal?

Thirty years ago this was still an inaccessible country, forbidden to foreigners. The highest mountains in the world, for centuries the natural protection of the Himalayan states against invaders, have attracted many hundred thousands of climbers and trekkers in the last decade. That has led to a fast and dramatic change: today tourism is the most important source of foreign currency. Nepal has become the 'Switzerland of Asia'. 'We know that our mountains offer an attraction for the world,' briefly remarked Birendra Bir Birkam Shah, the young king who rules Nepal with almost absolute power. 'The world is invited to come here and enjoy them.' I have been to Nepal a dozen times. I have learned to behave myself in this country as the inhabitants do. Only vis-à-vis the six-, seven- and eight-thousand metre peaks have I remained a European: ambitious and with singleness of purpose. In the evening Bulle and I go into the 'Everest View' to eat. This Japanese hotel at an altitude of close to 4,000 metres above sea-level has been a Mecca for prosperous European and American citizens for years. 'Experience the Himalaya', it says in the brochure. Standing close to the open fire, listening to conversation, we gaze time and again through the picture window at Lhotse and Everest. It is a terrific feeling to have climbed the world's highest mountain. We both did it in 1978 and wink at each other. 'Everest, an idyll!' In the hotel rooms there are oxygen masks; the building is heated. Outside in the rhododendron woods the wind whistles through the leaves.

Near us, the green-haired old woman brags: 'My grandchildren will marvel at me when they get my postcard from Mount Everest.' What tales she will have to tell when she gets home. When the hotel manager tells his guests that Bulle and I have climbed Everest we are overwhelmed with questions. To the first – 'Why do you risk such a dangerous adventure?' – Bulle says laconically:

'Everyone needs a little bit of exclusiveness in an age in which money buys everything.'

'How frightening is it really?' This question is directed at me. 'Fear is a constant companion', I say. 'You can't live life fully without it. When things get critical, your fear becomes even more intense. When I climb, I do so with hardly any doubts or worries. I make the decision about what I can or cannot do as I go along. Step by step. Day by day. Fear is an essential element in this, and I pay attention to it. It's natural. If you remain conscious that death is part of life, you cannot suppress your basic fear of falling, or of being overwhelmed by the weather.'

'Would you still climb eight-thousanders if the general public paid no attention to your achievements?'

'I started climbing at the age of five, and up to ten years ago only a few people had heard of me. In the first twenty years of my climbing career, I climbed at least 2,000 mountains in Europe and South America. No-one talked about it then, yet it gave me pleasure.'

'An eccentric hobby! What drives you to keep on trying harder and harder things? Are you trying to prove something to yourself?'

'As a kid I climbed the mountains around my home. I cycled into the Dolomites and later went by motor scooter to Switzerland, to the Eiger North Face and the Matterhorn. Today, to experience the same thrill, I must go to Everest or to the South Pole.'

'But aren't you chasing an illusion?' one of the hotel guests wants to know, a psychologist by profession.

'Perhaps,' interrupts Bulle, who has stood up and is about to leave. 'We must be off, we've got to get to Khumde tonight.' As a final riposte to the questioning pack, he adds, 'Every society colours its own decline with illusions.' Our inquisitors shake their heads. Bulle grins. We take our leave and go out into the night.

Kathmandu

'For these men days on the mountains are days when they really live. And as the cobwebs in their brains get blown away, as the blood begins to course refreshingly through their veins, as all their faculties become tuned up and their whole being becomes more sensitive, they detect appeals from Nature they had never heard before and see beauties which are revealed only to those who win them.'

The concepts of the first Everest pioneers are equally valid to us today, and for no one more than Bulle. The four weeks in Nepal have made him younger.

When we learn the following afternoon in Syangpoche that we are still only on the waiting list, we decide to walk to the next airstrip at Lukla, a two-day stage for trekkers. As we run part of the way it becomes strenuous. Our joints are painful. With battered limbs we arrive in Lukla. Exhausted – we have covered the last part of the way in the dusk – we sit down in the hotel of the 'Sherpa Co-operative'. We devour a couple of yak steaks and

The faces of Chomo Lonzo.

enjoy the comfortable warmth. Over a bottle of beer we talk until midnight by the open fire.

Early in the morning the following day we obtain two tickets for the first plane to Kathmandu. Our persistence gets on the nerves of the man with the

waiting list so much that he does everything he can to get rid of us on the first machine. We smile. Saved! Bulle and I are in such a hurry that we would have been ready to bid ten times the price for a ticket. I have to be in Germany in time for a lecture tour, and work is waiting for Bulle at the clinic.

As we wait for the plane on the stony terrace at the upper edge of the airfield, Bulle talks to two Canadian girls. During the flight they sit by us, relating their trip through Sherpa-land. As the scenery passes beneath us – freshly cleared woods, small villages, meandering streams with little footpaths alongside – we vaguely arrange to meet them that evening, but forget the rendezvous the moment we set foot in Kathmandu.

We have lots of things to do. Our flight to Europe must be booked, and we want to use the remaining time to take care of permits for further expedition plans. In Kathmandu there is a woman who knows practically everything about this region – Elizabeth Hawley, a journalist who has lived in the city for over twenty years. I visit her in her office at 'Tiger Tops', and she tells me at once that Naomi Uemura, the well-known Japanese mountaineer, has received permission for a solo ascent of Everest during the winter of 1980/81. This piece of news hits me like a shot. At first I am perplexed. How can it be true? It is my idea! It has been my secret for a year. What now? Within seconds a definite plan ripens. No, a whole string of plans goes through my mind. I must act quickly.

A few weeks after returning from

Naomi Uemura.

aware that this small, stocky man with frost-burned cheeks can do anything he puts his mind to. Our attitude to climbing, even to life generally, is similar. This time Uemura, this fox, has been the quicker. Much as I envy him, still more do I respect him for it.

I have to do something. At any price I too want to attempt this test, and to be the first to do so. A picture of the snow and ice covered West Ridge of Everest flares up uneasily in my mind while I am speaking with Liz Hawley. 'Is there any hope for a 1980 post-monsoon permit for the West Ridge?' I ask.

'I think so', she says.

The West Ridge is infinitely long, too exposed to the autumn storms.

There my chances are practically nil.

'What else?'

'There's nothing else.'

What about the north side? It lies in Tibet, and until now the Chinese government has only issued permits after

my solo ascent of Nanga Parbat in 1978 I had realized that a solo ascent of Everest was also possible. This knowledge then condensed into a fixed idea. Convinced that no one would be able to do it before me, I wanted to put off the actual attempt until the mid-1980s. Now I had to take the consequences. How was I to obtain a solo permit overnight? There's more to it than mere mountaineering ambition: after the failure of the expedition to Ama Dablam I am eager to push myself to the limit. The highest mountain in the world, in winter, alone – for a climber that is the absolute high point.

But how can I forestall the tough Uemura who has already taken a dog sled to the North Pole on his own and stood on top of five of the highest mountains in all seven continents? Naomi Uemura is not only one of the most successful mountaineers in the world, he is an adventurer, a daredevil, and as tough as any Sherpa. In 1976 we talked for a few hours in Tokyo. Since that time I have been

Everest, the middle part of the West Ridge.

25

laborious negotiations with senior politicians. I know that the North Ridge offers the best hope of ascent for a solo climber. The Nepalese so-called normal route – Western Cwm and South Col – is out of the question on account of the Khumbu ice-fall. To use Sherpas to overcome this dangerously crevassed ice cascade would negate a real solo ascent. The East Face is still inaccessible. But on the Tibetan North Ridge Englishmen nearly got to the top in the 1920s. A solo ascent there ought to be possible. I am as keyed-up about the prospect as if about to sit final examinations. This nervousness does not hinder me; it makes me alert. It conjures up pictures on the inner screen behind my forehead; it lends wings to my thoughts and steps. In this state of heightened concentration, snippets from old Everest books come into my mind again and again, as if I had learned them by heart. Learned them in preparation for this decision.

'A well-acclimatized rope can climb in six days from the Rongbuk camp to the summit.' That was Mallory's early assessment. Now it appears to me like

The Khumbu ice-fall.

a vision: 'A party of two appears insufficient, for if one man should become exhausted the other will probably want help in bringing him down.' Or, put it another way – two are too many! Yes, one alone is enough if he gets to the North Col, can bide his time and is prepared to accept the possibility that in the last resort, if things go really wrong, he will die.

'In the Himalaya everything is so much bigger that one must also reckon on longer times for the return of safe snow conditions. Once these giant peaks are in bad condition they need a corresponding length of time for the restoration of favourable conditions. There are worse possibilities against one than on lesser mountains. The sun burns hotter, the storms blow more furiously, the distances are further, everything is to excess.'

Previously nobody has sought unfavourable weather conditions on Mount Everest as an additional sporting challenge.

Only now, after the phase of conquest, after the ascent of the steepest faces, after the renunciation of oxygen equipment, must the first winter ascents follow. Thus the logical development of the idea: Everest in winter and solo. A new thought comes to me. Is not the summer, the time of the monsoon, the most unpleasant period for an ascent? During the monsoon, from the end of May to mid-September, it snows almost continually on the high peaks, avalanches thunder down, route-finding is impossible in the mist. Of course the winter is much colder, but December and

January, both released by the Nepalese government for future winter ascents for the most part bring glorious weather along with polar cold and violent storms. That is to say: little snow, little avalanche danger, and no parching midday heat. The monsoon period on Everest is far worse.

Of the twenty highest mountains in the world thirteen stand completely or partly within the boundaries of Nepal.

two, exceptionally four expeditions per year. One in the pre-monsoon period, one in the post-monsoon period, a third or fourth only if the teams choose different routes. And now, in the autumn of 1979, additional winter permits are to be given away. Why then not also a monsoon permit? An expedition permit for Everest costs at present US $1,200. That is little in an average total expenditure of US

Mount Everest from the north.

In order to be able to climb these peaks, one must first of all apply for a permit and then abide by the appropriate regulations. The regulations do not provide for monsoon expeditions. To be sure, in spring 1979 the government published a new list of so-called 'permitted' summits; the number of the peaks which are at the disposal of climbers has been expanded to almost 100. For the highest mountain of all the government normally permits

$100,000, but perhaps sufficient for the government to entice expeditions into the country throughout the summer. Nepal needs foreign currency, and sensational mountain ascents which will be discussed in the world press. Perhaps the Tourist Ministry is only waiting for my proposal.

Nepal is an undeveloped country with only a few road connections. A large part of its fourteen million population works as porters. These need

The summit of Everest from the north-east.

Then I act quickly. I must organize a permit for Mount Everest before winter 1980/81, when Uemura plans his climb. Accompanied by Bobby Chettri, the manager of 'Mountain Travel', the leading trekking organization in Kathmandu, I visit Mr Sharma at the Ministry of Tourism. As 'Mountain Travel' also organizes expeditions, I want to extract a yes-or-no before my departure for Europe in order to be able to entrust my friend Bobby with the most important preparations in Nepal.

No one will give me a permit for the monsoon period. They are, however, so interested in my idea for a solo ascent that I take new hope. In vain? Mr. Sharma promises me, somewhat vaguely, a permit for the Everest West Ridge in autumn 1980. I sign application forms and deposit data and sketch-maps. With an oral assurance of being allowed to climb Everest's West Ridge solo in the 1980 post-monsoon period I feel like a lad who has won a trip to the moon.

Naturally I know that the prospect of getting to the top by way of this long, difficult route, exposed to the west wind, is poor. Nevertheless I carry on as if I must try it above everything else in the world. During these days, in the toing and froing between the Tourist Ministry, 'Mountain Travel' and Liz Hawley's office, I surprise myself frequently with the 'illegal' thought of crossing over the Lho La into the Rongbuk Valley in Tibet and from there attempting the old classic English route on Everest. Liz Hawley can read thoughts, for she tells me at once that the Nepalese border with Tibet at Kodari is to be opened shortly.

work in summer too. If my monsoon expedition to the West Ridge should succeed, more groups would come in the future. Above all, summer climbs in the extreme north-west of Nepal would follow. Distances in Nepal are calculated according to how many days are needed to cover them, and distances are the measure of the wages. Expeditions often employ many hundreds of porters, even as many as a thousand or more. And the approach marches are long, they last sometimes several weeks. Thus there is no ground to refuse my application for a monsoon ascent.

I walk through the city, dream and reflect.

That would be still better and for sure the cheapest way to China, Tibet and Mount Everest! However, what would the Chinese government say to my non-ideological, non-political idea of a private highest solo venture?

Kathmandu is one of the cities which always make me inclined to saunter and loaf about. Everything is compact here, grimy, full of cheerfulness. I know no other city which smells so strongly of Life. In the old bazaar, which resounds with the tinkle of innumerable bicycle bells and in which from morning to night a compact multitude throngs leisurely, the smell of rotting fruit, spices and joss sticks mingles with the stench of excrement and urine. A white-flecked bull lies ruminating comfortably in the middle of the street, and I walk around him like everyone else as carefully as if he were a sleeping beast of prey. He is regarded as holy and each passer-by should beware of disturbing him, much less of driving him away.

In the shop called 'Two Snow Lions' I visit my old friend Gyaltsen, a Tibetan who fled from Tibet in 1959 with the Dalai Lama. He speaks pidgin English like I do. When he sees me he at once has tea brought, for he knows that as a passionate collector of Tibetiana I can seldom resist his treasures. The best titbits of all, however, he does not have in the shop but at home. This time it is two old Tibetan carpets, in natural colours and in fine condition. I am to come to his house in the evening and take a look at them.

His wife cooks *momo* especially for me, delicious pastries with a filling of meat and vegetables. The carpets are beautiful but expensive. 'It has become difficult,' says Gyaltsen. 'The Chinese allow no one across the border, and for smuggling indirectly through the Kingdom of Bhutan two merchants were shot only recently.' One of the carpets has as its pattern a mysterious tantra, occult signs and details on a human body. On the other I see all sorts of animals, a phoenix, snow leopards among clouds and mountain peaks. I fall in love with these works of art. I must have them.

The woollen mountain peaks on the carpet remind me immediately of my Utopian idea of a solo ascent. And as my journey to Lhasa is fast approaching I ask Gyaltsen: 'Are there still bronzes, carpets, old jewellery in Lhasa?' 'Yes', he says, 'In Tibet everything is much cheaper. One has only to get safely over the border with it.' He

Lho La from the south.

29

grins. 'You are a climber. The Chinese haven't placed any guards up there.' I have to laugh at the idea of crossing Mount Everest with a rucksack full of illicit goods. 'I want to go to Tibet officially. Across China with a permit, do you see? Then I don't need to smuggle anything out.'

'Do you think the Chinese will let you in?'

'I guess so,' I encourage myself. 'It is a question of time.'

'You must visit my relatives in Lhasa, no question about it, they can help you.'

Gyaltsen also talks as if I already had my permit for Tibet in my pocket. As I go back to the hotel, the two carpets under my arm, I try to picture Lhasa to myself. The firmament there must be even clearer than night-time Kathmandu. It is crazy but since I was a small boy and read Heinrich Harrer's book I have longed to visit Tibet. I have the feeling that I must go there, as if it is there my fate will be fulfilled. I must go to Tibet, as there my roots lie. Tibetans are convinced that we all originally stem from this high land enclosed by savage mountains, in which lies the heart of the world, the holy mountain Kailas. A strange thought comes to me: today, when we in the West are anxious about the last, all-destroying bang, is it perhaps time to return to the cradle of the world?

Like a Fairytale

During the night I have a peculiar dream. In a smoky alpine hut my mother reads to me from a slim volume the stories of the first Everest expeditions. It feels as if I were on the way with Bruce, Norton and Mallory. On awakening, the fairytale figures of my mother's story mingle with the historical facts. Suddenly I remember that my mother really did read me the Everest saga thirty years ago. On the Gschmagenhart Alm, where we children spent the summer holidays at that time, we listened evening after evening to this true story.

Mount Everest lies on the border between Nepal and China. Early attempts to approach it were frustrated by strict political measures in both countries, which forbade Europeans any access. Only in 1920 did the Dalai Lama, the Tibetan monk-king in Lhasa, give permission for the first time for an expedition to this myster-

'Storm on Mount Everest', a book for young readers by Herbert Hans Kruger.

ious mountain. All that was known outside the area about Everest stemmed from the employees of the Survey of India. Disguised as pilgrims, priests or merchants they had entered the country. Only under cover of darkness could they write up their notes on tiny rolls of paper, then hide them away in the innermost parts of their prayer-wheels: compass-bearings of peaks and rivers, heights which they had measured with boiling-point thermometers. None of them ever got within eighty kilometres of the mountain.

Mount Everest lies half-concealed behind another range of mountains, and no explorer had at that time set foot on the great glacier region at its foot. Its height and seclusion, as well as a report of an ancient 'Lamasery of the Snows', whose priests guarded the throne of the gods, stirred the curiosity of all climbers.

First of all, during his military mission to Lhasa in 1904, Sir Francis Younghusband had been able to extract a promise from the Dalai Lama that British expeditions should be allowed occasionally to climb in the Tibetan Himalaya. Thus it was Englishmen – as happened 100 years before in the Alps – who set their minds to the conquest of Everest. India was then part of the British Empire. The route from the south through Nepal would have been the shortest. But that Himalayan kingdom was totally barred to strangers.

Dr. Kellas, an experienced Himalayan climber, studied the possibility of reaching the northern foot of Everest from Darjeeling by way of Tibet, and in 1913 the young army officer John Noel travelled illicitly into Tibet.

Dressed as a native, he got to within about 60 kilometres of the peak. In 1921 the first expedition set out. By way of a great detour through Sikkim and Tibet the caravan made its way to Rongbuk, the monastery steeped in legend at the northern foot of Chomolungma (Qomolungma), as the Tibetans call Everest. Among the climbers in the group was George Leigh Mallory, at that time one of the ablest British alpinists. In the bazaar in Darjeeling they engaged local men, Sherpas from wild Nepal, who as porters would carry the expedition's gear through valleys, gorges and over Tibetan passes.

In mid-May the march began. The humid climate gave the Europeans a hard time. Landslides blocked the road in places. Roads soon gave way to paths, paths to mule tracks, which

Dr Kellas.

31

seemed to cling to the rocks high above. The Indian Army mules refused and Tibetan animals had to be substituted. Dr Kellas, the expedition doctor, succumbed to a heart attack when the group were still 600 kilometres from Rongbuk. The 'Lamasery of the Snows' was found eventually, one of the highest situated monasteries in the world, at that time a holy place, to which Tibetan pilgrims came on foot to pray, often taking many months over the journey.

Mallory and Irvine in Tibet.

George H. Leigh Mallory.

Above the monastery the team pitched camp. They were only thirty kilometres from Everest.

It was the task of the expedition to explore the mountain thoroughly. Their aim was to discover the easiest route of ascent. Only if there were an easy route could they hope for success.

'In the Alps nowadays, men look about for the most difficult way up a mountain. Every year hundreds ascend even the Matterhorn by the easiest way up. So men with any turn for adventure have to look about for the difficult ways. With Mount Everest it is very different. The exhaustion produced from the difficulty of breathing in enough oxygen at the great heights is so fearful that only by a way that entails the least possible exertion can the summit be reached. Hence the necessity for spending the first season in thoroughly prospecting the mountain.'

Thus Younghusband laid down the goal. This reconnaissance expedition was also too badly prepared for an ascent. First of all the main Rongbuk glacier was explored. From a high vantage point Mallory was able to observe the fearsome Khumbu ice-fall to the south. As the upper end was not visible he assumed that the crevasses he could see barred all passage to the hanging valley of the Western Cwm. The glacier calved in gigantic ice blocks and the broken ice made him

View of the main camp of the 1922 expedition.

shudder. It was two months before the expedition found a way to the East Rongbuk Glacier. They had failed to notice the narrow entrance which linked it to the main glacier and it was only after a detour of several hundred kilometres via the Kharta Valley – it was late in September – that the party reached the foot of the North Col. Mallory and two other climbers battled through violent storms to a height of 7,000 metres on the North Ridge. From there they could see a possible route to the summit. Mallory was satisfied – Everest would 'go'.

As soon as the expedition was back in London the Mount Everest Committee began new preparations, and in March 1922 launched the first attack. From Darjeeling they set in motion a small army. It consisted of thirteen Britons, 160 high-altitude porters and over 300 pack animals. Brigadier-General Charles Bruce led the expedition. Among his team were the cream of England's mountaineers: Norton, Somervell, Finch and, once more, Mallory. Bruce, the expedition leader, had forty years' mountaineering experience in the Alps and Himalaya. No one understood the local people better than he, for he had served thirty years in a Gurkha regiment.

Until the month of May, winter rules in the Everest region, yet by June the Indian monsoon storms are already not far off. The warm winds transform snow and ice into fragile death traps. The expedition, therefore, had very little time at its disposal. Each day, each hour was precious.

A string of small high camps equipped with tents, provisions and sleeping-bags was established on the route to the summit. Captain Finch had a bold plan: he wanted to attack the mountain using artificial oxygen, which would ease the climbers' breathing at high altitude.

Back home in England he had allowed himself to be shut in a low pressure chamber, and had made tests. The atmospheric pressure was regulated from outside. Finch sat in the chamber and the air was slowly pumped out oxygen removed all bodily uneasiness. Two doctors observed Finch during these experiments. The tests proved unequivocally that a person could survive at a height of 9,100 metres with the help of oxygen apparatus. The altimeter outside showed 8,000 and 8,500 metres, but inside the chamber with a rubber tube in his mouth feeding him oxygen Finch felt fresh and lively. Finch and his comrades now carried oxygen in portable light steel cylinders (each system weighing fif-

Members of the 1922 expedition: (front row from left to right) Mallory, Finch, Longstaff, Gen. Bruce, Strutt, Crawford; (back row from left to right) Morshead, Capt. Bruce, Noel, Wakefield, Somervell, Morris, Norton.

until the air pressure in the chamber equalled that at a height of 8,880 metres. He undertook two experiments, once with and once without an oxygen supply. Without oxygen his heart beat terribly fast. The pounding in his head and ears increased, and he became stupefied. The supply of teen kilos), into the mountains for the first time; oxygen which would relieve the almost unbearable agony of exertion in the thin air of the Death Zone.

The expedition needed a few days to overcome the ice-fall on the way to the North Col. They were able to pitch Camp IV at about 7,000 metres.

Directly after Camp IV came a comparatively easy stretch. Then new difficulties began. It was fiercely cold and at a height of 7,600 metres climbing became almost impossible, so powerful was the growing storm. Morshead was suffering from nausea; Mallory, Norton and Somervell felt themselves freezing. Nevertheless all of them except Morshead carried on. They reached a height of 8,230 metres, then lack of oxygen and the unbelievable cold forced them back. A few days later Finch and Capt. Geoffrey Bruce, a nephew of the General, got as far as 8,321 metres.

Reinhold Messner in 1977 during a test flight without oxygen mask at 9,000 metres.

'Though 1,700 feet below, we were well within half a mile of the summit, so close indeed that we could distinguish individual stones on a little patch of scree lying just underneath the highest point. Ours were truly the tortures of Tantalos; for, weak from hunger and exhausted by that nightmare struggle for life in our high camp, we were in no fit condition to proceed. Indeed, I knew that if we were to persist in climbing on, even if only for another 500 feet, we should not both get back alive.'

The second 1922 assault team descending.

Ascent to the Chang La (1922).

Under the North Col (1922).

Base camp, meanwhile, resembled a field hospital. Nevertheless Mallory and Somervell wanted to launch one last assault. As they climbed directly up the steep slopes of the ice-fall, there occurred a tragic and momentous misfortune:

'We met some of the worst snow. The scene was peculiarly bright and windless, and as we rarely spoke, nothing was to be heard but the laboured panting of our lungs. This stillness was suddenly disturbed. We were startled by an ominous sound, sharp, arresting, violent, and yet somehow soft like an explosion of untamped gunpowder. I had never before heard such a sound on a mountain-side; but all of us, I imagine, knew instinctively what it meant, as though we had been accustomed to hear it every day of our lives. Suddenly I observed the surface of the snow was broken and puckered where it had been smooth, for a few yards to the right of me. I took two steps convulsively in this direction with the thought of getting nearer to the edge of the danger that threatened us. And then I began to move slowly downwards, inevitably carried on the whole moving surface by a force I was utterly powerless to resist. Somehow I managed to turn out from the slope so as to avoid being pushed headlong and backwards down it. For a second or two I seemed hardly to be in danger as I slid quietly down with the snow. Then the rope at my waist tightened and held me back. A wave of snow came over me and I was buried. I supposed that the matter was settled. However, I recalled experiences related by other parties; it had been suggested that the best chance of escape in this situation lay in swimming. I thrust out my arms above my head and actually went through some sort of motion of swimming on my back. Beneath the surface of the snow, with nothing to inform the senses of the world outside it, I had no impression of speed after the first acceleration – I struggled in the tumbling snow, unconscious of everything else – until, perhaps, only a few seconds later, I knew the pace was easing up. I felt an increasing pressure about my body. I wondered how tightly I should be squeezed, and then the avalanche came to rest.

My arms were free; my legs were near the surface. After a brief struggle, I was standing again, surprised and breathless, in the motionless snow. But the rope was tight at my

The first assault team of the 1922 expedition.

waist; the porter tied on next to me, I supposed, must be deeply buried. To my further surprise, he quickly emerged, unharmed as myself. Somervell and Crawford too, though they had been above me by the rope's length, were now quite close, and soon extricated themselves. We subsequently made out that their experi-

ences had been very similar to mine. But where were the rest?'

Mallory's worst fears were confirmed: seven porters were dead. More climbing was out of the question.

Downcast, the party returned to Darjeeling. Mallory took the responsibility upon himself and answered the critics:

'. . . Mount Everest is beyond the range of a simple contract measured in terms of money; the porters had come to have a share in our enterprise, and these men died in an act of voluntary service freely rendered and faithfully performed.'

Now more than ever the whys and wherefores of such an undertaking were discussed in public. What, it was asked, was the sense in attempting to climb Mount Everest? Such attempts cost not only human lives, privations and sorrow, but a great deal of money as well, yet the usefulness to the general public was practically nil. The climbers tried to clarify what it meant to them.

'The most obvious good is an increased knowledge of our own capacities. By trying with all our might and with all our mind . . . we are getting to know better what we really can do. No one can say for certain yet whether we can or cannot reach the summit.'

And still more was said by way of justification:

'. . . a whole new enjoyment in life will be opened up. And enjoyment of life is,

37

after all, the aim in life. We do not live to eat and make money . . . And some of us know from actual experience that by climbing a mountain we can get some of the finest enjoyment there is to be had. We like bracing ourselves against the physical difficulties the mountain presents, and feeling that we are forcing the spirit within us to prevail against the material.'

The challenge to alter human limitations, the delight in winning through overcoming the most extreme ordeals, a strong relationship with Nature –

cumstances which endanger life. For the local people, participation in an expedition then as now means a highly welcome source of income.

Two years later, in March 1924, a new expedition from Darjeeling moved through the tropical valleys of Sikkim towards Everest. Once again the boyish, slender Mallory was there, for the third time. Bruce and Norton led the undertaking like a military operation. A chain of high camps was established, but this time the previously suitable and valuable expedition month of May surprised them

Amongst the ice towers on the East Rongbuk Glacier.

the motives of the Himalayan mountaineer have remained the same to this day. Likewise the dilemma has remained of whether to use local helpers, without whom a traditional expedition cannot manage, in cir-

with winter-like temperatures down to –30°C, and heavy snowfalls. The teams had to abandon complete camps twice and descend to base camp. These retreats amidst snowstorm and avalanche danger cost two porters their all camps up to the 7,000 metre-high North Col were once more occupied. The ascent of the ice chimney on the Chang-La face was a feat of the climbing art of the time. They even succeeded in establishing an assault camp at 8,145 metres. Most altitude physiologists had held such a thing at that height as impossible.

On 4 June Norton and Somervell departed in ideal weather for the summit assault. Somervell was suffering badly from a painful altitude cough; choking fits obliged him to give up and stay behind. Norton climbed on alone, and without oxygen got to 8,572 metres, a record, which was not to be surpassed for more than fifty years. Then he gave up. The expedition had failed.

George Leigh Mallory had been a

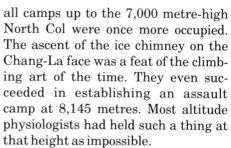

Lieut-Col. E.F. Norton.

lives. When in the last days of May fine weather finally set in, the expedition was in a weak state. Nevertheless

Ascent of the chimney on the Chang La face (1924).

Howard Somervell.

39

The highest point in the world to have been photographed at the time of the 1924 expedition: 8,500 metres.

still achieving something apparently impossible by means of our own strength and through the most extreme use of physical and psychological abilities. Mallory and Mummery were to me models, as later was Paul Preuss, who on the same grounds likewise condemned the use of pitons in rock climbing.

They all gave me the courage to put across my own philosophy, through my own example and through countless, often wild, discussions and provocative articles, to try to lead the climbing world back to mountaineering 'by fair means'.

Today, as those clever Englishmen foresaw, we all live more and more in a world of machines, in a world of technicalization. On our battered planet there is scarcely space left in which we can forget our industrial society and, undisturbed, put to the test our innate powers and abilities. In us all the longing remains for the primitive condition in which we can match ourselves against Nature, have the chance to have it out with her and thereby discover ourselves. And this is the real reason that for me there is no

great hero of mine since the 1960s, a time when I was realizing the great climbing routes of my Alpine career. I respected him as I did the English pioneer of Nanga Parbat, Albert Frederick Mummery, on account of his passionate discussions of the use of artificial oxygen.

At a time when technology had just begun to develop and when the use of technical aids would have been universally acclaimed as progress, both were prepared to argue for what we today call 'fair means'. They already recognized that by the use of technology we deceive ourselves in some essential – the joy, pleasure and happiness of

A rubbish heap at the southern foot of Everest.

more fascinating challenge than this: one man and one mountain. I refuse to ruin this challenge through the use of technological aids. In order to be able to survive in this epoch of depersonalization, concrete deserts, and the alienation brought about by being harnessed into the crazy machinery of manufacturing and administration, I need the mountains as an alternative world.

Anybody who fails to understand my despair and thinks that my 'by fair about their tragic end. And mostly it revolves around the question whether or not they reached the top before they died. Obsessed with the idea of perhaps seeing Everest soon from the north myself, I begin to arrange in my mind all that I know of this story. I am conscious of the hope that Mallory and Irvine fell or froze during descent and not ascent. I wish this even though Mallory himself wrote after one of his lecture tours: 'Success, that word means nothing here . . . '

Mallory and Irvine before departing for their last summit attempt (1924).

means' philosophy is an over-subtle indulgence should take a trip to the Everest Base Camp of today by the Khumbu ice-fall. When he sees the vast kilo--metre-square rubbish tip left there by previous mountaineers from the West with their throwaway technology, then he will understand me.

Mallory and Irvine

The next assault was to end in tragedy. The summit pair, Mallory and Irvine, were lost. Much has been written

On the morning of 6 June 1924 Mallory and Irvine started from the North Col. Each was carrying almost twelve kilos on his back. It was a beautiful day. Quickly they reached Camp V. There Mallory wrote in one of his notes: 'No wind here and things look hopeful.'

Next day they continued up to Camp VI. Odell and Sherpa Nema came up behind them to Camp V. On 8 June Mallory and Irvine left Camp VI for a last summit push. Odell moved up

41

Dear Odell
Herewith
Ang Tenjin
Tewang
Nima
Dareda
The first is anxious to go down to IV & as he has done well I should be glad if you could let him go.
The provision rucksack which he carries has been pretty well gone through by us.
No wind here & things look hopeful.
GM.

Dear Odell,
We're awfully sorry to have left things in such a mess — our Unna Cooker rolled down the slope at the last moment.
Be sure of getting back to IV tomorrow in time to evacuate before dark as I hope to.
In the tent I must have left a compass — for the Lord's sake rescue it: we are without —
To here on 90 atmospheres for the 2 days — so we'll probably go on 2 cylinders — but it's a bloody load for climbing.
Perfect weather for the job!
Yours ever
G Mallory

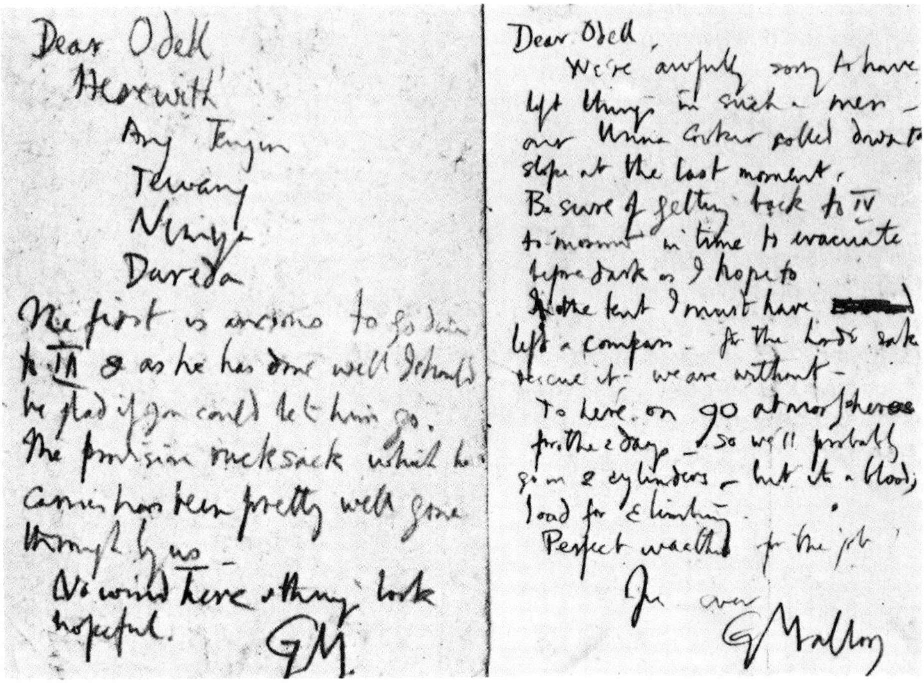

Mallory's notes to Odell.

alone into the camp vacated by them. It was shortly after midday when he saw two tiny figures high up on the ridge:

'There was a sudden clearing of the atmosphere above me and I saw the whole summit ridge and final peak of Everest unveiled. I noticed far away on a snow slope leading up to what seemed to me to be the last step but one from the base of the final pyramid, a tiny object moving and approaching the rock step. A second object followed, and then the first climbed to the top of the step. As I stood intently watching this dramatic appearance, the scene became enveloped in cloud once more.'

Odell was puzzled at seeing Mallory and Irvine still so low just before 1 p.m. However, he was not able to make out exactly whether he had seen them at the 'first step' or the 'second step'. Mallory had intended to be at the 'second step' by 8 a.m. at the latest. This lies at the foot of the summit pyramid and marks the beginning of the final short snow-covered part of the North-East Ridge. Also, Odell was not able to establish whether the second climber had been able to catch up with his companion. This initial report by Odell is one of the keys to the mystery of Mallory and Irvine. But it doesn't satisfy me. How am I to clarify the situation?

SUMMIT 29,002 ft

THE CITADEL

SECOND POSITION

FIRST POSITION

CAMP. Nº 6
26,700 ft

CLOUDS
COVERING
NORTH RIDGE

N.E. ODELL
CATCHES SIGHT
OF CLIMBERS

Odell sees Mallory during the ascent (reconstruction).

Andrew Irvine.

watching intently for some sign. The pale moonlight, reflected by the snowy peaks, which gleamed on the flank of the great peak, would have made it difficult to observe any light signals, and in any case no one knew whether the missing pair had actually carried lamps or torches on their way to the top. The only certain thing is that years later bits of signalling equipment were found by the next expedition in the tangled remains of the last camp.

During the night the wind rose and the cold deepened, and by morning the storm was blowing even more strongly. When nothing had been seen of Mallory and Irvine by midday, Odell went back up to Camp V with two porters, but by the next morning they were half-frozen and would not stir further. Only Odell went up, once more alone, to the top camp, gasping

Odell descended to the lower camp in order to leave room in the highest tent in case Mallory and Irvine should still return. Through the flying cloud streamers he caught fleeting glimpses of the ridge, saw a glowing sunset, and nothing else. During the evening strong gusts of wind threatened to tear the tents apart.

Mallory and Irvine could not be expected back all that early. The route to the summit was long. Perhaps they reached it at the onset of darkness, or perhaps by then they were already returning to camp. Slowly night fell. In the lower camps everyone was still

> Dear Noel,
> We'll probably start early to-morrow (8ᵗ) in order to have clear weather It won't be too early to start looking out for us either crossing the rockband under the pyramid or going up skyline at 8.0 p.m.!
> Yours ever
> G Mallory

Mallory's note to John Noel with the request to observe him on the summit.

badly without a mask. From there he climbed as far as 8,220 metres, in the fading hope of finding some trace of his friends. When the hopelessness of his exhausting search dawned on him he gave up. He wrote later:

'Then, closing up the tent . . . I glanced up at the mighty summit above me, which ever and anon deigned to reveal its cloud-wreathed features. It seemed to look down with cold indifference on me, a mere puny man, and howl derision at my petition to yield up its secret – this mystery of my friends. The summit pyramid of Everest is one of the most inhospitable spots on the face of the earth when the wind whistles across the gloomy flanks of the mountain. And how cruel that wind is when each step it hinders concerns lost friends.'

Odell still did not ask himself how and where the pair had perished. In a sort of lamaist resignation he accepted the fact.

'Had we violated a sanctuary?' But then he peered again at the summit and felt a breath of reconciliation:

'He who approaches close must ever be led on, and oblivious of all obstacles seek to reach that most sacred and highest place of all. It seemed that my friends must have been thus enchanted also: for why else should they tarry?'

Irvine and Mallory must have fallen or, as I think more probable, frozen to death. The question of whether they reached the top preoccupies me so much now that all night long I read the

Memorial cairn at base camp.

old Everest books which Liz Hawley has lent me.

Somervell noted in his diary at the time:

'Mallory and Irvine dead. That is the sad certainty. Have all our exertions and sacrifices been in vain? No, the loss of these splendid men is part of the price that has been paid to keep alive the spirit of adventure. But nobody can hold that lives lost in fighting Nature's greatest obstacles in the name of adventure and exploration are thrown away.'

The obstinate Mallory, a man who did more than any other to unravel the secret of Everest and whose iron will had been the driving force for three big

45

Irvine working on the oxygen apparatus.

expeditions, passed into legend. Who was this man? His comrades described him thus:

'Mallory was no common personality. Physically he always seemed to me the beau ideal of the mountaineer; he was very good looking, and I have always thought that his boyish face – for he looked absurdly young for his thirty-seven years – was the outward and visible sign of a wonderful constitution. His graceful figure was the last word in wiry activity and he walked with a tireless swing which made him a man with whom few could live uphill; he was almost better downhill, for his years of mountain training had added balance and studied poise to his natural turn of speed.

'But it was the spirit of the man that made him the great mountaineer he was . . . he lived on his nerves . . . it was almost impossible to make out whether he was a tired man or not, for he responded instantly to every call that was made on him, and while the call lasted he would remain the dominant spirit in any enterprise. The conquest of the mountain became an obsession with him, and for weeks and months he devoted his whole time and energy to it . . .

'He was undoubtedly fine in body. But in fitness to endure the cold and wind of Everest and in adaptation to high altitudes, he naturally could not compare with the men whose homes were at over 12,000 feet . . . They must obviously have excelled him in bodily fitness . . . But where he excelled was in spirit . . . his spirit drove his body to the utmost limit. He was not asked to make that last climb . . . But his spirit would not allow him; he must make one last desperate effort.'

It is said also that Mallory was impatient by nature. This is just as important to the understanding of the tragedy as his strong affinity with Irvine.

'Young Irvine was almost a boy in years – he was twenty-two; but mentally and physically he was a man full grown and able to hold his own with all modesty on terms at least of equality with the other members of our party ... he was a splendid specimen, as befitted an Oxford rowing blue, with the powerful shoulders and comparatively slim legs characteristic of the

best oars. His experience as a mountaineer was limited to the rocks of the British Isles and a climb ... in Spitzbergen.'

Mallory had also chosen him, presumably, on account of his suitability for the final assault. Added to that, no one knew better than Irvine how to operate the oxygen apparatus. At the beginning Mallory and Somervell had declined the use of supplementary oxygen. In 1922 Norton had got to 8,200 metres without this aid. They believed that natural abilities are more reliable than artificial help:

'What experience always teaches us is that the climber does best to rely on his

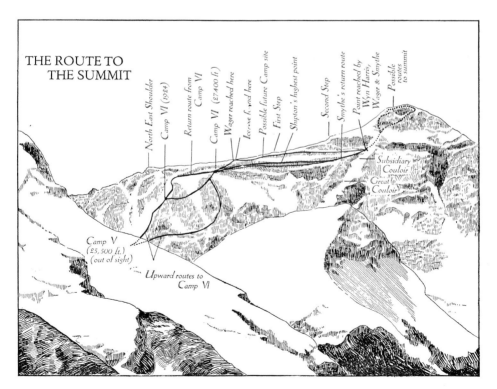

The route of the Ruttledge 1933 expedition and the heights reached.

Hillary and Tenzing in Camp IV after the ascent in 1953.

natural bodily abilities, which warn him in time whether he is overstepping the bounds of his strength. With artificial aids he exposes himself to the possibility of sudden collapse if the apparatus fails.'

In spite of this wise judgement Mallory wanted to make his last attempt with oxygen gear. Out of the maze of conflicting views he had developed a climbing plan, which united in itself the preferences of all opinions and which had been accepted unanimously.

When the survivors had returned to England there began endless speculations over the question of whether the summit of Mount Everest was conquered or not. Whosoever felt himself competent put forward his own theory, on the basis of diary notes, of Odell's eyewitness report, and of general information about high altitude problems and the difficulties of the north side of Everest. Almost all these theories contradicted each other.

Slowly the mystery of Mallory and Irvine began to interest me more than my planned solo ascent.

After the disappearance of Mallory and Irvine, eight years were to pass before the Dalai Lama gave permission for a new expedition to Tibet. The god-king and his counsellors disapproved of the harm, of the loss of human life connected with the expeditions of 1922 and 1924, and reverted to their policy of isolation. In 1932, however, the Tibetans gave way to the diplomatic pressure of the India Office and of the political agent of Great Britain in Sikkim and at last granted permission for a fourth expedition. It left England in 1933. Its leader was Hugh Ruttledge.

Although this expedition succeeded in placing its top camp almost 200

Ice axe belonging to Mallory or Irvine, found in 1933.

metres higher than that of Mallory, the summit team had to turn back exhausted beneath the 'second step'. Nevertheless, this party did get an exact picture of the 'second step' on the Mallory route. Smythe expressed himself sceptical about the possibility of overcoming it. The old Norton route, on the other hand, he held to be feasible. The discussion about the ideal route flared up once more.

In his book, *Everest 1933*, Ruttledge declared: 'Future parties will be well advised to leave it [the Mallory route] out of their calculations'. The number of experts who up to then had believed in an ascent by Mallory and Irvine became smaller. In 1933 Ruttledge's companions Harris and Wager discovered at a height of about 8,450 metres under the first step a Swiss ice axe which could only have belonged to the missing Mallory–Irvine rope. This does not exclude the possibility that Irvine, the weaker of the two, descended alone and thereby slipped and fell on the downward sloping rock slabs. And Mallory? Did he reach the top alone? Perhaps my wish for a hero is the father of this thought.

The mystery of the deaths of Mallory and Irvine fills my dreams; so does their intrepidness, Mallory's mental attitude to mountaineering:

'Have we vanquished an enemy? None but ourselves. Have we gained success? That word means nothing here. Have we won a kingdom? No . . . and yes'.

Only in 1953 with their ninth, perfectly organized expedition, this time on the Nepalese south side of Everest,

F.S. Smythe who succumbed to hallucinations on Everest in 1933.

49

did the English come away with proof of an ascent. Edmund Hillary and Sherpa Tenzing Norgay not only stood on the summit of the highest mountain in the world, they came back safe and sound. The mountain was climbed in 1953, that is certain. Not so clear-cut, however, is the answer to the question: were Hillary and Tenzing really the first men up there? Although Hillary found no traces of possible predecessors, the doubt remains.

Meeting with Nena

In my hotel room in Kathmandu I am reading one of the old Everest books:

'At great heights climbers have frequently noticed a lack of clarity of thought. Of course it is hard for a dulled brain to recognize stupidity, but still I hold it not impossible that Everest climbers try to drink their food, go backwards, or do other comic things. In thin air it is not only hard to think clearly, it is also extremely difficult to suppress the desire to do nothing. If something were able to rob us of success then in first place I would put the lack of will-power caused by oxygen starvation.'

Bulle comes to mind, and how he had bent back to look up the face on Ama Dablam when the stones were falling. There had been nothing stupid in his appearance, quite the contrary. With an odd tensed expression, as if he were holding his breath, he appeared to me more quick-witted than ever. His instincts were alert like those of a beast of prey.

Smiling, I put the book aside and glance at my wrist-watch: seven o'clock. I yield to a pleasant tiredness. Satisfied that I can remain lying in bed another half hour, I roll on my back, cross my arms behind my head and reflect. Now that I have returned from the mountains two things concern me: one is the office time at home, the other the solo project. With each expedition a mass of mail remains unattended to and with ever more leeway to make up, I face such a feeling of obligation on the return journey that I see no hope of being able to keep pace with it all. With the help that people now and again offer me I can deal with a part to be sure, but the main work I often put off for weeks on end.

My other concern is, as before, the notion of a solo ascent of Everest. I am obsessed with the idea of making an attempt in 1980, whatever the cost. Also, I want to be rid of the risk of annoying my business partner who expects more productive work from me than another risk-intensive adventure. Over breakfast, a German tourist sits down at my table. Early forties, medium build, overweight. He belongs to the type who would never set foot on a mountain, but nevertheless is unconsciously aggressive towards anyone who spends his free time without the aid of a well-organized travel bureau. We strike up a conversation.

'Why are you really travelling in the Himalaya?' he asks.

'Perhaps only because it is the Himalaya.'

'I saw a film of your K2 expedition. Climbing. Moving up, one little step at a time. Breathing in. Breathing out. Always the same. Loading something heavy on to your shoulders, groaning with exertion, then plodding ever upward, all the time with the risk that you may fall. And apparently you spend most of your income from writing on mountaineering. On such a senseless thing.'

I do not answer.

'I must say, I am sorry for your parents. First they send you off to study, only to learn that their son is doing nothing but climb all over the place. Divorced too, aren't you?'

'Is this a sermon?' I ask.

'No, I want to help you, by making it clear to you for once what you are doing with your life. Always higher, always that bit farther away from other people. No one can understand you any longer. How will it end?'

I look at him and can picture to myself that he feels better in the warmth of the masses, where he can

Nena Holguin.

forget his isolation. I finish my breakfast very quickly. How should I make this man understand the fascination of high altitude mountaineering? How should such a person, to whom pleasant well-being and the feeling of security in a society are important, understand that I have my most intense feelings of existence only when, through strain and most

extreme exertion, I achieve the bounds of human possibility, and attempt to push these bounds still further? That I can endure my loneliness better when I am far away from other people?

In the evening I meet Bulle in the old town for a meal, and talk to him about it.

While we are waiting for our steaks Nena comes in, an American whom we have already met in Tengpoche on the march in, and who turned up in our base camp after we had rescued Peter Hillary and his New Zealand climbing partner from the West Face of Ama Dablam. Now she is on her way to Canada, to look for work there. Immediately it occurs to me that after my return to Europe I am to begin a strenuous lecture tour, and out of the blue I ask her whether during this tour she would care to undertake the role of my technical assistant. I explain to her what it entails and as equally spontaneously as I asked, she agrees. Nena has recorded our meeting in her diary.

When I felt myself to be in a rather depressed state on account of a one-sided attraction to my New Zealand friend Peter Hillary, I was more than ready to change my life, to begin to live again, to laugh. On 7 November 1979 I said goodbye to Peter at the airport in Kathmandu. For me it was a definite leave-taking. I tried imparting all my positive feelings to Peter but there was little of our attraction left. When I considered the whole situation, I recognized that the cruel experience on Ama Dablam was not really a misfortune for him, but far more a big stride towards learning to know himself. Something he needed much more than me. As the machine took off, I felt both sadness and pleasure at feeling new and whole again.

Towards evening I say goodbye to my friends Merv and Ariane with whom I have been living in an apartment of the 'Himalayan Society' in Kathmandu. I go into town, seeking for something. I am not sure what I am really looking for but I say on departure, 'I'm going to town. Who knows, perhaps something will come my way that will change my whole life.' At 7 o'clock I enter the 'KC', a simple steak house. It is full, no single tables still free. I look around and, as I turn round and want to go, my gaze meets a pair of eyes which look at me full of meaning. The man smiles in friendly fashion, and at once I have the same feeling as that time in the Ama Dablam base camp. I cannot do anything about it. I remember what I thought then: 'There is tremendous power and energy in this man.' When I had gone up to him in the base camp, in order to give him a kiss as a thank you for his help, Reinhold took me in his arms. He had brought my friends down from the mountain when the position was already hopeless.

And now he is sitting in front of me. He says: 'Come and sit down here and eat something with us.' Bulle and two Canadian girls are with him. First I ask if I am not disturbing them but he quickly makes a place

between himself and one of the girls. I could not say no. There is an irresistible force which draws me when close to this man. We talk late into the night. I explain that I must return to Canada and look around for work for the winter. Reinhold proposes instead that I go on a lecture tour with him in Europe.

I think hard about it. I weigh up the good sides and the danger, which could be connected with it, one against the other. I have nothing to lose. At 11 p.m. I finally decide to do it. I don't know whether Reinhold is shocked by my decision, but I believe not. He seems to be a fairly uncomplicated person. After I have taken my leave of him and received a kiss on the cheek, I return to the apartment at one o'clock in the morning. I sit myself down, somewhat exhausted but very excited. I want to wake up Ariane and tell her what has happened. However, I get into bed instead and before I fall asleep thank God that I have always been one of those people who follow their impulses. I remember all the adventures which my mother had dreamed of but not been able to experience. She grew up in another generation. Times then were more difficult.

Oswald Oelz with Peter Hillary during the rescue on the West Face of Ama Dablam.

The summit pyramid of Mount Everest from the south.

As a child my mother had to work hard in order to support her family.

I spend the next day on travel preparations. In the evening I stroll with Reinhold through the colourful market, and we go for a meal. Only once am I startled by him: on the way to the restaurant in the taxi Reinhold pulls me close and says: 'I love you.' That's strange, I think, you hardly know me.

Two days later we fly from Kathmandu to Munich. I still haven't told Nena much about my new plan. Only now and then do I give vent to my determination for the Everest solo climb. Perhaps it is the weight of work at home, hectic Europe, and the new relationship that push my scheme into the background. The obsession of my days in Kathmandu has become weaker. To be sure I tell friends of my idea, but in lonely hours and before sleeping doubts come to me. I need time.

Strength grows slowly in the heart of a lone wolf. It must grow, until it bursts upon me, it must grow like love. If this passionate strength fails, all action becomes calculation, determination only a matter of judgement. And what has reason to put up against the deadly risk of avalanches, crevasses and exhaustion? Too little.

Firmness, especially severity towards oneself, cannot be learned overnight. Concentrated energy stores itself up only in the long period of waiting, hoping. Only when an idea has become a passion does it become independent and seek an outlet, at any price. But all passion fizzles out without willpower, and this will-power must become perseverance, a toughness not paralysed by altitude.

53

Kangchung –
Taboos and Mysteries

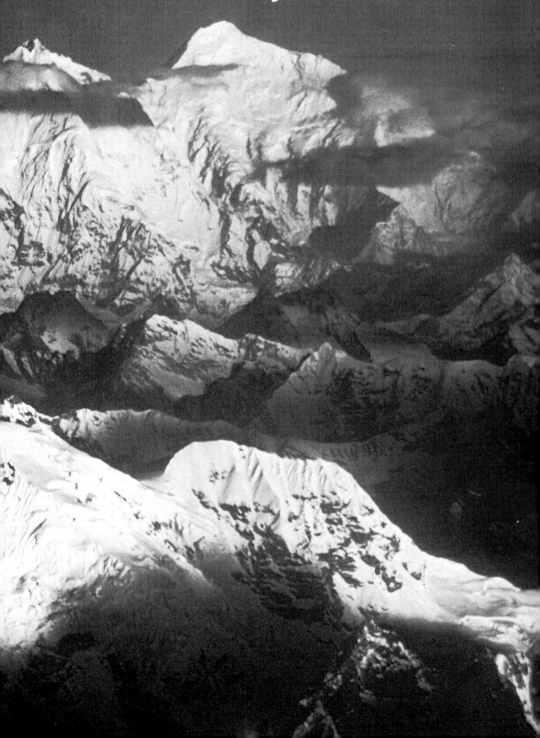

Foolish are you, who in the midst of life
do not sense the coming of death;
for all that you do and hold great
is worth nothing in that moment.

From Dardò Thödol

Kangchung –
Taboos and Mysteries

Back in Europe

Neon lights flare and go out again. The sky over Zurich-Klothen is inflamed. Bulle is seized with a feeling of helplessness. Each time he returns from the mountains and is thrust back among crowds of people he feels a longing for human intimacy, but does not know where to find it. This time a sort of bodily pain overtakes him in night-time Zurich. Imprisoned suddenly in the noise of the modern metropolis, it is as if he were paralysed.

The same evening in Munich a period of hard work begins for me. Of course I am not alone – Nena is with me – but forty lectures without a single free day, and a book that is to be edited at the same time, are too much after six weeks in Nepal.

As a climber I have a strong affinity with Bulle; now each of us goes his own way. What do I know of Bulle's private life, what do I see of it, what lies beyond our common adventure? Little. I only know that he also takes up his work again, pursuing it with the same great enthusiasm he has for climbing, but with the ulterior motive of departing as soon as possible on the next expedition.

Someone who, like him, has grown up in the mountains can live all the year round in the town, as a scholar works and develops his thesis, but there is one thing he cannot do: remain there for ever. When he sees the sun

break through the clouds and feels the wind in his face, he dreams like a young lad of new mountain adventures. With me, it is the same.

In the first few days I don't identify with Europe – as if I had transferred my future to Nepal. At Customs they search through all my crates for dope and through my passport for indications that I may be a terrorist. My hair, too, is somewhat longer than usual. The fact that I do not return like any normal subject costs me a hour's waiting in passport control at Frankfurt. Yet I am in a tremendous hurry. My lecture chase across the most important cities of Germany, Austria and Switzerland is due to start the day after my arrival. Each evening an illustrated lecture about my solo ascent of Nanga Parbat, each day a 100–400 kilometre car journey. After each lecture a public discussion – for me by far the most positive and interesting part of the work. On 11 November in Cologne I am describing my ascent of the Diamir Face and the history of the peak. The questions from the public, however, overstretch these bounds. I am pleased and give out information patiently.

'Do you want to climb Mount Everest solo too?'

'I'd rather not say at this time.'

'Is it your intention to climb all the eight-thousanders?'

'I haven't planned it.'

'On your K2 expedition, why did you switch over to the Abruzzi Ridge? You said once that you'd rather fail on an unknown route than repeat an existing one.'

'Yes, I did say on one occasion that I would rather give up an eight-

Reinhold Messner lecturing.

thousander than climb it by a known route. 'Known' however means for me not only that the route has been done but also the method, and the tactics. I left for K2 with the intention of climbing a new route. Bad weather and accidents during the walk-in obliged us to give up this plan. We then switched to the Abruzzi Ridge. We conquered this too but in a manner in which it has not been repeated to this day: without high altitude porters, without oxygen, with a bivouac at a height of 8,000 metres.'

'I have read somewhere that you want to give up mountaineering.'

'I have never said publicly, or in front of journalists, that I would renounce climbing for ever. I did once say – at a press conference and, as

generally happens, someone twisted it – I would gladly renounce an eight-thousander if I were to get the opportunity to cross Tibet or the Gobi Desert. By that I only wanted to point out that such a thing interests and attracts me just as strongly as climbing the Eiger North Face or ascending Nanga Parbat. Whether I shall ever give up climbing I cannot say, because I still want to do it and I shall always do what I want, so long as our government, the world political situation and my means permit me.'

'You are against technical aids in climbing. Where do you draw the line?'

'Everybody uses technical aids in some way. My boots, clothing, ice axe, cooker to make tea, these are all technical aids. Each person can do what he wants. I dispense with substantial technical aids. By that I mean oxygen gear, expansion bolts, helicopters – in short, gear with which the impossible may be made possible. I would rather cope with the possible with my own abilities and not with the help of technology.'

'Doesn't ambition alone lie behind that?'

'I have always been accused of wanting to climb without oxygen, just to satisfy my ambition, but this is only

'In 1978, after the Nanga Parbat solo climb, I said to myself, mountaineering-wise I have achieved more than I ever wanted to achieve. I had certainly dreamed of a solo ascent of an eight-thousander, and the success did my mountaineering ambition good. Meanwhile I have grown older. But I still feel strong, I still have the desire, and fortunately today I could even afford to travel to Tibet. For ten years, since I began my expeditions, I have had to deny myself great

Reinhold Messner and the public.

partly true. I do have a fair amount of ambition and it seems to me that I am one of the few mountaineers who stand by their ambition. In general, however, ambition leads to pretence and not the reverse.'

'Have you still got mountaineering pipe-dreams?'

journeys.'

'Does your enthusiasm hold good only for mountaineering?'

'By and large I do everything with enthusiasm, as long as it doesn't concern bureaucracy, which I hate like the plague.'

'Is there another climb to come?'

'I would like to travel to Tibet, to South America, I would like to experience so many countries, get to know so many areas. I can't step up my performance any more. I know that in recent years I have reached my limit several times, if not overstepped it. I would be a fool if I did not recognize this.'

'How do you explain not having suffered any brain damage from that?'

'Thank you for the compliment! There are people who say I am obviously not quite right in the head.'

In the often half-hour discussions we don't only talk about climbing. I sense that my way of life attracts more people than the 'sensation' with which my evenings are sold. There are sociological, political, above all critical questions.

'I think you are running away, or in the mid-life crisis', says a man of similar age to me in Vienna.

'If being for activity and against bureaucracy, for uncertainty and against middle-class sufficiency, for the last wild places on earth and against the exploitation of nature constitutes flight, then, gladly, I am on the run.'

'And what do you do for the community?'

'Nothing. On the contrary I love experiments, adventure, I am therefore a danger to this industrious, timid and unimaginative society.'

When the discussion spills over into politics I always feel unhappy. I hate sterile ideological debates, meaningless proposals for world improvement. The consciousness of the individual must alter. All other political commitment is lost time, wasted strength.

'You are passing reality by,' people often say to me.

'I don't consider myself to be enlightened but are you sure you see reality as it actually is? I am seeking and I suppose it is immaterial what I do. The only important thing is that I remain in motion and don't become settled.'

The mood of the listeners tells me that I have come up against a fundamental point there. Is it this impulse to seek, to venture the leap into the unknown, which many perceive and which so few follow? Is my generation in Europe therefore sick, because it lives in conflict, hungry for adventure but instead locked up in a little house and garden? Some are shocked, others converse excitedly about my answers. Not only with my talk but also with my music have I distracted people this evening. In some parts of the lecture I fade in music: 'Oxygen' by Jean Michel Jarre, because these synthesizer tones render especially well the atmosphere of great height and thin air, and 'Single Man' by Elton John, because therein I recognise my solo feelings. For the traditionalists among the climbers, all this is too progressive.

'Rubbish, utter rubbish, this music belongs on the rubbish heap. It is not worthy of your splendid adventures,' a woolly-clothed Alpine friend with blazing eyes says excitedly. And, 'We are not in a disco here!' an indignant lady reproaches me. Ah yes, I have forgotten once again that the mountains are to be presented solemnly. They won't grasp that I of all people, who come from a South Tyrol mountain valley, cannot identify with the clangour of an organ and Sunday yodelling.

Shortly before midnight I finally fall dead tired into my hotel bed. But I find no peace there either. The heating is on full blast and the dry air parches my throat. Why must I be afflicted with this stifling heat after having endured so much glacial cold, I ask myself, before I fall asleep exhausted.

Frequently, when I leaf through the local newspaper in the morning and find an article about my lecture, the quotations are freely invented or so deformed as to be unrecognizable. Often I get proposals, even prescriptions for my conduct, because by my activities I am apparently a questionable model. I am accustomed to other mountaineers knowing better than I myself, what I should have done in this or that situation. However, it is hard for me to believe that my lecture public can demand that I adapt myself. And because I do not fulfil this demand

I am often disowned. Adjustment has always been very difficult for me. I try in a few months of the year to earn my livelihood and finance the next expedition. Sometimes when too many target dates accumulate I lose peace of mind and fail to make clear decisions. I then become chronically absent-minded and it takes all my concentration to produce an exciting and generally understandable lecture in the evening.

Also, my fans give me a great deal of trouble. It has always been inexplicable to me what point autographs have. In the lecture intervals I sign them until my fingers ache. Were I to refuse, no one would understand and I find it tedious to debate the sense or nonsense of my signature each time. I am a circus horse and keep to the rules of the game. With a skittish sideways glance at Nena, who is slaving over

Geschichte der Expedition zum K 2

Reinhold Messner – Abenteurer des zwanzigsten Jahrhunderts

1200 Menschen hören den berühmten Bergsteiger in der Kantine der Hoechst AG in Bobingen

Bobingen (lf). Etwa 1200 Menschen besuchten am Samstagabend in der Kantine der Hoechst-Werke Bobingen den Vortrag Reinhold Messners über die Besteigung des zweithöchsten Berges der Welt, des K2 im Karakorum-Massiv. Dieser namenlose Berg, von keinem bewohnten Ort sichtbar, wurde zum erstenmal 1856 gesichtet. Unter begeistertem Beifall aller Besucher konnte Direktor Laber von den Hoechst-Werken Bobingen den berühmten Gast begrüßen. Die Karten für diesen Abend waren schon vor Monaten bei der Skischule Käufl, dem Initiator des Abends, ausverkauft gewesen. Käufl sollte Reinhard Messner selbst seine ganz eigene Anerkennung: Mut, sagte er, habe schon dazugehört, diesen Abend vor seiner Expedition vom Mount Everest zu buchen, denn die Chancen seiner Rückkehr von diesem seinem gewagtesten Unternehmen, dem Alleingang ohne Sauerstoff, seien in der Tat gering gewesen.

Als der magere 36jährige mit den asketischen Zügen auf der Bühne die ersten Worte spricht, verstummt jeder Laut, er spricht gut artikuliert, mit ausdrucksstarker Stimme, ohne jede Prätension, mit karger Geste. Man spürt: wenn er auch gerade eine gedrängte Vortragsreise fast hinter sich hat, sogar sich allabendlich der Diskussion stellt (,,jeder soll in diesem demokratischen Staat das Recht haben, mich mit Fragen zu fordern, ich stelle mich jeder Diskussion; ich sehe überhaupt meine Vortragsreise als Konkurrenz für Fernsehen und Rundfunk, wo der Zuschauer passiv bleiben muß . . .''), so spürt man doch, daß er eigentlich ein

Friedl Mutschlechner nach Askole zurückgetragen werden.

Die Expedition bewegt sich, geleitet von den sieben Europäern, langsam auf dem Batroro-Gletscher, der sich wie eine überdimensionale Autobahn durch das Gebirgsmassiv zieht, langsam vorwärts. Der Aufstieg beginnt nach einem etwa 60 Kilometer langen Treck zum Basislager und steht schon am 9. Juni unter einem schlechten Vorzeichen, als sich ein Träger entgegen einem sicheren Rastplatz entfernt, in eine Gletscherspalte fällt und aus 15 Metern Tiefe nur noch tot geborgen werden kann. Die Sherpas rebellieren, wollen

Zermürbendste und Deprimierendste, was die 8000er zu bieten haben, weil du dir vorkommst wie ein kleiner Ohrenkäfer, der aus einer Badewanne zu krabbeln versucht.'' Steckenweise ist diese Schneewand so steil wie ein Kirchdach. In der Tortur äußerster Erschöpfung machen sie weiter, jeder hoffend, daß der andere aufgibt, nur gebunden von diesem verbissenen Ringen miteinander. Später gestehen sie sich, daß die kleinste Andeutung des Aufgebenwollens für den anderen genügt hätte. Plötzlich bricht die Sonne über sie herein, sie haben den Gipfel erreicht. Erschöpft, aber glücklich sehen sie sich um; Reinhold Messner spricht durch Funk mit dem Basislager — wieder wie so oft bewegt ihn die momentane Sehnsucht für immer auf dem Gipfel zu bleiben. Sie reißen sich los, um den Abstieg rechtzeitig zu schaffen. Er ist leichter, als sie ihn sich vorgestellt hatten, sie erreichen das Biwaklager in zwei Stunden. Die Nacht im Zelt ist sturmdurchheult, Schlaf ist schwierig in solchen Höhen. Messner und Dacher wälzen sich ruhelos auf ihren Matten, die Kälte durchdringt sie. Sie erinnern sich oft gegenseitig ans Trinken und Essen. Die

Newspaper critique of lecture: 'Reinhold Messner – Twentieth Century Adventurer'.

the projectors, quite strange women make me the most remarkable offers. Quite strange men, not likewise motivated, want me to drink a beer with them. They can all produce a reason for wanting to talk to me. I believe the main reason for it is the longing of frightened and lonely people to experience through me some fantasy in their own lives. I am confronted with loneliness and used as a substitute for what they are missing. It makes me tired and burdens me.

Halfway through the lecture tour the 'Spiegel' reporter Joachim Hoelzgen, a friend from Hamburg who was on K2 with me, slips into my hand the 'Peking Review' of 20 November 1979. It states that eight mountains in China will be made available to foreign alpinists. From this moment on I know that I shall travel to China.

Peking

It is immediately clear to me, after this official announcement, that the race will be on for China's mountains. For too long too many ambitious climbers have waited for this opportunity. The applications will pile up. In order to have the slightest chance in the negotiations I must go at once to Peking [Beijing]. But how? The fact that the Chinese have put a high price on their co-operation must not be allowed to hinder me. I must find someone to help me in getting hold of this presumably vast sum. I reflect, I need a sponsor, and it must be a sponsor to whom I can offer something in return for his commitment. The sale of film rights occurs to me.

Reinhold Messner signing autographs.

Eight mountains in China accessible
to foreign alpinists
From 1980 onwards, eight Chinese peaks
will be accessible to foreign alpinists:
- ☐ 8,848 metres high Chomolungma
  (Mount Everest), the highest summit in
  the world, on the Chinese-Nepalese
  border, the north side of which lies in the
  Chinese Autonomous Region of Tibet.
- ☐ 8,012 metres high Shisha Pangma
  (Xixabangma) in Tibet.
- ☐ 7,546 metres high Muztagata in
  Sinkiang (Xinjian).
- ☐ Kongur and Kongur Tiubie Tagh in
  Sinkiang, twin summits 7,719 and
  7,795 metres high respectively.
- ☐ 5,445 metres high Bogda in Sinkiang,
  the highest elevation in the eastern part
  of the Tian Shan Range. It consists of
  seven summits and at its foot is located
  the world famous Tian-Chi Lake
  (Heavenly Pool).
- ☐ 7,590 metres high Minya Konka
  (Gongga Shan) in Szechuan (Sichuan).
- ☐ 7,160 metres high Anye Machin
  (Anyemaqen) in Chinghai (Qinghai).
- ☐ The Chinese Mountaineering
  Association will concern itself with the
  transaction of the formalities with
  foreign mountaineers, such as
  contracts, permit, fees and assistance.
- ☐ In south-west and north-west China
  there are many high peaks. With the
  growth of foreign expeditions more
  peaks will in future be made accessible,
  in the interest of the promotion of
  international alpinism and the
  strengthening of the friendship between
  the peoples of China and other
  countries.

During our involuntary, and as it turned out thrilling, Ama Dablam expedition we shot a film for Bavaria-Film-Gesellschaft, and the collaboration with the people at 'Bavaria' was excellent. So I call up Jürgen Lehmann, the producer responsible then. He understands at once what it is all about and is ready to join in. The unknown, hidden Tibet of today and my solo attempt on Everest fascinates him as much as it does me.

He moves heaven and earth and a few weeks later we are sitting in the plane for Peking like two excited trailblazers on a hot scent. High above the clouds I tell Jürgen how I saw Tibet for the first time. I was standing on the summit of Manaslu and gazed down on the country of my longing. In spite of my exhaustion a wave of excitement rose in me. Beneath me a sea of rocks spread out far and wide, high tablelands and snow mountains. An unending, unspoiled landscape over which clouds moved in grotesque formations. My whole being became so deeply immersed in them, it was hard to tear myself away again. From then on I have been waiting for a new opportunity to enjoy them more intensively than through a view from the summit of an eight-thousander.

In Peking we are picked up at the airport by a friendly delegation from the CMA, the Chinese Mountaineering Association, with whom the German Embassy has meanwhile made contact for us. Sepia-brown, the city stretches endlessly into the distance, little houses as small as boxes crammed together, now and then a prosaic concrete block, everywhere dust. On the broad asphalt streets rolls a dense stream of black bicycles ridden by blue-clothed Chinese. Many women protect their faces from the all-penetrating dust with filmy scarves and look like wrapped-up dolls. At the crossings giant placards exhort the populace to cleanliness and order. In glaring colours regular cleaning of is accessible to everyone. Amidst garlic steam poor Chinese from the provinces press their noses flat against the glass in order to gaze in wonder at the unimaginable jewels of the imperial concubines. If things are better for them today compared with yesterday, the Chinese are still poor, despite Mao's long freedom march, despite strenuous attempts at industrialization, despite the radical sacrifice of each individualistic impulse. I have

Peking.

teeth and washing of hands before eating are taught. In dreadful contrast to the catastrophic need for living space, in the centre of the city the Great Square spreads out, grey, deserted, a gigantic parade ground for ideological march-pasts. In the middle Mao's mausoleum: an enormous house for a small corpse.

The square is flanked by the red walls of the 'Forbidden City'. Today it time only for fleeting observations, for it is filled with endless negotiations with the Chinese Mountaineering Association. There, restraint, ceremony and courtesy determine relations with me, the stranger. The functionaries speak of friendship and at the same time want to charge me an astronomical price for an expedition permit. The tourist, as well as the 'extremist' like me, is to become one of the most important of China's sources of foreign currency, that much I understand after a few hours.

These are the days in which in Peking the pictures of Marx and Engels disappear once more from the walls. It seems to me, with the overthrow of the group around Mao's widow, that the writings of Lenin and Mao are also defunct. Mao's successors are now trying slowly to resolve the inner contradictions in their country which plague all socialist systems. More trade, more self-responsibility means foreign currency. The interaction of supply and demand is to have an effect again. The new China seems certain to remain communist in the future – the means of production belong to the people as a whole and not to private individuals – but the economy is to obey other laws: free markets with competition for consumer goods, varying rewards for work of varying quality. Peking seems to me like a big laboratory. The transposition appears to advance very cautiously and in small steps. In front of the doors of the state shops I see small stalls with fresh meat, vegetables and fruit, run by street traders and peasants. Already private traders supply restaurants with ducks and poisonous snakes which rate as delicacies.

Finally the CMA grants me a permit for the solo ascent of Chomolungma. I learn of the extremely high transport and accommodation costs in Tibet and spend the whole night in my hotel room anxiously adding up figures. Result: the expedition will cost me US $40,000 to $50,000. Next morning I sign a protocol, a sort of expedition contract.

The summer park of the Emperor of China.

It is done! I am, therefore, to be given a second time on Mount Everest. Again without oxygen, but this time also without a climbing partner, without a fixed chain of camps, without porters, and over a new route on the Tibetan side.

On the evening of 3 April, the day of the contract signing, Jürgen and I dine in company with senior personalities from the world of sport and of the CMA, twelve of us in all, in a separate room of a restaurant, served by studious waiters. It is a tradition at such meals that each person gives a speech. Each of these speeches is ended with a 'Gánpéi', which means more or less 'finished', and on this command all empty their schnapps glasses. A strenuous tradition and when my turn comes I say: 'I give thanks for your friendliness. This is the most expensive expedition permit of my life,

Protocol concerning the ascent of Chomolungma by the Italian mountaineer Reinhold Messner

The request of the Italian mountaineer Reinhold Messner to carry out an expedition in China is granted by the Chinese Mountaineering Association. This expedition serves to promote the friendship and understanding between the Chinese, Italian and German peoples. In friendly consultation the representatives of the Chinese Mountaineering Association and Herr Reinhold Messner have committed themselves to the following:

1. Description of the expedition:
   First solo ascent in summer 1980 to the summit of Chomolungma by Reinhold Messner
   Total number of participants:
   Two (R. Messner and one medical attendant)
   Leader of the climbing team:
   Reinhold Messner
   The accredited representative in Peking of Herr Reinhold Messner:
   The Embassy of the Federal Democratic Republic of Germany in Peking.

2. Programme of the ascent:
   Aim:
   Ascent of Chomolungma
   Route:
   North side
   Approach route:
   Peking–Chengdu–Lhasa–Shigatse –Shekar (Xegur)–Base Camp
   Scientific Research:
   Meteorological observations of temperature, atmospheric pressure and amount of precipitation in the rainy season

Duration of ascent:
From June to 31 August 1980
Arrival mid-May – Departure beginning September.

3. The Chinese Mountaineering Association will nominate a liaison officer and interpreter, who will accompany and advise Herr Messner during the expedition. The CMA will place two yak drivers and two yaks at Herr Messner's disposal.

4. Transport obligations of the Chinese Mountaineering Association:
   For the journey from Lhasa to Chomolungma main camp, a jeep with seven places; for the return journey from main camp via research on Shisha Pangma and then Lhasa, a jeep with seven places.

5. Provisions:
   On reaching main camp the Chinese Mountaineering Association takes over provisions for all Chinese participants. R. Messner and his companion will provision themselves as from arrival in main camp and will provide 100 litres of petrol for the Chinese attendants.

6. R. Messner shall, before 31 May 1980, send to the Chinese Mountaineering Association a list of the items of equipment and the ascent fee for Chomolungma and the research fee for Shisha Pangma (4,080 Yuan) and the estimated costs (ca. 33,000 Yuan).

In Behai Park.

7. The CMA shall, before the end of April, forward to Herr Messner the measurements and shoe sizes of the Chinese participants.

8. Herr Messner shall observe the instructions of the Chinese Mountaineering Association for the carrying out of foreign expeditions in China. He shall settle the costs in accordance with the directions of the CMA. Account 81-89013199/Bank of the People's Republic of China in Peking.

9. During the discussion the Chinese Mountaineering Association has noted that Herr Messner wishes, in spring 1981, to undertake the ascent of Shisha Pangma. That will be negotiated in July 1980.

10. The foregoing specific points were dealt with in detailed consultations. Changes or supplements to this protocol can be made by both sides by mutual agreement.

11. This protocol shall be signed on 3 April 1980 by Herr Messner and Mr Shi Zhanchung, representative of the Chinese Mountaineering Association in Peking.

This protocol shall be drawn up in two copies, in the Chinese and German languages. Both wordings are equally valid. The protocol comes into force on the day of signing.

Reinhold Messner   Shi Zhanchung

                    Vice-Chairman of
                    the Chinese
                    Mountaineering
                    Association

Peking, 3 April 1980

purchased on capitalist principles in a communist country. Gánpéi.'

'If you haven't eaten Peking duck, you don't know Peking', runs a proverb. It was served to us in twelve different ways – roasted, in jelly, minced, in sauce, in pastry . . . If much has been lost in the way of culture in the epoch of the revolution, one thing stands fast: nowhere is cooking more imaginative and nowhere are the meals so truly works of art as in the poor People's Republic of China. Here a tradition of the decadent world of the emperor is cherished with full devotion, and I can not believe my ears when during dessert a waiter proudly declares to me that the little marzipan cakes were a favourite dish of the Empress Se-chi. On my return to Europe I rave about this tremendous gourmet evening in the Middle Kingdom for a long time.

Jul, a South Tyrol friend, is one of the first people I tell about my new permit. We sit late into the night in my

67

Messner's 1980 expedition brochure (Everest – South, Everest – North, Everest – Solo).

house in Villnöss, fool around, and he tells my fortune by the cards. These foretell quite other things: 'You believe that you have settled up with some people. But you have overthrown them without tasting the content of their goblets. You must be wary that you do not overturn the good friends, who at this moment support you, who stand behind you, through a high-handed stroke. They will help you to cross a river, if you move into a completely new, if also outwardly old, house.'

I love the Tarot oracle, full of riddles, and Jul's interpretations. And I really have the feeling of crossing a river. Jul thinks I'm mad because of my 'solo' idea. To want to climb alone up the highest mountain in the world, he thinks, can only occur to a madman like me. So I tell him that long before I came along, there was such a madman. He was called Maurice Wilson.

Maurice Wilson

The first person who wanted to climb Mount Everest alone was the Englishman Maurice Wilson. He was no mountaineer, rather a religious fanatic. He firmly believed that a person who was purified through belief and fasting could overcome everything in the world, even the highest peak on earth. Like Columbus and Thor Heyerdahl he wanted to prove a theory by a deed. Columbus knew that the world was round. In order to prove it, he tried to sail round it. Maurice Wilson knew that with God's help man can do anything. To prove it he wanted to climb Mount Everest. With that belief began one of the most bizarre chapters in the history of Everest. But how did Wilson arrive at his conviction?

Born in 1898, the son of an industrious man who by his own efforts had built up a small woollen mill, Maurice Wilson grew up in Bradford as the third of four sons. He was a diligent pupil, and by the age of twelve spoke fluent French and German. In 1916 he enlisted in the army, one day after his eighteenth birthday. He became a lance-corporal, then lieutenant and was decorated for his bravery and devotion to duty. Shortly afterwards, badly wounded by machine gun fire in the left arm and chest, he was invalided home. Like many of his generation he could not forget the horrors of the trenches, and was unable to fit into civilian life again. Fruitlessly he asked himself what the sense and purpose of his life was. His father's factory with its monotonous work quickly oppressed him, and he went to London. There he fared no better and like so many other ex-soldiers who could not find their way, he emigrated. At first to New York, then San Francisco and finally to New Zealand, where he remained for several years. He sold vehicles, then a quack medicine, tried his hand at agriculture and went at last to Wellington where for a time he owned a small ladies' dress shop.

Acting on a sudden impulse, he returned to England on a mailboat. Until then, he had been neither successful nor a failure; but he was unlucky. And still the big man, strong as a bear, had no aim in life. On board ship he met some Indian yogis who impressed him with their teachings about self-discipline.

Back in London he visited his parents and got to know new friends,

Maurice Wilson.

among them Leonard Evans and his wife Enid, on whom he at once developed a crush. Frustrated and depressed, his physical condition also deteriorated. He lost weight and was racked by coughing spasms. He declined conventional medical treatment and one day he vanished without trace. When he turned up again he was better. Secretly he had undergone a mysterious cure, fasted for thirty-five days, drunk only sips of water now and then and prayed constantly. Thereafter he was well and happy – and he had found his purpose in life.

He had discovered a panacea for all ills but he knew that with his conviction he would be only one prophet among many. If he wanted to make the human race pay attention to his new-found healing method he must light a beacon.

After this period of suffering and fasting he took himself off to the Black Forest. And here, in a small café in Freiburg, he read quite by chance an old newspaper cutting with a report of the 1924 Mount Everest expedition. He read about the Sherpas and yaks which carried the loads, about glaciers, storms and insurmountable obstacles. And he asked himself whether with fasting and faith one really could overcome everything. He was convinced of it and wanted to prove it. He would climb Mount Everest, alone, relying only on the power of his faith. Everest! Now he knew what he had to do and nothing could keep him from it. At last the world would pay attention.

It was a fantastic, mad idea. Wilson did not know the first thing about mountaineering. Returning to London he at once began his preparations. He studied all the reports of previous expeditions. These should have convinced him that his plan was hopeless, but he remained determined to realize his undertaking without the cumbersome transport and string of camps of his predecessors. When he heard of the Houston flight over Everest, planned for 1933, his first thought was to persuade the team to take him with them, and to make a parachute jump over

Everest. This idea was quickly abandoned. Instead he wanted to fly to Tibet himself, make a crash landing on the East Rongbuk Glacier and set out on foot for the summit. The fact that he entertained such thoughts in itself proves that he had not the slightest notion of the region. No notion of Everest, no notion of mountaineering, no notion of flying. His friends were horrified. However he only smiled and said: 'I know. But I can learn all that.'

He bought himself a three-year-old second-hand 'Gipsy Moth', a biplane, had 'EVER WREST' painted on its fuselage and took flying lessons at the London Aero Club. After the first joint flight it was already clear to his instructor that Wilson would never make a good pilot. But the eccentric pupil possessed two qualities with which he made up for his deficiency: courage and determination. Nevertheless the flying instructor considered Wilson had no chance of reaching India alive. To fly more than 8,000 kilometres in an open biplane over what at that time were still totally undeveloped regions would have been a master performance even for experienced pilots. For an inexperienced pilot it was a risk that must end in catastrophe.

Unperturbed, Wilson carried on. He bought himself equipment for his mountain adventure: tent, sleeping-bag, light clothing. He purchased an altimeter as well as a lightweight camera with a self-timer. With it he wanted to photograph himself on the summit.

Then he began to train for the climbing. Several times he walked on foot from London to Bradford and back, in nailed boots, heavily loaded. Then he went climbing. For five weeks he scrambled around in the Lake District and Snowdonia, without at any time asking anyone about technique or safety. Instead of letting himself be shown by a Swiss guide how to use crampons and ice-axe, and training in the Alps for great altitude, he climbed eccentrically and naïvely up Snowdon or other relatively harmless mountains in Britain. To test his nerves he made a parachute jump over London.

Meanwhile the press had become aware of his fantastic project, and a fierce controversy raged concerning his actions. Wilson had a special fuel tank built into 'EVER WREST' for long-range flights, and in addition fitted a more robust undercarriage. He provided himself with maps, and carefully marked in the legs of his course. From Freiburg he wanted to fly over the Alps to Milan, Palermo, across the Mediterranean and on to Tunis. Because he wanted to fly without using oxygen, he settled on a ceiling of 3,000 metres. Wilson determined the departure date as 21 April 1933, his birthday. In mid-April he went down with severe tonsilitis. His plans began to totter. But he fasted, prayed, and was soon completely fit again.

On his first flight he had to make an emergency landing. Wilson was lucky that he did not perish. Valuable time slipped away.

Meanwhile the Houston Flight-Over-Everest Expedition had set out and two machines succeeded in flying over Everest. A major expedition under the leadership of Hugh Ruttledge had installed itself in the base camp. If Ruttledge should succeed Wilson would arrive too late to be the first on the summit.

When the 'EVER WREST' was once more ready for take-off the Air Ministry wanted to stop it. Wilson tore up the telegram that forbade him to fly.

On Sunday 21 May 1933 Wilson said goodbye to friends and reporters. He tried to take off down-wind and it was an eternity before the machine rose into the air. Then he flew into the morning sun, became smaller and disappeared. Only a few of those present believed that they would ever see Wilson again. A week later he landed in Cairo. Another week and he would reach India. But in Cairo he was forbidden to fly over Iran. He had to make a direct flight from Baghdad to Bahrein, a flight which with a distance of over 1,000 kilometres tested the most extreme performance limit of his machine. There finally he was denied fuel by the British consul, and had to procure black market petrol. He managed to reach Gwadar in India. In two weeks he had put almost 8,000 kilometres behind him, dramatic proof that he could accomplish impossible-seeming things through will-power. But he would not rest. He must go to Everest.

After this performance he was at last taken seriously. A special correspondent of the *Daily Express* had a lengthy interview with him in Karachi. In Lalbalu near Purneah the journey was temporarily ended. The authorities refused him permission to fly over Nepal. Wilson was in despair. Weeks passed, the monsoon period began, and he saw his chances dwindling. His money ran out. Then he learned of the failure of the Ruttledge expedition, sold 'EVER WREST' for five hundred pounds and made his way to Darjeeling.

As so often, the authorities there refused him permission to cross Sikkim and Nepal on foot. So he contemplated how to reach Tibet illegally. Then he got to know Karma Paul, a Tibetan, who had taken part in the Everest expeditions of 1922, 1924 and 1933. To start with Karma Paul was

had worked as porters with the Rutledge expedition. They were goodnatured and discreet, obtained a horse for the journey, and sewed provisions and equipment into wheat sacks. Wilson gave out that he was going on a tiger hunt, paid for his hotel room six months in advance, and during the night of 21 March 1934 the four of them slipped carefully out of Darjeeling. Nearly a year had elapsed since

Wilson with his 'Ever Wrest'.

enthusiastic about Wilson and promised to accompany him to base camp. Soon, however, the eccentric Englishman began to seem sinister and Karma Paul withdrew.

Meanwhile, it had got to January and Wilson looked around for other help. He needed someone who could take him safely through Tibet, and he found this support in the three Sherpas Tewang, Rinzing and Tsering who

Wilson's departure from England.

So as not to be recognized, the four men travelled at night, Wilson disguised as a Tibetan monk. Thus they made good progress. The Sherpas were excellent guides and solicitous companions. Bypassing towns and villages, the small party marched about twenty-five kilometres each night, through icy streams and scorching heat, through snow drifts and hail showers. They struggled on past Kangchenjunga and at last topped the pass of Kongra La: before them lay Tibet! Vast mountain chains disappeared into the far distant horizon, a sea of brown, violet, olive and white – a moon landscape. Wilson discarded his disguise and at last felt himself free again. They still avoided people and villages but journeyed now by day. Bravely they battled through the daily snowfields blew in strong gusts into their faces. The thin grass disappeared. Rocks, scree and glacier led Wilson up into the world of his dreams. In the valley, that seemed to lead nowhere, the monastery suddenly emerged. Its massive walls appeared dwarfed by the tremendous mountain which formed the back-drop to this world: Mount Everest.

The High Lama of Rongbuk Monas-

Shekar Dzong, two days from base camp on Mount Everest.

sandstorms until finally, on 12 April, Wilson could write in his little diary: 'Saw Everest this morning!'

From a 5,200 metre-high ridge he had an almost unreal view in the crystal clear air of its snow-covered East Flank. It was ideal climbing weather. And two days later the four of them finally reached Rongbuk. An icecold south wind coming down from the tery, regarded by the Tibetans as a highly revered reincarnation, invited Wilson, Tsering, Tewang and Rinzing to an audience. He received them in a richly painted room with elaborately carved door frames and windows with panes of real glass. Wilson's courage and determination impressed the Lama, and he gave Wilson and the Sherpas his blessing.

That night Wilson lay awake for a long time in his tent. Again and again he gazed up at his peak, at Everest, then wrote in his diary: 'Am starting the job tomorrow.'

When on awakening the following morning he heard the deep chanting of the 300 monks of the monastery, he was convinced that they were praying for him. In the most beautiful weather he set off; laden with more than 20 kilos he climbed slowly up the valley to the East Rongbuk Glacier. As all the reports which he had read about this terrain were by outstanding mountaineers who preferred understatement, he was horrified at the bewildering labyrinth of ice towers, crevasses and rock boulders which towered in front of him that day. Laboriously he wandered around in it; exhausted by his load, he made slow progress. Now he had to pay dearly for the fact that he still had no idea how to move on ice. He had no crampons with him, nor could he cut proper steps. By some marvel he avoided falling into any of the countless crevasses. On 16 April, exhausted, he reached Camp II of the earlier expeditions, at a height of 6,035 metres. It began to snow. Weakened, he chewed a few dates and some bread. After an icy night in the tent he set off again. After two further laborious days he finally slumped down at 6,250 metres in the snowstorm. It did not cease snowing, the provisions were at an end. At last he determined to retrace his steps over the dreadful glacier to the safety of the monastery at Rongbuk.

Limping painfully, he got back to Rongbuk again three days later. His eyes were inflamed, his throat dried

High Lama of the Rongbuk Monastery.

up. While Rinzing and Tewang warmed a bowl of soup for him he wrote in a barely legible scrawl in his diary: 'I'll not give up. I still know that I can do it . . . ' Accommodated in an adjoining room of the monastery, Wilson slowly thawed out. When he had consumed his first hot meal for ten days, he began to relate to the Sherpas confused stories about the loneliness, hardship and disappointment on the Rongbuk Glacier. Never before in his life had he so longed for company and friends. Then he slept for thirty-eight hours.

Although after that he was still too weak to get out of his sleeping-bag, he worked out a plan with Rinzing and Tewang for the next attempt. Tsering was suffering from stomach pains and could not accompany them. The two other Sherpas were to climb with him this time as far as Camp III, which lies

On the East Rongbuk Glacier.

under the ice-fall which descends from the North Col. With sufficient provisions they intended to remain there until, in good weather, Wilson could undertake the final spurt for the summit alone. For four days Wilson lay in bed. When on the fifth morning he got up for the first time he was shaky, his feet were swollen, his left arm and his left eye were painful.

Not until the end of the month was he better. On 30 April he wrote:

'Feet and eyes very much better, another few days should see me on the job again. Have lost weight tremendously, but have developed many new muscles since leaving Darjeeling. Soon be fit as ever. The trek to Camp III should be comparatively light this time. Shall take crampons, and will have the boys with me to make something hot. Hope to be off in a few more days.'

On 1 May, however, his left eye was heavily swollen and the left side of his vision partially impaired. He fasted and soon felt better in himself. During his convalescence he frequently took part in the religious rites of the monastery. The serene state of quiet self-contemplation in which the monks lived fascinated him. Farther up the valley lay Chamalung, the 'Sanctuary of the Birds', a small monastery that was hidden amongst steep moraine slopes. It consisted of a row of primi-tive cells where hermits led a life of total seclusion and meditation. The living conditions of these recluses, who hoped through enlightenment to escape from the terrible cycle of rebirth, were for a European scarcely imaginable. One of these monks had already lived there for 15 years, sitting motionless in meditation in a grotto. Once a day his fellow monks handed him a cup of water and a handful of barley flour through a head-sized opening in the cell. It is not very surprising Wilson sensed an inner affinity with these people.

On the evening of 11 May, with Everest covered in mist, Wilson ended his diary entries with the words: 'In any event we're off tomorrow, come what may. Shall be glad to get the job over.'

Tewang had to promise not to sell the little horse and in the case of Wilson's death to hand over a letter to the authorities in Darjeeling. In this

Everest from Rongbuk.

letter he declared that no blame should be attached to the three Sherpas for the forbidden journey through Tibet.

As it was fine on 12 May, Wilson, Tewang and Rinzing left the monastery. The Sherpas were familiar with the terrain of the East Rongbuk Glacier, and after three days they reached the site of Camp III. Nearby they found a food dump left by the Rut-

upper snow-fields of the East Rongbuk Glacier. Even for the most experienced climbers of the time this obstacle had presented great difficulties. Even so, Wilson quite naïvely wrote that evening in his diary: 'Summit and route to it can be seen quite clearly now. Only another 8,000 feet to go.'

On 16 May the three were surprised by a blizzard which pinned them down in Camp III for five days. Freezing,

Hermitage above Rongbuk.

tledge expedition which, by comparison with their scanty victuals, offered a veritable store of delicacies. While Rinzing cooked, Wilson went a bit further, to reconnoitre the route to the North Col. He saw the shattered slopes of the ice-fall, a steep, rugged, constantly changing ice cascade, which soared up some 500 metres above the

they squatted in their tents. The hurricane tore at their nerves, and the high altitude gave them a lot of trouble. When on 21 May the storm had at last blown itself out, Wilson set out anew in the direction of the ice-fall; Rinzing accompanied him a bit further to show him the route which Ruttledge had chosen. Soon their progress was a gasping crawl. Rinzing opted to return to Camp III. Wilson battled on alone.

Four long days his despairing battle with the ice-fall lasted. Not the slightest trace of the Ruttledge expedition remained to guide him. He spent the nights on tiny ledges in the most exposed places. Fighting for breath, he hacked steps in the hard ice, he placed ice screws, he scraped and scrabbled himself higher. When a ten metre-wide crevasse barred his way, praying, he ventured across a thin snow bridge. Finally he stood at the foot of the last ice step below the top of the North Col. But this ice wall, less than 100 metres high, was vertical and without holds. After a bivouac, Wilson tried to climb it via a smooth chimney. Again and again he climbed a few agonizing metres, only to keep slipping down again. On the evening of 24 May, still at the foot of the chimney, Wilson must have realized that Mount Everest could not be conquered. More dead than alive he slipped and skidded back down the ice-fall to sink into the arms of the anxiously waiting Sherpas.

The next two days Wilson lay debilitated in his sleeping-bag in Camp III. Even then – one can hardly credit it – he wrote: 'Tewang wanted to go back, but persuaded them to go with me to Camp V. This will be last effort and I feel successful . . . '. In reality the Sherpas considered such a plan completely mad and tried to persuade Wilson to go back. Wilson would not listen to them and on 29 May set out alone once more. Too weak to make any real progress he camped not far from Camp III at the foot of the North Col.

On 30 May he remained in the tent. Too weak to leave his sleeping-bag, he scribbled in his diary on 31 May: 'Off again, gorgeous day'. Completely exhausted, quite alone, frozen to the marrow, Maurice Wilson died soon after.

A year later, in 1935, Eric Shipton and Charles Warren, on their way to the North Col, found his body dessicated by the wind. The knees were drawn up and he was clothed in the shreds of a pullover and green flannel trousers. A boot was missing and the protecting tent was long torn away by the winter storms. The climbers wrapped Wilson's corpse in what was left of the tent and buried him in a crevasse on the glacier. Shipton took away with him only the diary.

From these notes and the reports of the Sherpas who waited a long time for their employer before they returned to Darjeeling, the up to then most audacious attempt at an Everest ascent could be reconstructed. 'The way is the goal' is a Buddhist saying, and mad as Wilson might seem, I have taken this persevering Don Quixote, who always carried with him in his rucksack some mementoes of the for him unattainable Enid Evans, to my heart. He is dearer to me than the legion of all those who anxiously build their little houses and preserve their lives for the old-age pension.

The idea of climbing Everest alone must, I think, have occurred to more people during the past fifty years than Maurice Wilson and me. And soon, in the pauses between training, packing and bureaucratic red tape, I stumble across new material. I stumble across Denman and Larsen.

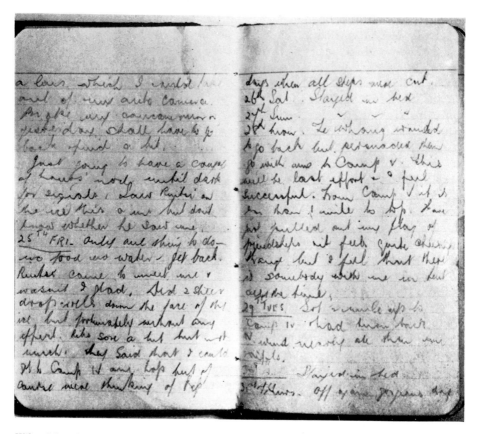

Wilson's last diary entry.

Denman and Larsen

'I was travelling extremely simply, and with the barest of essentials for survival ... I was, in fact, so utterly poor that I could not afford a watch for myself! Tenzing had one, but I did not.' It could have been Earl Denman's motto, the motto of a man who was the second person to make a solo attempt on Mount Everest. That was in 1947. Born in Canada, he had had a hard childhood in England: a bed-ridden father, a mother who slaved for their sons. Denman was very ambitious, and had many pipe-dreams. One was of Africa. When he finally got there he was the first to climb, barefoot and in shorts, all eight Virunga volcanoes. Only a few natives accompanied him. This accomplishment filled Denman with pride. 'No one will ever climb these mountains again with such primitive means.' And soon this pride gave birth to new desires. The mountain of mountains came into his mind – Everest. But how to climb it?

'[The difficulty] ... of attempting a task of such immensity with only one fiftieth of the money that had been spent on at least one previous Everest expedition . . . '; thus ran his self-imposed challenge.

He declined to use any oxygen gear because he believed in the adaptability of man to altitude. 'It has been proven that it is possible to survive without oxygen at a height of about 8,500 metres on the mountain. It is therefore ridiculous to maintain that no one is in a position to reach 8,800 metres or somewhat more.' Denman knew the Everest literature too. He knew of the disappearance of Mallory and Irvine and was convinced that they had perished because their supply of oxygen had run out at altitude and that without that they were not sufficiently acclimatized. Denman wanted to make a solo ascent because he was a lone wolf, and because he wanted to prove something to himself. Of Wilson's attempt he knew nothing.

He was to come to learn of that first in Darjeeling.

With only a sleeping-bag filled with goose down, two tents made of war-time barrage balloon material, a rope, handmade crampons, gloves, snow-goggles, dried meat and £250 cash Denman shipped out on 7 February 1947 from Mozambique to Mombasa. He arrived in Bombay and travelled on to Calcutta. He learned to know India as follows:

'Men lay on the pavements, some with blankets or sacks drawn over their bodies, but none bothering to seek shade. A wrinkled beggar woman slapped her bare hollow stomach and whined for food. One of several sacred bulls wandered into a shop and came

Climber with oxygen mask.

out just as leisurely. A cab horse, little more than skin and bone, had collapsed in its traces opposite a branch of Lloyds Bank and could not be brought to its feet, though a small crowd gathered to pull, push and kick.'

Denman was sickened and at the same time moved by so much poverty. The monotonous rattle of the train to Darjeeling sounded in his ears like a refrain: '*You fool, turn back. You fool, turn back.*'

In mid-March he got to know the then thirty-two year old Tenzing Norgay. The wiry Sherpa was by this time already a well-known man. He had been to Everest several times, and also had accompanied Smythe, Shipton and Tilman on other Himalayan expeditions. His performances had earned him the distinction of a 'Himalayan Tiger'. Besides his native tongue he spoke fluent Tibetan, Sikkimese and Hindustani. He even spoke broken English.

Tenzing Norgay (second from right) in 1977.

Naturally, Denman had learned of Tenzing through Karma Paul, the obsequious servant of all Everest crack-pots, and Karma Paul had also another companion at hand for Denman. He was called Ang Dawa. Although both Tenzing and Ang Dawa knew that Denman possessed no permit for a journey into Tibet and no money with which to pay them properly the pulling power of Mount Everest was so great that they were unable to say no.

On 22 March 1947 they set off. First by bus, then with Sikkimese mules, later on foot. Denman went barefoot as in Uganda. They finally reached Tibet by way of the Kongra La. They travelled across desolate, windswept, barren southern Tibet and lived from hand to mouth. Like a fugitive, under constant strain and under the most primitive conditions, Denman got to Rongbuk.

Denman, who had come across many monasteries on his journey through Sikkim and Tibet, found Rongbuk bigger and more beautifully painted, but was dismayed when the lamas brought him not mystical charms but their defective flashlights and alarm clocks to repair. The locals were as curious as children. They laughed over Denman's shabby appearance. With other 'sahibs' they were accustomed to relative riches and exciting luggage. They were astonished by Denman's eccentric repudiation of material things.

The first sight of Mount Everest, which soared up above the monastery, was also for Denman overwhelming. He understood at once why the monks had sought out this secluded, sterile little patch of land for their settlement. The old, English-speaking High Lama was dead. In his place sat a small lad motionless and cross-legged on the richly carved seat of meditation – the new abbot. The lamas believed him to be the reincarnation of the man who had set previous expeditions on their way with his blessings. Denman was allowed to use the monastery buildings as base camp. One of Tenzing's sisters, who was married to one of the monks, helped with the organization. Denman watched the pilgrims in the monastery. Impassive of face they ran strings of beads like rosaries through their hands, at the same time incessantly moving their lips. Others turned their prayer-wheels, little cylinders of copper or silver in which were enclosed prayers written on tiny rolls.

Karma Paul, interpreter for many Everest attempts.

Denman was far removed from being a second Maurice Wilson. Long ago he had decided to take the two Sherpas with him to the summit.

On 10 April the three of them set off. They took the traditional route over the easterly of the three Rongbuk glaciers in the direction of the North Col. Denman was suffering from the cold to such a degree that after the first night he moved into the Sherpas' tent. As he still could not sleep for extreme cold he crept into Tenzing's sleeping-bag. Also, the altitude oppressed him. Nevertheless they reached the old Camp III, and the two Sherpas led him safely up the Chang-La face. On the North Col, however, fierce storms dashed all hope. Worn out, Denman realized how insufficiently equipped they were for a summit assault. The storm would not let him sleep at night, eating was agony, thirst a constant nightmare. Denman could see that he was beaten. He surrendered.

Returned back home, his ambition awakened afresh. Within a year he reappeared in Darjeeling, better prepared, with good equipment, full of new daring; but this time no one was ready to travel once more with him secretly to Tibet. He went back to Rhodesia, wrote a book and turned his back on the mountains for ever.

Only four years were to pass before the next adventurer got the idea of climbing Everest alone. This was the Dane, Klavs Becker-Larsen. He too dreamed of Rongbuk and the north side of the mountain. In the meantime, however, Tibet had been occupied by Chinese troops. So for the time being Larsen travelled to Darjeeling. Who else should he meet there but Karma

Paul. With his help he took on four Sherpas. To force their way secretly through southern Tibet to Rongbuk had become too dangerous in view of the Chinese occupation, so Larsen resolved to get from Darjeeling to Rongbuk illegally through Nepal on the traditional route of the salt caravans. He ascended the Dudh Khosi valley to Namche Bazar in Sherpa country and first attempted the cross-fall as well as being very difficult. The lama who is supposed to have crossed it without rope or pitons must have had wings. Klavs Becker-Larsen turned round and travelled to Thame, bloodied but not beaten. Then he attempted the almost 6,000 metre-high Nangpa La, over which the Sherpas had fetched their salt for hundreds of years from Tingri in Tibet. It too was snowed up. Nevertheless he crossed

The Khumbu ice-fall, with the Lho La to the left.

ing of the Lho La into occupied Tibet. According to local reports by the Sherpas a lama had once gone from Solo Khumbu to Rongbuk over the Lho La. But Larsen, who neither had at his disposal divine assistance nor was able to manage with axe and crampons – for he too was no mountaineer – had to give up halfway to the top of the pass. The Lho La lies at a height of 6,000 metres, and the descent to the south is dangerous on account of stone-

the border and succeeded with the Sherpas, who safely showed him the way, in getting as far as Kyetrak. Once across the Lamna La the little caravan switched over to Rongbuk where they arrived six days after their departure from Namche Bazar.

Just as Larsen had been able in Namche Bazar to borrow a rope from the camp of the Tilman–Houston expedition, so he now persuaded the young High Lama to lend him stuff from the

84

stores left behind by the pre-war expeditions. In spite of the ominous prediction of the monk that he would not reach the top of Everest, Larsen managed to traverse the East Rongbuk Glacier in three days and reach Camp III. With the two strongest Sherpas he wanted to climb from there to the North Col and erect a fourth camp as the starting point for his solo assault on the summit. On 9 May they had already two-thirds of the ascent to the col behind them when a storm came on. Additionally threatened by stonefall from the Changtse face the Sherpas refused to climb further. All Larsen's insults and oaths were in vain; without their help he too was compelled to abandon his solo attempt. Sadly he returned to Rongbuk. Chinese soldiers who had learned of the stranger were already there, however, on the lookout for him. The monks concealed him but it was high time he left the monastery. Over the same route by which he had come Larsen returned to Nepal. After five long days of marching he was once more in Namche Bazar.

In 1953 Mount Everest was 'conquered by an army' as Denman expressed it. Beside Edmund Hillary, Tenzing Norgay stood on the summit. On his head he wore Denman's balaclava. Thus a piece of him also reached the highest point in the world.

'Sometime this mountain will also be climbed alone and with simple means,' prophesied the anti-materialistic Canadian. Since then more than twenty-five years have passed. Denman's dream has remained alive, come to life in other minds, in other hearts. Now it is my turn.

Nangpa La from the Tibetan side.

The Motive

Now, after making the literary acquaintance of Wilson, Denman and Larsen, I cannot help thinking hard precisely about my own motives. For Larsen, the driving force for his solo attempt was clear: 'I wanted to prove myself to myself and others by doing something which would take everything I had to give. I also wanted adventure. I was brought up to believe that I could do anything I believed I could do – that my own reason was the best judge as to what I could cope with and what not. With this sort of code it is not quite as difficult for one's dreams to materialize.' He wrote this on board ship as he travelled back to Europe. Denman expressed himself thus: 'I am an impecunious child of my time and learn slowly that ambition, if it cannot actually be quelled, must subordinate itself to the amount of money available.' To put materialism in its place was one of his motives, the

85

Reinhold Messner and Edmund Hillary in 1978.

inability to form a deep human relationship the second. He attempted to quash his isolation through friendship with the native peoples with whom he felt himself more kindred than with his 'white' contemporaries.

By his act, Wilson wanted to prove that there was a higher power which would come to his aid. With his belief in an outside force he differed basically from Larsen and Denman who hoped to find strength within themselves.

And what about me?

I want to get there before Naomi Uemura. I want to be the first who has climbed the highest mountain in the world alone. I want at last to go to Tibet, land of my childhood dreams. But that alone is not it. 'Why do you want to go to Everest again?' asks my sorely tried mother as I tell her of my plan. 'You've climbed it once already!' I explain to her how wonderful this mountain is on the northern side, how very much I wish to see Rongbuk and to find out what the Chinese have left of this mysterious monastery, the myth that surrounds the Tibetan side of the mountain and how the earlier expeditions are part of alpine history. As I tell her all this I know that also it is only a part of the truth. While my mother pushes wood into the cooking range, at which she has spent a large part of her life, in order to feed her nine children, she says: 'If you're not planning an expedition you're restless. You can't settle down to daily life.' She is right. I cannot imagine anything more terrible than an everyday existence as it occurs in middle-class life. I know that that is unjust but I am not ashamed of my refusal. The peasants in our valley have no time to think about the meaning of life. They are fully occupied doing essentials. I on the other hand am a tormented child of a generation which has to ask itself what sense there is in following an unloved profession in a world which through a materialistic mentality daily becomes more hateful. To my existence no meaning will be given, I must find it for myself.

I have no fixed beliefs, and the passive resignation to fate of the people in my valley often drives me to despair. Only quite seldom can I overcome my separation from the world, can I feel myself at one with the cosmos – when I am climbing. And then only if through extreme stress, and concentration on the greatest difficulties, I reach a state in which my ego dissolves itself. To these moments, however, I am addicted.

In order to experience this feeling of oneness with the world, I must go to the limits of my physical ability. Soloing a difficult face, at great height, only by the greatest physical expenditure and exhaustion can I achieve it.

Tenzing Norgay in 1953 on the summit of Everest.

My worst enemy on the way to this goal is fear. I am a timid person, and like all timid people I long to overcome my fears. Victory over fear, that is also a happiness in which I am close to myself. Three times I set off alone for Nanga Parbat, three times I turned back out of fear, before I had the power to overcome it and climb to the summit. I want to have the feeling of being stronger than my fear, that is why again and again I place myself in situations in which I meet it in order to overcome it.

But while I am attempting to resolve my isolation through experi-

A classic-style expedition with groups of porters on the Chang La face.

do I take enough time for the people whom I meet. Something in me constantly makes me uneasy after a short time, as if I had a train to catch. It gives me no peace. Torn between flight and quest I am condemned to climbing, and it does not surprise me that recently in one of Uschi's dreams, appearing as the 'Flying Dutchman', I sailed across the unending sea of a shattered glacier in a ship of shredded canvas.

Success of the Japanese

In the middle of May I read in the newspaper of the success of a Japanese expedition. It has climbed Mount Everest from the north by two routes.

For the Japanese Alpine Club, as for me, the ascent of a mountain lying on the northern Chinese side of the Himalaya was a long-cherished aim. In February 1979 proposals for a major Japanese Mount Everest project were submitted to the Chinese Sports Federation. In June 1979 came the official permission of the Chinese Mountaineering Association. Thus the Japanese were the first group of foreign mountaineers allowed to undertake an expedition in Tibet since the creation of the People's Republic. The Japanese plan was to attack Everest simultaneously up the North-East Ridge and the North Face. A live television transmission – the first in the history of expeditionary mountaineering – was to enhance the sensation.

In September/October a reconnaissance party examined the possibilities of two routes on the northern side. On that occasion three Chinese were killed in an avalanche under the North Col and a Japanese climber injured.

ences at the limit of human ability and to become master of my fears, I live. I live with an intensity which I can find nowhere else. And so every descent from the mountain is for me less a return to life and much more a descent from a piece of life lived to the full, a small death.

Uschi, the woman I was married to, thinks that these journeys into self experience distance me ever more from other people and lead to a sort of morbid preoccupation with fantasy. Perhaps she is right. It hurts me that during my expeditions neither on the outward nor on the homeward journey

The expedition consisted of three teams: the North-East Ridge group (12 members), the North Face group (12 members) and the newspaper and television reporters (13 members). Leader and co-ordinator of the project was Hyoriki Watanabe.

In support of the undertaking, 56 Chinese were signed on: two liaison officers, three translators, two managers, 22 high-altitude porters, four radio specialists, six cooks, three drivers, a bookkeeper and 13 yak drivers. The high-altitude porters were to work like the Sherpas in Nepal and carry loads to a height of 7,500 metres.

At the beginning of March the 100 men arrived at base camp at the lower end of the Rongbuk Glacier at an altitude of 5,150 metres. Two advanced base camps – one at 6,500 metres on the East Rongbuk Glacier, a second at 6,200 metres on the Central Rongbuk Glacier – were established. In mid-March the North-East Ridge party began the ascent. On 25 March they reached the North Col, where the fourth camp was erected. The fifth camp, 7,600 metres high, went up on 6 April, the sixth, over 8,000 metres high, on 23 April. The Chinese supply team carried up the equipment and provisions, doing most of the work. On 29 April four expedition members, together with six auxiliaries, left advance base camp for the decisive assault. On 2 May they erected a seventh camp at 8,200 metres above sea level.

The four departed for the summit on 3 May. Not until 7 p.m. did two of them – Kato and the cameraman Nakamura – get to the snow ridge which leads to the highest point. As Nakamura felt ill, Yasuo Kato climbed the last 200 metres alone. He reached the summit just before 9 p.m. During the descent both of them bivouacked at a height of 8,750 metres, without oxygen. A tremendous performance, certainly, but no solo ascent by Kato who by this success is the first climber who has ascended Mount Everest from both the Nepalese south side and the Chinese north side.

A solo ascent of Mount Everest begins where the climbing starts: at the foot of the Khumbu Glacier or at 6,500 metres under the North Col, according to which route one chooses. The ideal route for a solo ascent is certainly the North Ridge, because there the yaks can approach to within 2,500 metres of the summit. But this last 2,500 metres without outside help are and remain the real problem for the true soloist.

The second Japanese party

The North Face and North-East Ridge (left) of Everest.

ascended the North Face. The 60 degree steep flank was interspersed with bare ice. On 20 April the Hornbein Couloir was reached, into which the new Japanese route merged. From Camp V, 8,350 metres high, the summit was to be climbed.

The first assault stuck fast in deep snow. The second party set off a windslab avalanche as they climbed up to Camp V. Akira Uge's rope broke; he fell and was not found again. After this tragic incident all members of this group descended to advance base camp.

There followed a third attempt with Tsuneo Shigehiro and Takashi Ozaki as the summit team. Early on the morning of 10 May they left Camp V, reached the snowfield in the upper part of the Hornbein Couloir, traversed to the West Ridge and, although their artificial oxygen had run out, climbed to the summit.

After they had descended as far as 8,700 metres they had to bivouac on the West Ridge like Kato of the North-East Ridge group a week before. With this first ascent of the North Face perhaps the most beautiful route on Everest fell to the Japanese.

A few days earlier a Spaniard with a Sherpa had climbed Everest by the South-East Ridge from Nepal, and some ten days later came a new announcement of success from Kathmandu:

'Two Polish mountaineers succeeded in climbing 8,848 metres-high Mount Everest. They conquered the mountain by the hitherto unclimbed South Buttress. The two 32 year-old engineers used no oxygen sets for the final section. They stayed 50 minutes on the summit. Altogether 107 climbers have so far reached the summit of Everest.'

To the two Poles, therefore, fell the first ascent of the South Buttress, to which Peter Habeler and I had aspired in 1978. Great as my respect for this first ascent is, my interest is soon completely captivated by the northern side, by the planning of my Tibetan journey, by equipment and catering problems. I am in a fever of anticipation for my most audacious mountain adventure.

My Valley, the People

'One day you'll go climbing and stop before your slippers do.' This common South Tyrolean saying, meaning 'You'll kill yourself one of these fine days', is shouted at me by a peasant who stands by the roadside as I go panting past him. Once again I am running regularly up the steep road from Bolzano to S. Genesio, to train heart and circulation. I used to love this stretch which is about 7 kilometres long and rises some 1,000 metres. Then one day the surface was paved, later concreted. Since then it has deteriorated in several places: I am always losing my rhythm.

Slowly I wander back into the hollow of the Bolzano valley – I don't want to damage my joints by running downhill – and go into the old town. In a bar, over a cup of Espresso coffee, a friend holds an article from 'Tandem' under my nose, in which Alexander Langer, an active South Tyrol politician, has written about me. I scan the lines quickly.

'Although made well-known by the mass media of many countries and often idolized, Reinhold Messner has succeeded in resisting his fame, his picture, his image.' Langer begins.

Then he quotes me:

' "Today I have a good understanding with my neighbours, above all with those closest, and I am accepted here in the valley. There used to be tension, it was more difficult. For people I was at school with, it was harder, perhaps, to forgive my international celebrity. The worst aggression came from those of my own age – and manifestly reflected dissatisfaction with themselves. I was seen perhaps as an exhibitionist, even the Tibetan prayer flags in front of the house were taken as a provocation. Yet I liked them simply because they radiated peace and pleased me aesthetically.

"And then naturally they took offence that I did not stand up and be counted for my valley and for South

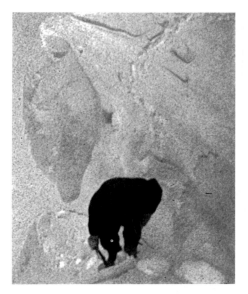

Peter Habeler in 1978 on the 'Hillary step'.

Tyrol – or possibly even for the People's Party. I did not care for the notion that in sport, one should always be useful to someone, to a fatherland, to an idea – as in war. That must alter one very much, above all in the conscious." '

Langer quotes accurately. I am surprised and read further.

'Reinhold Messner, with whom this dialogue thus begins, is surely – in his way – one of the many South Tyrol dissidents who do not fit into the stereotype of the predominant power block. Not for nothing has he repeatedly traded arguments and polemics with official representatives of established power, setting store by distancing himself firmly from them. A critical top sportsman?

That is not on – and so the local media prefer to laud paragons like Gustav Thoni, while at the same time working off their hostility on Reinhold Messner. It is small wonder, therefore, that a few years ago his car was defaced. Among the many letters he receives there were also anonymous writers from the homeland who demanded: "You dirty pig, get your hair cut!"

But a victim of political persecution Reinhold Messner certainly is not, and he feels himself socially and politically no more committed than formerly, when after matriculation he was active at community level and interested himself – above all during his engineering studies in Padua – fairly strongly in social questions. Today he thinks more of an inner revolution and looks with interest to

91

the Orient and its worldly wisdom, which he has come to know more intimately in the course of many journeys. He rejects communist self-effacement and the emptiness of the cult of the individual – at least as practised today. He follows events and developments in South Tyrol from a

The Messners wanted their children well-educated. Reinhold attended school in Bolzano, later he studied in Padua and Munich.

"Naturally one sometimes feels cramped in South Tyrol, but I don't feel driven to exile. Perhaps I would not have developed the same – almost

Reinhold Messner on a training run.

distance, but is well-informed about fundamental problems.

"The best proof that I do have a commitment to this country and to Villnöss is the fact that I still live here. Of our family of nine children I am the only one who has stayed in the valley. I bought this house at auction from the parish – formerly it was a parsonage, then a schoolhouse; that is why the rooms are so big."

pathological – need for remoteness, if I had grown up in Germany or in the U.S.A. To be a South Tyroler is something like climbing: one must learn to get along alone."

To his homeland Reinhold applies a severe verdict; he characterizes South Tyrol as "the least tolerant country that I know, even Bavaria is more tolerant and for that, surely, intolerant policies are largely to blame.

"Nowadays mountaineering is my life – to the exclusion of everything else, but I could no longer get along without it. Not because I see it as something outstanding or special, detached from the rest of my life, but rather a simple, intense knowledge of myself which I would like to advance still further. For others it is often the beautiful in relation to the non-beautiful life – but if this were the choice, that would mean that something is sick!'

Reinhold also climbs for a living, for to finance his expeditions and to support himself he must inevitably commercialize himself. Photos, books, sponsors, lecture tours, exclusive reports, a climbing school in Villnöss ... But he has and wants no agent because he does not want one day to fall victim to the self-motivation of such exploitation. A housekeeper from the Pustertal, Veronika, deals with part of his correspondence and contributes to his "public relations", so far as the strands can be sorted out in Villnöss.

But for Reinhold Messner writing and photography are not just means of earning money, rather principally they are a form of expression. Among the living writers of South Tyrol he is one of those who have published the most; over a dozen books, many also translated, in which the talk is not only of the mountains, but also about himself, the people and countries he encounters, about life and death.

"I write not so much from the need to tell a tale, but because I want to express, to fashion, to design. My reading public – like my lecture public – is remarkably diverse: from the extreme

climber to the complete sit-at-home. The average citizen compensates for something he lacks, that he will never experience."

Reinhold Messner has taken part in or privately organized 30 expeditions, has under his belt first ascents under extreme circumstances in all parts of the world, has time and again brushed against death – and in 1970 lost his brother Günther on Nanga Parbat – what does he still seek? With him, it seems to me, it is all about the challenge of new, strange, perhaps also mysterious experiences, countries, sensations and possibilities. Not because he would like to be a hero, "although I shall be seen, described and marketed as a hero. It is not so easy to resist that, even though one remains self-critical, when one's story (actually that of an anti-hero) is strictly speaking an epic tale."

Reinhold Messner sees in his attitude no contempt for others or for society – "I need society too, without it I would not be able to live" – but his individuality, his personal originality is just the way he is. "If you take away a person's individuality, he is no one. The individual in me has come increasingly to the fore in recent years – parrots of any kind do not interest me."'

I am pleased that after a conversation with me somebody has taken the trouble to put something into words without utilizing my statements for his own ideology. How often in South Tyrol have words been put into my mouth, how often have party functionaries and politicians made banner headlines of my activities without looking to see

Messner-Everest-Solo-China-Tibet-Lhasa-Qomolangma

Everest Solo Expedition 1980 greetings card.

whether it was appropriate . . .

Fortunately I am not dependent on the goodwill of the leading political power in the country, or even sponsored by anyone. It would have meant giving up either my climbing or my individuality. So the danger of falling is limited to my mountain trips.

The fact that I have spoken with Alexander Langer, who is a comrade-in-arms of the red 'Lotta Continua' already brings reproaches from the established power blocks in South Tyrol. There is a discernible aloofness. Why should this be? Soon I shrug it off. Anyone who takes seriously the concepts of life of those who stand outside the South Tyrol trinity – People's Party, church, national-minded press – has to reckon with aggression, withdrawal of recognition or even being

ignored. That I have known for a long time. Why, then, do I find it so hard to adapt? With the blessing of the bigwigs, how much easier everything would be.

To be a member of the ruling clan carries with it a condition: one must echo their creed without criticism. Sometimes when I am in South Tyrol for months, listening to the speeches of our politicians, reading 'our' daily paper or hearing from the locals what the parson has said in church, the world becomes very small again – just as I remember it as a child.

I travel back to the Villnöss valley and ask myself when I arrive at my parents' house in St Peter, whether the narrowness of this valley could actually be what awakened my desire for wide open spaces. The Villnöss valley is similar to the famous Grödner valley but the majority of holiday makers don't know that. There are few historical objects of interest and scarcely any ski lifts. It is a peaceful Dolomite valley of harmonious beauty, sunny, wedged in between high wooded ridges and steep mountains. Often it seems to me as if these delicate limestone cliffs have absorbed all melancholy, harshness, isolation from the place.

Here, on a hill at the back of the valley, I am studying old maps of Tibet. My life has no other goal at this moment than this journey to Mount Everest. For me, the year 1980 is a new interval; a year without firm ties, without exact plans for later. The preparations this time last only a few weeks. For all that they are all the more exhausting. Through tension, hope and anxiety I am like a cat on a hot tin roof. Nena also, who is to accompany me as far as base camp, is full of excitement from the moment that her participation is certain. She begins a diary that she wants to continue during our Chinese journey:

I am glad to be going to China. It would have been crazy to say no. I love to see other people, to live amongst them. I would have liked to see the real China. But I am excited when I imagine myself travelling with this man. To go with him, to laugh, to cry, to experience the mountains with him and to share a part of my life with him. I am pleased about so many things which we shall do together.

Since Reinhold's divorce nearly three years ago he has erected a wall around himself in order to protect himself. It is difficult

Ascent of Everest's south side in 1978.

1922 sketch map of Mount Everest.

to penetrate it. Only now and then does he permit small glimpses of the real man behind the wall. I believe my inner strength begins to flag. I don't know why the idea dawns on me to tell him certain things, although I know he has a good heart.

Nena before departure.

Tibet –
The Yak Nomads

The Potala is the paradise of the Buddhas,
Palace of Chenrezi,
To the east, west, south and north
There is only one Potala on this earth.

Tibetan proverb.

Tibet – The Yak Nomads

Departure for the Land of Snows

After a journalist has begged us to take small walkie-talkie radios with us to Everest, Nena writes in her diary on 7 June:

I can imagine exactly what people think of me.

I am not the conventional little woman. Being able to speak with Reinhold on the walkie-talkie each evening won't make me feel safe and sheltered in base camp. To be able to give him courage and the certainty that he makes good headway is not everything.

Reinhold does not know me as I really am. I don't know how I know but I know what I shall feel. We have lived together for six months and yet he considers taking a radio with him on his solo trip for my sake. I have my own ideas about a walkie-talkie on the summit of Everest. To my mind it is not a true solo, one is not completely alone, if one can have daily contact with base camp over the radio. Perhaps one can compare the security which one receives from this device with the taking of oxygen. For laymen it may be of slight importance, whether someone climbs Everest with or without artificial oxygen. But actually there is a big distinction. With oxygen flasks on one's back the feeling of security increases. Similarly the radio set could also promote the consciousness of safety. As long as a person has it with him – whether he uses it or not – he knows that there is always the possibility of contact.

I shan't change my mind about this. I do know how exciting it would be for the masses to hear or read thoughts spontaneously recorded on the summit. Just as it was on the first moon landing. The men could share their emotions with humanity. I want neither the one nor the other. I prefer not to speak with Reinhold when he climbs to the summit, for many reasons. I can put myself in his shoes, and I believe that it is more important for him to be without contact. Without connection with the world below, to climb alone up there must remain a deeper experience. To gaze at the surrounding mountains and horizons is not all; to reach the summit through one's own will is more important; to stand up there and to look inwards; to understand and to accept all that is beautiful and hateful in our make-up; to see ourselves as the people we are and not the illusion which we make of ourselves.

Reinhold seeks self-experience. I am sure that he will be happier *en route* without, rather than with, a walkie-talkie. His advisers overlook not only the weight of the apparatus, but also the intrusion into the possibilities of experience.

There are, however, egotistical considerations which concern me alone. The adventure will be bigger for me if Reinhold goes off and leaves me alone. Naturally it will be hard to watch him leave. Perhaps I shall be afraid that I will never see him again. Already now, while I write this, I must fight the cowardice in me which urges: 'Talk to him over the radio.' How easy it would be to anaesthetize fear. I can imagine the alarm which comes with waiting. But at the same time my ego is telling me that I shall grow if I endure all that.

And there is something else: when Reinhold is up there alone on the mountain and thinks about us, his feelings for me could clarify. Brief halting words over the radio could disturb him. I believe that it is very important for our relationship. We can also share our experiences without radio contact. If Reinhold does not sense my presence from base camp to summit – where is our friendship then? Can I then ever venture to speak of love?

A week or more later Nena and I travel from South Tyrol to Munich. Whilst travelling I dream of the 'Land of Snows' as the Tibetans call their country. 'Miles from nowhere . . .' sounds from the loud speakers of my Porsche, which I shall sell today. A few fragments of Cat Stevens' song penetrate my consciousness and I become wide-awake. Nena translates the lyric for me:

Miles from nowhere
I think, I leave myself time
Oh yes, to get there
I gaze up at the mountain
Which I must climb,
Oh yes, how to get there?
My God, the body is a
Good friend,
But I shall not need it,
When I reach my goal . . .

For a long moment I am far, far away. And for a long moment I know not whether Everest lies before or behind me.

In Munich my publisher gives me a critique of my planned solo climb to read. Sebastian Leitner has written it for the Vienna 'Kurier' under the title 'Peak-bagging: Sheer waste of courage?':

'I ask myself what this Everest is really all about. It was climbed for the first time in June 1953 by a certain Mr Edmund Hillary from New Zealand who was then knighted for his efforts.

Since then I don't know how many teams have scrambled to the top, with ever more similar experiences: the air there is damned thin, it is bloody cold, the view is fine only in good weather (and always far more restricted than from a high-flying jet-liner), the ascent and descent are costly and a danger to life. Only two years ago the South Tyrolean Reinhold Messner ventured and pulled off a new (and literally breath-taking) feat. He was the first to climb the highest mountain in the world without oxygen – that is quite something, although the view may not have been any better for it. The purpose of the undertaking could only have been that it would be harder that way. Why do it simply, when it can be done with complications? That's what Reinhold Messner wants – to make it as complicated as possible. Now, we hear, he is to attack the mountain again, from Tibet and, because he considers it the worst and most dangerous season, in the monsoon period.

In this he is in competition with the Japanese mountaineer Naomi Uemura who has similar aspirations – a winter ascent of Mount Everest: this Japanese – you've guessed it – considers a winter ascent to be the greatest of all tests of courage.

Whether winter or monsoon – one of them will win . . .

And what then?

Will Mount Everest be a totally deflowered mountain, of no more use? Will it become a meaningless pile of stone, only good to look at – from below?

I believe that we under-estimate the imagination of the peak-bagger: how about a first ascent by night and without torches?

Or, instead of straight up, spiralling round the mountain to the top? Or perhaps a trip with bare feet or shackles on our joints, or (when all that has been tried) with a black bandage over our eyes?

I know (I ask, therefore, for pardon) it is not only to do with the mountain.

It is about, so Messner tells us in a *Profil* interview, the "last cryptic motivation", about "resistance against the challenge of death" – the measuring of man's courage against Nature.

That, by your leave, I hold to be sheer waste of pluck and daring. For human courage is too valuable to be squandered in this fashion just in the mountains; it is needed elsewhere far more urgently – in the valleys, towns, villages – in its most insignificant form: courage of one's convictions.'

I am both amused and shocked at the same time. Leitner is not all that far out. How is he to understand my motive?

Nena and I leave the publisher's and hasten to 'Bavaria Film', where Jürgen Lehmann also has something for me. It is a telex from the German Embassy in Peking, and it doesn't sound all that welcoming:

'Mountaineering Association regrets unable to grant extension through September for Reinhold Messner. Alternative proposal: 15.7. to 31.10.1980.' [Instead of June to 31.8.80, laid down in protocol.]

Shortly before, I had asked for an extension to my permit. What should I do? I can't upset my plans now. A later departure is out of the question. We fly as planned.

'I shan't believe we are really on our way to China until the jet takes off from Frankfurt for Karachi,' Nena had said while still in Munich. Now, on 17 June and only a half hour away from Peking, she writes in her diary on the aeroplane:

It is still hard to believe that I am on the way to Everest with Reinhold. These past months the preparations, the helping with packing were agony. I was almost bursting with enthusiasm. But daily I had to listen to Reinhold saying: 'I made a big mistake when I decided to take you with me. I wish Ursula Grether were here'. She accompanied him to Nanga Parbat in 1978. But in the long run practically no one matches up to Reinhold's ideals. I was never able to fully embrace the joy of our forthcoming trip. Never sure whether I would accompany Reinhold to Everest, I was constantly tortured with doubts. Scared of being blown away like a cloud by the first false move, I felt paralysed. He even went so far as to suggest an agreement that I should promise to disappear from his life after our return. Then that struck him as comical. What notions this man has of a relationship! What, have we planned everything together for the past six months only to smash it all up!

At any rate things are never boring. He keeps my energy level constantly at the highest pitch. Shouting, laughing and dreaming, we get on together somehow or other.

Dead tired we arrive in Peking. A minibus takes us from the airport into the city. As if in a trance I see trees and houses passing by outside. The walls at the side of the street are covered with billboards. Gigantic paintings and signs swing past. I cannot make out whether the colourful pictures are party propaganda or advertising. Not once can I decide whether it is morning or afternoon outside. The air is stifling.

In June the sky over Peking is gloomy and grey, the air so hot that one doesn't care to walk a step. Nevertheless the streets are extremely lively. I wonder at the countless women and men who pedal past on their bicycles. Upright, proud even, they tread the pedals. I have since found out that these ubiquitous black bicycles are for today's Chinese a status symbol just as a Volkswagen in the fifties was for us. It is often not all that

life into the street. Under lanterns, old men sit on little bamboo stools and read their newspapers. Others play checkers on the pavement. A woman plaits her daughter's pigtails. The mothers lavish all their longing for finery and individuality on the children. The little ones are colourfully clothed and adorned with large hair

Peking.

easy to distinguish the men from the women. Both wear blue or olive-green suits. Mao was the most influential fashion designer of all time.

A stroll after dinner through the streets in the vicinity of the Bei Wei Hotel brings us new impressions. In order to escape from the constriction of their families crowded together by the catastrophic lack of living space, many Chinese shift their evening private

slides. In order to control the population explosion, each family is only allowed to bring one child into the world. Those who do not keep to it are punished by wage cuts. I sense the constriction, the feeling of being shut in in this city. No one stares at us, no one pays any attention to us. Then we discover a gigantic, garish-coloured film poster. A gloomy looking man has his arm round a languishing woman, above them float fairies in white dresses. The latest Chinese film. That we must see. But no one whom we ask in English for directions to the cinema can answer us. All respond with embarrassed tittering. So, as no one here speaks English, we do not find the cinema. Nevertheless, I enjoy being once more a real stranger in a strange country. Dead tired we sink into our hotel beds with the explosively coloured padded silk covers.

19 June. We both wake up with a feeling of emptiness. Our psychological condition is miserable. Nena writes:

Depression! We are living through unaccustomed solitude. It is not rational. For years we have both been accustomed to travelling and living in extreme situations.

This, however, is our first big trip together and by force of circumstance we are as isolated as on a lonely island. We have told ourselves we must learn to live with each other. Being cut off linguistically from the world around us strikes us for the first time; the possibilities of understanding between us are also restricted. We speak English to each other, so Reinhold is not in a position to carry on sophisticated conversations with me because the possibilities for expression fail him, and what I say he understands only if I restrict myself to a simple vocabulary. That increases our loneliness with each other. It will not be easy but nevertheless I shall be glad of our isolation over the next three months.

What with sleeping, eating and bureaucratic discussions with the CMA we are forever going through the streets of the city. We buy a few

Behai Park in the vicinity of Peking.

provisions in the 'Friendship Store', a kind of luxury shop, in which we meet practically all the foreigners living for the time being in Peking. In China there are two types of money: the 'old' yuan for normal domestic use, and the 'new' yuan that is issued against currency, i.e. tourist money which you need if you want to shop in the Friendship Store. These small points heighten our feeling of being outsiders and make us feel ill at ease.

By day a business-like atmosphere lies over the city, cool, relentless. In the evenings the mood is sad, lifeless. People push and shove their way to the bus stops. Usually Tsao, the interpreter forced upon us, trots along near us. His English is lamentable; he is largely self-taught because he has had the opportunity to meet foreigners. And now he uses his capabilities to ask us unceasingly about pop music, money and sex. That's what we Westerners represent for him. It makes one despair. Thus we issue forth to where we seemingly belong. A taxi takes us to the 'International Club'. For 14 yuan – that is about 20 DM, the weekly wage of a Chinese worker – we can enter this mixture of disco, billiards, bar and bowling alley. To our astonishment the majority of the guests are young Chinese. We establish that here also there is an 'upper class', privileged persons who, in colourful clothes of Western cut and stylishly coiffured, try to look like men and women of the world. For all that, the atmosphere is fusty. Can this be the new China of which we have heard?

With the never-ending negotiations over trifles with the CMA, we come up against the traditional behaviour of communist functionaries every time. Friendship between our nations is of course constantly spoken of and they make protestations of heartfelt hospitality, but in spite of all that I sense the wall which stands between us. These people have been indoctrinated with the ideology of class warfare for too long. Everywhere about us is a vacuum. We long for the day of our departure.

Before that there is another opulent dinner to which the CMA has also invited the Chinese Mount Everest expedition of 1975. Finally I get the chance to hear more of this undertaking about which the Western world has heard so many rumours.

Success of the Chinese

When the Chinese occupied Tibet in 1950/51, the northern side of Mount Everest fell to them too. What could be better than the highest mountain on earth for a demonstration which would prove to the world that, with united communist strengths, everything is possible? By 1960 the Red Guard of the People's Republic had already organized an expedition to this end. Mao Tse Tung was symbolically named as expedition leader. But the Chinese were unlucky. When the first announcements of a summit victory reached the rest of the world no one believed them. The few inadequate documentary photographs, on which really nothing concrete could be identified, were not taken seriously. That gave the offended Chinese no peace. Mao had said:

'Within the mass of the people lives an unlimited creative power, they can organize themselves and can develop their strength in every place and every direction where it is possible for them to achieve an advance.'

By 1975 all was ready again. To the praise of the party the biggest expedition of all time departed from Lhasa on the long march. A road had been specially built for the convoy of lorries to Rongbuk at the foot of the mountain. In the ruins of the monastery, from which the last monks had been driven in 1967, more than 300 Tibetans and Chinese established themselves for a long siege. By the route reconnoitred 50 years before by the English, as many comrades as possible were to reach the summit. So that equal rights should not remain an empty word women had been included in the team, of whom more than 20 reached heights above 8,000 metres.

The Chinese laid a telephone line from Rongbuk into advanced camp at 6,500 metres above sea level. Edifying speeches resounded daily from the loud speakers, morning gymnastics trained their bodies and ideological discussions their spirit.

A herd of yaks transported the supplies up the East Rongbuk Glacier to advanced base camp. With admirable team-work the Chinese built camp after camp and secured the second rock step – that 'second step' which, with the disappearance of Mallory and Irvine in such a tragic manner, has become so famous. Aluminium ladders were installed. More than 200 men provided the basis for the nine who finally reached the summit. They were the key-stone of a collective pyramid.

The Tibetan woman Phantog was

Column of Chinese climbers on the North Col.

not only deputy leader of the whole undertaking, she was the second woman after the Japanese Junko Tabei to reach the highest point on earth, which she did on 27 May together with eight men. There had never been such a mass ascent of Mount Everest! This time the Chinese took care that no one in the world could doubt their victory. On the summit they erected a survey tripod with Mao's flag and shot a film of the entire undertaking.

The team had taken sporadic bursts of oxygen during the ascent, but the summit team had stayed on the highest point for an hour without this aid.

As the Chinese mountaineer at that CMA dinner came to the end of his story I looked at him thoughtfully. What must this man, drilled with the maxim 'the individual is nothing – the community is everything', make of my decadent ego-trip? He smiles at me and raises his glass: 'Gánpéi!'. World of the East – World of the West. For me mountaineering is not sport, rather a

Just beneath the 'second step'.

game, not battle, rather adventure. The 'sporting' ingredient is the travelling through a wide, wild country. I drink a glass to my friend Bulle Oelz. He once called mountaineering 'the sport of suffering'. Next morning we fly from Peking to Chengdu in the province of Szechuan, the next stage on the way to Lhasa.

Lhasa

Despite our impatience to get to Lhasa we are sorry that we have to leave Chengdu so quickly. After the dusty brown-grey of Peking the province of Szechuan appears to me like an oasis. It looks just as I imagined China as a

child: endless green paddy fields, in between thick, high bamboo copses with reed-thatched peasant cottages. The fields are subdivided by many narrow dykes, some of which are under the water. In them sparkles a silver grey sky. On the dykes, barefooted peasants wander along with poles over their shoulders, on which wooden buckets hang front and back. Under the flat straw hats only the long Chinese pigtail is missing, replaced nowadays by a radical military haircut. Here is the China of a beauty which stirs me deeply. Here, at first sight, everything goes on unscathed.

Slowly, our old propellor machine

winds itself up off the airfield, and the green landscape beneath us becomes gradually hilly. The hills grow into mountains, the first snow shimmers on the horizon.

We approach the mountain ranges of eastern Tibet. The outstretched, isolated brown mountain ridges speckled with little houses fly by in a bizarre sea of rock. Like colossal white-caps, seven thousand metre peaks appear

hours by jeep and we shall be in Lhasa. I can scarcely wait.

Finally, we have our rucksacks stowed in the vehicle, have organized the transport of our remaining luggage, and we are off. Behind us two minibuses transport precious tourists.

And so we approach Lhasa, the mysterious city in a legendary country that has been for centuries the longing and goal of adventurers, scientists and

The Chinese in 1975 with the survey tripod on the summit of Everest.

time and again; iced-up faces, glittering glaciers. My heart pounds. Our pilot changes course for the Tsangpo, the long river which winds its way out of Tibet in a sandy yellow bed to India and is there called the Brahmaputra. Ever further we fly up the Tsangpo. Beneath us lies Tibet!

At last we land on an airfield in the Tsangpo valley. It lies at a height of 3,600 metres. Impatiently I hop from one foot to the other. Only two more

religious mystics, like so many who have tried before us. Like in a different way, Heinrich Harrer, fleeing from an Indian internment camp with his friend Peter Aufschnaiter in 1944, after a march lasting many months and full of privations, miraculously reached the city of the god-king alive, and spent seven years there. Like in a different way, too, the Swedish explorer of Asia, Sven Hedin who tried to reach this wonderful city in the

In Chengdu Tibetan and Chinese cultures meet.

most adventurous disguises, as a pilgrim, as a shepherd dressed in skins, and as a respectable Ladakhi merchant, in the course of three journeys under unimaginable conditions. He never saw Lhasa. The tourist bus behind us seems to me a frightful affront to all these persevering travellers.

Our little motorized caravan winds along the valley of the Kyichu River, followed by a great cloud of dust. Out of the sparse grey-brown plain rise ranges of stony hills, pale violet coloured. Time and again there are spots of green, little groups of willow or poplar trees, through whose tender green leaf tracery the sun shines as through the hair of a blond woman. Now and then a tiny, whitewashed village. Frequently it delights us to discover brushwood stacked on the flat roofs, on which flutter bright prayer flags. Above the valley, a hawk circles in the clear air. I am glad. I had read somewhere that there were no longer any wild creatures in Tibet because the occupying troops had killed them all off. A big yellow dog trots across the grey gravel of the river bed and disappears slowly into the arid grass. After more than an hour's journey on the bumpy road the Kyichyu valley broadens out. In its centre rises a hill on which – like a Fata Morgana – golden roofs glitter in the sunshine. The Potala! A gigantic white fortress which seems to have grown from the hill and, punctuated by innumerable black window apertures, tapers upwards like a waterfall to culminate in the red-coloured part of the building which is crowned with pagoda-shaped golden roofs. Like a mighty stone ship full of mystery the Potala is enthroned on the Marpori, the red mountain.

Although I am no believer, I can suddenly perceive how pious pilgrims feel when they catch sight of the dome of St. Peter's or Mecca for the first time. The word Potala means 'safe haven' and the word Lhasa 'place of the gods'. As we approach ever nearer to the place of the gods, I am more and more irritated by aluminium tanks and barrack-like concrete facades. Behind them, what is left of old Lhasa?

Directed by liaison officer and interpreter our jeep sheers off left at the edge of the city into a small alley, and after we have passed two turnpikes we draw up in a bungalow settlement, a hotel town encircled by the military, the government rest house. Once again we are in a ghetto. After we have dumped our belongings in the spacious and prettily furnished rooms, we are

The airfield in the Tsangpo valley.

despatched to a meal in the dining room. Under a suspended roof we take our places at the white covered tables. Plastic flowers stand in glass dolphins. 'Welcome to Tibet.' We look into noisy white tourist faces. Hastily we down

The Potala.

our meal. Then there is no more holding us. Curiosity drives Nena and me into the city while our liaison officer and interpreter, to our great relief, return to their rooms. They want to accustom themselves to the altitude in peace. Lhasa lies at 3,700 metres.

We cover the 3 kilometres from the hotel to the edge of the city on foot. We have an ancient sketch-map, and at first we look for the Lingkor, the famous pilgrim road which surrounds the holy district of the city. But, alas,

Potala like a hateful frill, we lose ourselves in streets which become smaller. The dreariness becomes animated. And suddenly we are standing on the Barkhor, the innermost ring of streets which surround the Jokhang Temple, Tibet's holiest place. Old Tibetan town houses with carved window frames fence it in. In front of its walls traders have spread out goods on the ground; materials, shoes, wool, tin-plate ware. A dense, gaily coloured crowd strolls clockwise around the

Lhasa, view from the Potala.

asphalt, concrete and hooting lorries have taken the place of pilgrims crawling in the dust and statues of Buddha. Past shuttered banks and administrative buildings, which encircle the

ring. After the closed faces in the vacuum of Peking, the liveliness takes our breath away. Pilgrims from the whole country throng here. Tall men from the rebellious province of Kham, who have pinned up their black pig-tails with red woollen bands, Amdo-Tibetans who are recognized by their round hats, nomads in greasy sheep-skins. In the dust of the street is an old woman who measures the Barkhor with her body length. When her fore-head and arms, protected by little wooden sheaths, have touched the ground, she rises, only to place her feet where her hands were, once more to prostrate her outstretched body on the ground. In earlier times there were pilgrims who covered the whole way from their village to Lhasa in this fashion.

In Lhasa, cut off for centuries, for-eigners are still something like crea-tures of fable. In an instant we are so pressed around by people that we can hardly breathe. We stare into laughing eyes, half fainting from the odour of fat, smoke and urine, which surrounds us. Almost everyone holds some sort of amulet, a jewel stone or a shred of cloth under our noses which he wants to barter with us. I am happy: at last we have arrived. Under the ancient, dried up willow tree dotted with prayer flags in front of the Jokhang Temple pilgrims and beggars have sat themselves down with their whole families. The scent of joss sticks ming-les with the smell of the butter lamps. On the stone flags in front of the entrance to the temple the faithful lie outstretched. Through their hands slide strings of rosary-like beads, their lips murmur prayers. 'Om Mani Padme Hum', 'O, Priceless Jewel in the Lotus' is the ever recurring formula.

As I know that all religious expres-sion was forbidden by punishment to the Tibetans by Mao's Red Army until the overthrow of the Gang of Four, I am most deeply moved by the pious

Bazaar in Lhasa's Barkhor.

fervour which surrounds me. I begin to divine that Buddhism has given the Tibetans strength to hold out and to survive unbroken all the atrocities, which have been done to them by the Chinese 'liberation'.

When on 9 September 1951 the first Chinese troops marched into Lhasa they behaved initially, to the amazement of the population, like a true 'army of liberation', namely peaceably. A treaty was signed which it is installed alongside the Dalai Lama. The dissolution of the Tibetan army was followed by the first onslaughts on the might of the monasteries.

As the occupiers began to confiscate land, to empty monasteries, to arrest and humiliate monks and big landowners, the province of Kham rose in open rebellion. A guerilla war which was to last 15 years spread to the whole country. The young Dalai Lama stayed in the country and tried to

The 'Wheel of Life' (or 'Round of Existence') in the Jokhang Temple, Lhasa.

true took away from the Tibetans all rights in foreign policy, but at the same time guaranteed them internal autonomy. The powers of the Dalai Lama were not to be touched. Soon, however, a different wind blew. Ever more soldiers were stationed in Lhasa, the food supplied to the army by the Tibetans was not paid for; and the Chinese-raised Panchen Lama was mediate. With ever more brutality the Chinese tried to intimidate the obstinate Tibetans. Monks and laymen were tortured or murdered, women raped, children forcibly deported to China. In March 1959 there was a people's uprising in Lhasa, and the Dalai Lama fled to India. Tens of thousands of Tibetans followed him into exile. After the official fall of the Tibetan government the Chinese military took over the administration. Their 'reforms' led to misery as never before. Thousands upon thousands starved. Murder of monks and destruction of the monasteries continued. Monks were put into labour camps. In order to overcome the guerillas a prohibition on travel was imposed over the whole country. Brainwashing and re-education, forced labour and religious prohibition were part of the agonizing everyday life.

Scornfully, Tibet was declared an 'autonomous region' on 9 September 1965; a puppet government danced to the tune of the central committee in Peking but the Red Guard held the tormented people in check. In 1966 a new wave of violence – Mao's renewed cultural revolution – destroyed what still remained. Thousands of monasteries were razed to the ground, the golden statues and treasures transported away to China. The god-king state, the last ancient civilization on earth, was destroyed and was colonized by Chinese settlers. In Lhasa alone, beside 40,000 Tibetans there now lived 120,000 Chinese. Mineral resources and forests, essential wealth of the land, were exploited without restraint, the Tibetans made wretched by hard work and crushing taxes in communes. Only one thing the Chinese could not root out: the belief in Buddha in the hearts of the Tibetans and their loyalty to the distant Dalai Lama. So it does not amaze me that the trader in front of the temple who offers for sale photographs of the Dalai Lama is besieged by a bunch of people. 'Jishi Norbu' they still call their beloved god-king, the 'Priceless Jewel'.

Also, free trading in the markets was forbidden to the Tibetans until 1980. Now they haggle again and enjoy this new, small freedom. Yak butter, vegetables and pressed brick tea make a roaring trade. Under the traders' sales tables sleep dozens of dogs which have sought shelter there from the heat of the day. Even permission to own a dog is an innovation. The Red Guard had killed them all in the pursuit of their purge, and only someone who is aware of the Tibetans' love of animals knows what that did to them. Buddhism abhors all taking of life. Thus in old Lhasa the butchers had their own shunned district in the city, and whosoever wanted to atone for some sin gladly bought a condemned animal in order to save it from death.

Nena and I join the queue of pilgrims round the Barkhor, and let ourselves be lulled by the shuffling of the feet, the rattle of the prayer

Chinese soldiers in the Potala.

115

wheels, the scents of fragrant woods which are burned on small altars at the street side. Now and then a green military cap with red star emerges in the surging of the crowd, but generally a friendly Tibetan face looks out at us from underneath. Not many Chinese are to be found on the Barkhor.

Tired by the many impressions and and squealing children. We avoid the imposing zigzag of the entrance steps and attach ourselves to some nomads who are taking the steep, winding path on the rear side. Here long cords of yak hair run from tree to tree on which a sea of colourful prayer flags billows. At the entrance a Chinese woman guide in a ridiculous white sun

Bazaar in Lhasa.

exhausted by the unaccustomed altitude we return to the hotel where we politely consume our evening meal.

Next morning we visit the Potala. Tsao, our interpreter, has obtained permission for us. In the lake at the foot of the monks' palace women from the old town wash laundry, carpets hat awaits us. She is obligatory. Unpleasantly disturbed by the way in which she pushes aside the pilgrims scurrying in the opposite direction to us with their little butter lamps, we try again and again to make ourselves independent. It's no use. Straightaway a Chinese attendant in sun-glasses detaches himself from some corner and holds us up until she has caught up with us again. And so in the half-light we are driven past the shimmering bronze statues of the Buddhas, through solemn chapels and libraries, ever deeper into this wonderful ant-hill of the monk-king. The Potala is 365 metres long, 109 metres high and

dhas and Bodhisattvas, a wealth which filled even the poorest nomads in the land with pride. More than 1,000 rooms are to be found in the Potala. Today they stand empty, but even in the worst times no one dared to touch them. We see the statues of deceased Dalai Lamas entombed here in elaborately decorated chortens.

Steps leading up to the Potala.

The thousand-roomed Potala.

335 metres wide. Formerly, the high officials of the state lived and carried out their official duties in the unconsecrated white part of the building. In the red part, seven floors high, the monks lived and meditated in the twilight of their butter lamps before the jewel-bedecked statues of the Bud-

The Tibetans believe that the Dalai Lama is a Bodhisattva, an enlightened one who, already freed from the fate of re-birth through his goodness and wisdom, has returned to the world, to redeem suffering humanity. At the same time he is the reincarnation of Chenrezi, the God of Compassion and

A Chinese soldier on the steps leading up to the Potala.

begetter of all Tibetans. When a Dalai Lama dies, this Bodhisattva is born again in the form of a child. The state oracle and high lamas had to seek him out and could recognise him by infallible signs.

Above the chorten tombs of the buried Dalai Lamas, on top of the Potala, there are small pagodas with golden roofs. Past mythological wall paintings the sun-hatted Chinese woman leads us along by way of idyllic interior courtyards and steep ladder-like staircases to the roof of the Potala. What we notice there at once fills us with joy. Everywhere is being rebuilt and painted, rubbish removed and wood repaired. The Potala is being renovated. The Tibetan women peasant workers have happy faces. Perhaps they hope that their god-king will soon return to his hereditary

kingdom. I know that in 1978 the 14th Dalai Lama was asked to return by the Peking government. Since then three delegations have travelled from exile in 'Dharamsala Tibet' in order to inform themselves on the spot about the situation of their countrymen. Their upsetting reports have made the god-king hesitate. Despite the new revisionist policy in Peking it will take years of laborious negotiation before the Tibetans have once more their 'Priceless Jewel'.

Lost in thought, I gaze down into the old city full of nooks and crannies and across the corrugated iron roofs of the dreary architecture of the invaders. Nothing can represent the situation of Tibet better than this view of the disfigured but ever-living Lhasa.

Back in the hotel, I try to converse with Tsao about my impressions. He is

sad and thinks that I should try to
understand the Chinese point of view
too. Shyly he gives me a propaganda
notice.

Tsao cannot understand why I cannot stomach any more. I know that in
old Tibet not everything was for the
best. Not for nothing had the young
Dalai Lama instituted a programme of
reform years before his flight. But I
also know that the feudal masters had
many social obligations which they
complied with. In the old Tibet, starvation such as occurred after the annexa-
tion by China would have been
unthinkable.

Communism is an ideology, which
originated in Europe at the beginning

Inside the Potala.

The Potala, which is being restored.

Chinese Tibet

The Autonomous Region of Tibet is situated on the south-western border area of China. Here are snow-covered mountains, green steppes and ancient forests. Here live over a million industrious and valiant Tibetans, as well as members of other nationalities.

As a result of the feudal bondage system, before the liberation Tibet presented a wretched picture of political corruption, scientific stagnation and cultural backwardness . . . The three great feudal overlords – the reactionary local government of Tibet, the monasteries and the nobility – who made up less than five per cent of the total population of Tibet, but who possessed all the land and most of the draught animals, exploited the broad mass of the people of Tibet up to the hilt. The serfs, on whom multifarious taxes and duties were levied, were exposed to the most diverse, most horrible tortures: beating, whipping, cutting out of tongues, poking out of eyes, skinning . . . The old Tibet was a hell on earth!

Since the peaceful liberation in 1951, especially after the democratic reform of 1959, massive changes have taken place in Tibet. Thanks to the leadership and welfare work of President Mao and the Communist Party of China the million Tibetan serfs have destroyed for all time the reactionary, backward system of feudal bondage, and have introduced a socialist reconstruction on the basis of democratic reforms. Former serfs have now become masters of the land and have taken their destiny into their own hands. Industry, agriculture and cattle breeding are constantly developing: culture as well as education and health organization make great progress; the living conditions of the people are quickly improving. Through democratic reform Tibet has changed from a feudal society of bondage to a socialist society, thereby skipping several centuries. In common with all the other nationalities of China the Tibetans march forward now with giant steps on the road of socialism.

of the industrial age. To impose it forcibly on a people who until the middle of the twentieth century lived in an asiatic civilization of mediaeval form, is to put on this people a hat which cannot fit.

The talks with Tsao make me sad. As he has not learned to think dialectically I do not have the right to take something from him for which I can give nothing in return.

Shekar, Wonder of the World

On the morning of 27 June we leave Lhasa. The sun has not yet risen, the air is fresh and cold. I cast a last glance at the twenty-year dormant Potala on top of the Marpori and at the remnants of the ruined school of medicine of Chokpori which is now a prohibited military area. Tsao, Nena and I sit in the jeep, behind us travels the military lorry hired by us, with Cheng, the liaison officer. Both vehicles are chauffeured by Chinese drivers with white cotton gloves. Our expedition luggage fills scarcely a quarter of the lorry.

The arterial roads of the city are already crowded. On foot or on bicycle people hurry to work in the surrounding cement factories. Peasants carry fresh vegetables to market. Pilgrims move towards the Barkhor in order to make their morning incense offering.

We take the road towards the west. To the right of us in the blue, cold shadows of the mountain side lies Drepung, one of the three state monasteries from which the Tibetan state church ruled its empire. More than 7,700 monks lived here; in the centre lies their medium, the famous state oracle. Black window apertures stare from the white walls of the Drepung, which means 'Rich Heap', abandoned to decay.

After about an hour's travel we cross the guarded bridge on the Kyichu river. On the gravel bank a shepherd refreshes himself in the muddy water, and nearby an old boat is rusting away. Time and again we meet travellers on the dusty road on the way to Lhasa. With wild hooting, our driver frightens them to the side. The bumping and rocking of the jeep lulls me into a half-sleep, from which I first awake when I begin to feel chilly. We have gained height and it becomes perceptibly cold. Below the serpentine bends of the road I see ruined villages. Often, the remains of the temple in their midst are freshly whitewashed. In the grey-brown of the stepped slopes lie tiny freshly tilled fields like green Easter eggs. There are scarcely any trees here. Widely scattered small black dots move about – grazing yaks. We wind higher and higher, the wind becomes cuttingly cold. We have reached the top of a pass and get out.

The top of the pass between Lhasa and Shigatse.

The mountain ridge is crowned by a massive stone mound. In the belief of the Tibetans the passes are inhabited by spirits, so in order to placate them pious travellers place stones for them, and formerly elaborate prayers were often carved on them. Tall dried rice and bamboo canes stand on this mound, on which hang prayer flags and shreds of sheepskin. Even a tattered brocade cap flutters in the wind.

Far below me lies an enormous turquoise-blue lake. Its numerous arms and bays are surrounded by brown mountain slopes. Now and then a toy-size straggly village appears, and terraces of fields which seem to be laid out for dolls. Beyond the brown slopes rise mountain ridges in all colours from violet to aubergine, while in the distance the horizon is delimited by the sharp teeth of white peaks. A clear deep blue sky stretches over all, across which drift isolated snow-white clouds like creatures of fable.

On none of my journeys have I been so torn apart inside as this one. Now, for a moment, I am entirely happy.

Tsao urges us on. We must get to

Shigatse today, and Shigatse is a long way off. As our jeep roars down the winding road and hastens to meet the motionless turqouise-blue of the lake, where it increases speed, I despair of this method of travel for the first time. I would prefer to go on foot, to enter this countryside at a speed with which my soul can cope.

We cross the lake at its right-hand end over a dam, which for a large part is flooded with water. Time and again highway maintenance depots appear on the edge of the road, over and over small bands of workmen are engaged in repairing the stretch. Sound roads are a prerequisite for the controllability of the country. Here, the Chinese have performed a singular work of development in the previously almost completely roadless Tibet.

Now and then, lorries pass us which are often decorated with fresh bamboo on the driver's cab. Tsao explains to me that they come from Nilarmu, a valley on the Nepalese border. The drivers have brought with them into the sparse upland a little bit of green from the luxuriance there. There is an exchange of goods between China and Nepal but I do not find out exactly what is handled.

We stop in front of a barracks. Tsao and Cheng greet the commandant, and lead us proudly forward like rare animals. We drink tea out of enamel cups, which are painted with panda bears. The commandant is a young Han-Chinese, who has lived here for 10 years and seen his family only twice in that time. His room is shabby but tidy – an iron bedstead, two chairs, a red table, a wash bowl, a telephone – that is all. On the wall hanging on

nails are two caps in white wrapping paper. One in cotton for the summer, one in fur for the winter. The man is friendly and polite. He comes from the south of China and hides his infinite homesickness behind rational words. He offers us sticky sweets on a tin plate, and his gesture is of a peaceful friendliness which conjures up the old China. For the first time in my life I am moved by a military commandant, for I sense that here suffers someone who has never been asked about his feelings. He and his soldiers have the task of supervising the scientific development of the country, Tsao explains to me, and with these words I land back in the present.

The road takes us ever further westwards. Here are villages with freshly ploughed fields, grazing yaks and cows in soft green meadows. Like small oases they lie between irrigation ditches bordered by earth dikes. Often a new village is built not far from a ruined one. Generally we see straightaway somewhere above the place a ruined monastery or a gompa, as the Tibetans call their small temples.

Where the land is not yet cultivated we see collective farm gangs ploughing the fields in the vicinity of the villages. The graceful archaic ploughs are drawn by yaks. On their horns these yaks wear red wool pompoms lovingly attached as decoration. The yokes of the team are decorated with the red flags of the People's Republic, yet in the animals' coats I discover again and again little prayer pennants which are to protect them. Children run towards us screaming, and each time when we stop we are immediately surrounded by people.

Then dark faces stare through the windscreen and call out to us some sort of joke which we do not understand.

The fertile oases in the river valleys alternate with broad plains of sand and steppe grass. Like rock towers, weathered ruins soar up into the clear sky. Here, Mongolians and Nepalese burned and plundered centuries ago.

After a journey of eight hours across passes and valleys, feeling sweaty and dirty, we approach Shigatse in the

The highest pass between Lhasa and Shigatse.

A ruined monastery by the wayside.

broad valley of the Tsangpo. Military barracks, corrugated iron roofs, barbed wire protected walls. Above the depressing cement grey something in warm red and gold shimmers at me: the monastery of Tashi Lhunpo. A bird of paradise on a concrete nest. Above it all – how else should it be – the ruined remains of the mighty fortress. Shigatse is Tibet's second largest city. Here, once, were celebrated silversmiths and carpet weavers; today it still grows the best wheat. Here was once the residence of the Panchen Lama, his summer palace, where he always spent his holidays when he

was not in Peking attending to his duties as a delegate.

Nena and I are unloaded at the only rest house in the city and we are no longer surprised that it lies inside the barracks. We are dead tired. On a little table stand two tin basins for washing, and warm water in flashy-coloured thermos flasks, without which here no single household is imaginable.

We sleep deeply until at 5.30 a.m. a penetrating croaking from loud speakers wakes us. The city is being called to

Shigatse Dzong, destroyed during the Cultural Revolution.

123

work and reminded not to forget the most important principles of the government of the People's Republic. The whole thing is accompanied by dreadful music. I hear the assiduous pattering of feet and it makes me think of my years at boarding school. Half asleep, I see the Tibetans as Peking's boarding school pupils, and traumas from my time at school blend themselves with

whirls up sand and rubbish. Despite the sun being up the sky is dull and cheerless. To the west is a wall of cloudy yellow dust. I close my eyes tight, hunch my head between my shoulders and turn away from the wind. The children, who play amongst large-wheeled wooden carts, remain unimpressed by the squall. They notice neither dust nor cold. As the

Tibetans in Shigatse.

the new reality. To endure all this for 150 DM per night per head! Am I mad, then? The Chinese know perfectly well that no Westerner will turn back at this point. I look irresolutely at my tin chamber pot with the goldfish pattern and then brace myself to go across the dusty barrack square to the dirty latrine.

After Nena and I have choked down some slushy breakfast rice we stroll into the city. A sudden gust of wind

wind roars afresh, one of them spreads out his arms as if he wants to capture it. Then they all run towards us with flying hair. They seize us by the hands and lead us to the monastery.

Whereas formerly there were 3,000 monks, now some 500 once again inhabit the small town of cells around the sanctuary in which is stored a nine storey high statue of Buddha. We go up some steps, through low passages and suddenly we are staring into a gigantic golden face. It is of the most beautiful symmetry and surmounts a body which I inspect one storey lower down. The whole Buddha is clothed in shimmering brocade, draped with *kata*, white luck scarves. At its feet stand enormous silver butter lamps. Nearby sits a small boy in a red monk's cowl. He is the first novice I have so far come across.

We return to the city. Sven Hedin waited here in vain for six months for permission to proceed to Lhasa. Apart from a few soldiers I see scarcely any Chinese in the alleys. Hardly any of them will live here voluntarily. The Tibetan plateau, with its average height of between 4,000 and 5,000 metres gives them a great deal of trouble health-wise. They cannot acclimatise themselves sufficiently in the long term. The rate of miscarriages and child mortality among Han-Chinese in Tibet is high.

In Shigatse there is a small market too. A peasant has spread out the undefinable remains of a yak on a grimy tarpaulin. The flesh is crawling with flies. Nearby lies garlic, of which we buy a supply for base camp. Then I discover a small Lhasa Apso. These are the little sealion-like dogs which formerly were only allowed to be bred by the honourable monks in the Potala and by nobles in Lhasa. Only at the beginning of this century were the first examples sent to Europe as gifts for hostesses. I have two of these dogs at home, and for a moment I am homesick. In the area of Munich alone I believe there are more of these animals today than in all Tibet.

The next day we have to cover more than 300 kilometres. Our next des-

Tashi Lhunpo Monastery.

tination is called Shekar Dzong. To right and left standing like ostriches in the desert countryside are blue flowers which children have stuck in the sand. During the journey we bind scarves over our mouths and noses, the better to endure the all penetrating dust inside the jeep.

The fortress of Shekar was prized by the old Tibetan travellers as a sort of wonder of the world. The dzong, as a

Monks by the walls of Tashi Lhunpo Monastery.

Shekar Dzong today.

Shekar Dzong before the Cultural Revolution.

fort is called in Tibet, was a bold, secular building. On a cone-shaped rock outcrop some 300 metres high, joined to the underlying monastery by an embattled wall of savage steepness, the 'Castle of Glass' once stood.

When we arrive it is already night-time. In the bright moonlight the ruins of the destroyed castle reach into the sky like outstretched fingers. With battered bones we crawl into the beds which are housed in a mass dormitory.

The reason for my panting my way at any price up the steep path to the topmost battlements of the dzong the next morning is well-founded; in earlier times the Tibetans brought their offerings of incense here to a special goddess – the 'Goddess Mother of the Snows', Chomolungma. One can see her from here. She stretches out her white arms on both sides, a goddess in the form of stone and ice. Europeans named her Mount Everest.

I gaze towards the snow-white mountain range and am as excited as a young lover.

In the last Village

A Tibetan woman in a ruby-coloured blouse and a long black hand-woven wrap-over dress, held together by a colourfully striped woollen apron and a big silver buckle, brings us breakfast in the rest house at Shekar. Groggy with the stay at the still unaccustomed height and the short night, we eat beans, dumplings, fish and pickled vegetables. In the morning greyness we climb into the jeep.

The scenery here is softer in form than between Shigatse and Lhasa. But the nearer we get to the chain of the Himalaya, the frontier wall between

Ascent to the top of Shekar Dzong.

View from Shekar to the south.

Tibet and Nepal to the south, the more sparse becomes the plateau. After two hours' journey we reach the top of a pass at over 5,000 metres. The eight-thousand metre peaks of Makalu, Lhotse, Mount Everest, Cho Oyu and Shisha Pangma soar out of a sea of dense clouds.

In the ruins of Shekar Dzong.

Chomolungma, Mount Everest.

We climb out the jeep and a wild figure with a rifle over its shoulder stares at us aghast. It must be a Tibetan hunter. Where he comes from, where he is going, is not evident. Perhaps he lives in one of the nomad tents far below the road. Excited by the unreal picture of the ice giants rising out of the clouds I relate to Nena how the Tibetans believe the world was created.

Tibet's story of the creation begins with emptiness, a dark emptiness. Out of this nothingness a wind arose. It filled the emptiness softly and peacefully at first. It blew from all four corners of the sky. With the passing of years it became stronger and ever harder and fashioned a great bolt of lightning. Out of the lightning came clouds which were heavy like the lightning and the wind. From the clouds gushed rain with drops as big as waggon wheels. When it stopped raining there lay the primaeval ocean. When its surface had quietened there came a wind once more. It tossed the water and turned it into foam, thick as cream from which butter is made. Thus was the earth created.

In its midst was a great mountain made of precious stones, the home of the gods. Around it spread out a lake and around the lake a circle of golden mountains. Beyond these golden mountains lay another lake, also ringed round with mountains, and beyond that still another ... seven times earth, seven times water. Behind the last mountain stretched the outer ocean out of which four worlds rose like islands, each of a different form. The world of the south like an upside down cone; the westerly world which was circular; the prosperous land of the north which was square; the easterly world in the form of a half-moon. This whole universe was plunged in darkness, for the gods needed no light. Each of them carried his own light within him. One of the gods came across a juice that flowed out of the earth. All drank from it and left behind their powers, their light; they lost their immortality.

So out of the gods came people. Although dependent on sun, moon and stars this world was ever full of riches. For each person there grew each day one fruit. Until one day a greedy person discovered two fruits on his tree, plucked both and ate them up. Next morning there was no fruit there for him and he became hungry – so hungry that he took the fruit of another. As this person now had no nourishment, he plucked someone else's fruit. Soon everyone was driven to take what did not belong to him. Thus work was created. For all must now plant in order to have enough to eat if someone stole from them. These gods who became people were men. But through their squabbles over the fruit they had altered their feelings and thoughts. One of the men tore his genitalia from his body and became a woman. Children came and soon the world was full of women and men who begot more children . . .

From the airy height of the pass we gaze at this wondrous world. No Tibetan ever came upon the idea of climbing one of these gigantic summits, for the belief is deeply rooted in them that the mountains are the home of the gods. Long before the first expeditions came into the country the inhabitants undertook pilgrimages to them. Rongbuk was one of these places of pilgrimage, Chomolungma a mystery, a mystery in the original sense. The root of the Greek word 'musterion' means 'close lips or eyes'.

In spite of its height, the top of the pass is teeming with butterflies and small animals. The monsoon is long since due but the valleys are still without rain and the summit pyramid of Mount Everest is snow-free and dark. The eternal north wind has swept the uppermost 1,800 metres almost clear. The thought that I have already stood on top of this mountain once makes me feel peculiarly strange.

The road constructed by the Chinese nearly 15 years ago between Shekar and Rongbuk winds first 1,500 metres upwards, and then down the other side into the valley of the Arun which opens up to the south. There is still the old road to the Everest base camp which leads from Tingri over the Lamna La to Rongbuk, but in Peking we have been strongly advised against using it during the monsoon period. A little below the pass I observe a young woman who, with mattock and shovel, is making good the holes in the road. Her brown, tanned forehead is bathed in sweat. She is about twenty years old and has been detailed to work the road here quite alone for weeks. Eight hours a day, six days a week she wields her shovel. At night she sleeps in a tent by the roadside. She has never been to Lhasa in her life. As I look into her imperturbable face I know at once that legendary Shangri La which we occidentals have always sought in Tibet, is not to be found in the scenery of the old, still less in that of the new, Tibet. The Tibetans carry it in their heads, in their souls, in their hearts.

In each Tibetan monastery hangs a drum.

The worker who is called Tashi invites us into her tent for a cup of chang, home-made barley beer. In the tent are bed covers, cooking utensils, an old worn out carpet. In front of a figure of Buddha, which is covered in a fatty layer of soot, burns a tiny lamp.

The valley which leads to the Rongbuk monastery lies far beneath us. Hills in subdued colours and without plant life hem it in. Only the small village of Chodzong appears as a green speck in the wilderness. We travel on. When we reach a height of about 4,600 metres I am surprised by the sight of wood carriers. Wood is scarce in Tibet, and holy also. Tree felling is for the buddhists synonymous with killing. They have always heated with dried yak dung which has been collected in summer and dried in round flat cakes by the house walls.

Chodzong on the edge of the high mountain desert is a poor village. Even the river looks wretched when one considers from what mighty glaciers it springs. The village is bordered by brown limestone humps and old moraines like railway embankments. The houses, built of mud or grass bricks, are windowless; light enters only through the open door or the smoke hole in the roof of the room.

At the edge of the village our lorry gets stuck in the mud; it must have rained here recently. In an instant we are surrounded by some 100 people who help us. How the peasants and shepherds can survive up here is a mystery to me. Barley can be ripe for harvest in 60 days at the earliest. Turnips, potatoes and mustard are irrigated by a fantastically graceful ditch which is scarcely a hand-span deep, and many kilometres long.

When I ask about the gompa, the temple, a few children lead me to a ruin on the edge of the village. Everywhere I see tumbledown dwellings. Inside I find not much more than ragged beds with little tables and meagre utensils. Where stones have fallen out of the wall they have simply covered the places with corrugated iron. The few new houses have not been built in the old style. Here I see the first sacrifice of traditional designs which seems still sadder than the flaking paint and unsightly colours everywhere.

I cannot find out what has happened to these people. They are distressed to such an unusual degree. Perhaps poverty has made them apathetic.

We buy a sheep in order to have some fresh meat in base camp. While a young man from the village slaughters, skins and disembowels it, the mayor tells me about the lack of income in this awful hole. Tsao passes my English on to Cheng in Chinese who finally translates it into Tibetan. Here people earn even less than in other parts of Tibet. Per year per head it is 60 yuan (about 80 DM) and 200 kilos of corn. All the Chinese developments are far away from here. What will become of this poor Chodzong when the planned Everest sight-seeing tourism wrenches it out of its lethargy; when the inhabitants are confronted with what will seem to them unimaginably rich travellers from the West, whose money still flows lump-sum to Peking? The Tibetans do not wave as we leave their village. Soon there opens up a view into the basin of Gyachung Kang, and at the next bend of the road appears a white shoulder which can only be the west summit of Everest. A little bit further and the familiar form of the mountain emerges at the same time as the Rong-buk monastery. We have arrived!

Yak dung stacked by a house wall.

The Monastery of the Snows

In spite of its size, Mount Everest seems at first sight remarkably self-effacing. It is partially hidden behind other mountain ridges, enveloped in thin clouds. I catch only a glimpse of the North Flank when the veil of mist

On the journey to Chodzong.

A sheep is slaughtered.

131

Nuptse and the west shoulder of Everest.

ridges. In a moment its contours are as familiar to me as if I had always lived here. Ghost-like, as in a dream, I experience the visible reality. The mountain seems to grow as I gaze towards it. Ever more mightily it towers up before me; far above the summit appears dark. I cannot see the glaciers at its foot for they are hidden behind the hills.

clears. I have the feeling that the mountain shifts with the moving clouds and I follow it on its imaginary journey. The cloud curtain is blackest around the summit. I stare through my binoculars as if to pierce this curtain.

Suddenly the grey of the mist dissolves, snow-fields glisten through the murk, fragments of the mountain link up. Like a jigsaw puzzle Mount Everest comes together. The mountain builds itself up from its walls, glaciers,

Shivers go through my body, although I do not find the mountain terrifying. I stand before one of my former loves, whose power of attraction is still a puzzle to me. My senses are over-strung, worn down by the strain of the long approach journey and no longer capable of processing quickly enough the impressions which assail me. I simply gaze in silence. Nena too says nothing. The Rongbuk Valley might have been created simply as a frame for Chomolungma. It runs for a length of nearly thirty kilometres, rising only 1,200 metres, and at its end the mountain stands like a mystical colossus – matter which seems intangible.

Summit pyramid of Everest.

The over 3,000 metre-high North Face is flanked by two mighty wings. To the left the North-East Ridge sinks like a roof from the summit, to the right the steep North-West Ridge which with its enormous length emphasises the height of the mountain. Nowhere does one discern toothed ridges or towers, only smooth lines.

Centuries ago monks built the monastery of Rongbuk here. Now I understand why. The monastery is familiar to me from old pictures, and the name has always evoked peaceful and contemplative ideas in me. 'The Monastery of the Snows', a name out of an old fairytale.

First, Nena and I decide to put up our tents, by the well east of the monastery walls so that we have a protected standing camp. Then we go through the ruins of the former town of monks and want only to get away out into the mountains, further into the wilderness, away from here. The ruined monastery has not only been a rubbish heap for a half dozen Everest expeditions, it is so empty and cheerless that I get depressed in its vicinity. The only thing from earlier times which still stands is the chorten in front of the main entrance, but its top, too, already leans precariously. All the wood from the famous temple carvings has been burned or carted away. The remains of the fine paintings crumble from the walls. The expelled monks have erected a new monastery on the other side of the mountain in Nepal, called Tutunchuling.

The Upper Rongbuk Valley used to be a holy district in which no animal could be killed. The limit of this nature

In the ruins of Rongbuk.

Tutunchuling Monastery in Nepal.

133

reserve was a gigantic Mani wall at the valley entrance by the village of Chobuk. This wall of heaped stones and incised prayers has disappeared as well.

The monks were supplied by the pilgrims who brought with them abundant barley meal (tsampa), tea, yak butter, warm materials and other gifts. While Nena and I deliberate where we want to put our camp I hear a rifle shot. I run round and see Cheng, who is hunting a hare. I am furious, for I have decided that we too shall kill no animals up here.

Late in the afternoon we depart, to travel with the jeep a further 5 kilometres up the valley. There we shall erect our camp. Frightened by the noise of the motor a small dun-coloured wolf trots away on a moraine. At a safe distance he peers curiously at us. Everest is now almost completely visible. Its whiteness looks glassy as if it were lit from within. I have the jeep stop in order to orientate myself. To the left of us rises a row of unclimbable rock bluffs which are over 1,000 metres high. Their dull rust red reminds me of mountains in the Dolomites. In front of us lie lower moraine banks and far behind bluish ice glistens in the desolate grey glacier tongues.

Time and again we have to stop to remove pieces of stone from the road. The bumpy jeep track leads past a handful of deserted hermitages. Here lived the monks who once so impressed Maurice Wilson. Bodily life in its most abstract form, motionless perseverance over years, alone with themselves and infinity, such was their sojourn in a mysterious region between heaven and earth.

It makes me think of a poem that the hermit Milarepa wrote in the 11th century. It is called 'Snowstorm on Chomolungma'. (See opposite)

We build our main camp exactly at the spot where the early British expeditions camped on the Rongbuk Glacier at a height of 5,100 metres. We have good drinking water, a little bit of green, and flat places for the tents. Five hundred metres further on I discover the graves of the Japanese who had died on Mount Everest shortly before. Meanwhile Chomolungma is again covered in cloud, and above us dark banks of thunder clouds threaten: I suspect that the monsoon wind has already set in in full strength.

Mount Everest lies at the narrowest part of the over 2,000 kilometre-long Himalayan chain. It is especially

The remains of walls of a hermitage.

Snowstorm on Chomolungma

To the wilderness, to Chomolungma's glacier walls, I went, craving solitude.

Heaven and earth conspired to send the snorting wind as messenger; wind and water, the elements, boiled with rage, the dark clouds of the south formed themselves into a ball.

The exalted pair, sun and moon, were held captive; fettered were the eight and twenty constellations of the lunar stations, the eight planets into an iron chain beaten, the false Milky Way all concealed, the small stars quite by vapour veiled.

And when the vapour clouds covered everything, it snowed for nine days, nine nights, steadily for eighteen days and nights heavy snow fell in fleecy clumps, floating like birds it came down.

When the thickness of the snow has surpassed all measure, up above the white summit of the snow mountain rises against the sky, down below the groves of trees lie pressed down.

A white robe envelops the black mountains, ice smoothes the billowy, reflecting lake, and in the subterranean hell a blue stream hides, the ground, high or low, smoothes itself away to the plain.

Between the whirling snow, which fell from up above, between the wind in the fullness of the winter's New Year and the cotton robe of Milarepa, there raged a battle on the summit of the soaring, white snow mountain. The falling snow melted away in the distance to water, the wind howled loudly, laid itself nonetheless aside, and the cotton robe burned like fire . . .

Absolutely have I defeated the snow faced demon.

exposed to the first thrusts of the south-west monsoon. This rainy wind from the Bay of Bengal arrives earlier in the year than the westerly streams from the Arabian Sea. Thus there exists at end of July to early August the hope for a break in the bad weather. I know that it is impossible in this wind to make headway at great heights, but I hope for a break in the monsoon, as German meteorologists have predicted for me.

On the first morning in base camp I immediately have to climb up for an hour to reconnoitre the mountain and its world. Nena has sent Tsao, who has altitude sickness and has complained all night, back to Shigatse with the vehicles. Now she is sorting out our provisions.

In the Alps we use the principal glaciers as quite obvious, more or less pleasant, access routes. Here, things are different. The Rongbuk Glacier is so churned up that I don't at first attempt it at all. Like a brown-grey storm-whipped sea its rubbish-covered ice humps lie beneath me. I ask myself how we shall make headway further up above.

The first real approach to a big mountain is always exciting. There are so many unknowns: the weather, the possible course of the route – the way I myself will react in the face of this self-imposed task. Every time Mount Everest becomes visible, I am seized by a feeling of hopelessness, a whole new experience of weakness bordering on impotence. After climbing 30 or 40 metres, I have to rest. I am still not sufficiently acclimatised and cannot yet rightly see how I am to cope with the stresses higher up. The air is thin, I keep trying to breathe deeply. On the way back I ask myself, not for the first time, why I don't stay below, why don't I just stay below as the hermits did? Why not take up my quarters in one of these secluded districts, which so attract me, for the rest of my life? I know that I could not do it. I am inwardly just as dependent on the civilized Occident as on my expeditions.

One of the many reasons I need these expeditions is because I have a terrible fear of otherwise wasting away bodily. I cannot forget the old man, whom I saw some time ago making circuits of a hotel garden. On unsteady legs, he tottered about on the grass, his pale belly held in by an enormous pair of bathing trunks – a wealthy wreck. One wreck among many whose squandered lives my friend Bulle daily has to support. The intensive care unit in his clinic is filled with the flotsam and jetsam of an affluent society – rusted away at desks, corroded by nicotine and alcohol. The futile struggle against heart attacks and cirrhosis has awakened in Bulle too a horror, which has become the spur for keeping him unremittingly active. It makes him jog round the university campus at lunchtime, drives him to evening runs in the woods, to climbing on Sundays and on expeditions in the holidays.

The reverse solution – of becoming one of the contemplative residents of Rongbuk – is not possible for a Westerner like me. For that I would first have to have put many rebirths in the East behind me.

On Foot to the Nangpa La

We are still not acclimatized and the weather is terrible. I believe that not only this summer of 1980 but all summers to the north of Mount Everest are grey, windy and unpleasantly cold. We are suffering from the inclemency of the weather. Low pressure troughs which have built up in the north-west pass over the Rongbuk valley and it rains almost every day. Even in the foothills it is cold and damp. Each weather disturbance manifests itself

Arrival at base camp.

Base camp 1980.

in an endless succession of storms and downpours.

For the time being we can only sit around up here and wait. So as not to get out of form and because we are full of curiosity, Nena and I decide to march out of the valley westward to the Lamna La.

As we pass Rongbuk a column of smoke rises, and large birds of prey circle over the monastery. Some dark forms disappear behind the walls. We are fascinated. Is, by chance, a so-called sky burial taking place here? It used to be the custom in Tibet to throw the corpses to the vultures and ravens. In an old book I read of such rites taking place to the east behind the hills of the Sera monastery. We are not allowed to approach; by their savage

Tibetan recluse.

137

appearance alone the Tibetans drive us away. The carrion crows make tight circles in the air or wait on walls higher up the slope. If my conjecture is correct, then even now a lifeless corpse is being laid face down on a rock up here, the skull split open, and heart and liver thrown to the vultures. The bones are burned. We have too much respect for this ritual to want to anger the people. An old woman making tea

small bridge and struggle up the steep slopes to a pass left of the Lamna La. We see many Tibetan hares and beneath us an almost unending landscape of hills.

It slowly becomes clear to us what we have let ourselves in for. All the villages on our way are abandoned or empty. We had reckoned on being able to buy food as we went, but we have already been going for seven hours

Messner, Cheng, Nena and Tsao at base camp.

keeps guard. We carry on. Poor Tibetans previously often threw the bodies of their dead into the river or burned them. The bodies of the lamas were buried intact or their ashes sealed in urns walled up in chortens. In the Upper Rongbuk Valley we have found so many such chortens that we believe that this holy place is used for burial now as formerly.

A dim sun shines weakly through the clouds as we descend the gravel track on the right bank of the Rongbuk river. After three hours we cross it by a

without meeting a soul. We are deadbeat. We have not had enough to drink, and far and wide there is no water. As we cross the top of the pass it begins to snow, but an hour later the air is clear again and we can see far to the north and the west. The high summits in the background seem to be within easy reach, but that is an optical illusion, as ever in the Tibetan landscape where the air is more transparent than elsewhere in the world.

On the pale green of an alpine pasture I can see below something which looks like five enormous black bees. On approaching we discover them to be nomad tents. It is the thick ropes of tarry coloured yaks' wool tethering the awnings that gave the impression of bees' legs. Around the tents big stone walls are piled up, pens in which sheep huddle together. Further away some yaks are grazing: their shaggy coats reach almost to the ground.

We put up our tent about a stone's throw away and I approach the camp cautiously. Out of one of the tents comes a man who whistles to the two giant dogs who approach threateningly with bristling backs. Then he looks at me calmly. I ask in gestures for milk.

'Dudh', I say for I have learned the word from Tibetan Sherpas in Nepal. The man laughs and invites me into the tent. I call Nena.

Around a fire of dried yaks' dung sit men, women and children who I can scarcely make out in the half-light. We receive butter tea in a bowl made out of root wood decorated with silver. Before she pours the tea out the housewife – if one can actually call a nomadic woman who spends her life in tents thus – garnishes the bowl with a little pat of butter.

Meanwhile, my eyes have become accustomed to the half-light. I can see that the men are stitching soles on to boots made of felt, or spinning wool. In a corner a pile of yak dung cakes is stacked up. Hides, covers and wool carpets complete the furnishings. Here, too, is a small picture of the Dalai Lama with a butter lamp in front.

Of course red flags flutter on all five tents, but for nobody in Tibet has so little been altered through the annex-

Bridge over the Rongbuk river.

ation, as for the nomads. In earlier days the land belonged to the feudal lords, today it belongs to the state. They themselves have always been without property.

We try to converse with each other and our sign language is accompanied by much tittering. Over and over again I say 'Lamna La' and point in the direction from which we have come. Each time the nomads raise their hands as if parrying and laugh. Slowly

Yaks.

139

it dawns on us that we have taken the wrong route. How about that for play acting?

I like the salty rancid butter tea. The salt comes from the lakes in the north of the country, the butter from a plump leather skin bag. Roasted barley meal, sheeps' cheese hard as stone, occasional dried meat if an animal has met with an accident; self-woven material or hides as clothing, a tent that, together with household goods and weaving stool, is fastened on the backs of the yaks when the land yields nothing more, so simple is this harsh life.

As we return to our tent it snows lightly. The yaks look odd in their thick cloaks of snow. Imperturbably they lie in the wind-driven snow and munch away to themselves.

Nena and I sleep deeply. Once a dog barks and I look out of the tent flap. It has stopped snowing, a bright moon shines on a silver scene. I crawl back into my sleeping-bag and for a long time listen to the peaceful munching of the yaks.

Next day we carry on. We go first down into the plain of Tingri and then up the valley in the direction of the Nangpa La. Mount Everest shows itself in clear beauty. We have been travelling for some four hours when a small yak caravan crosses our path. Seven yaks, a donkey, a dog and two drivers who drive their animals with a soft, almost tender whistling. For all they appear so thick-skinned, yaks in reality are extremely hypersensitive and if they are alarmed it can be hours before they can be captured again and quietened down.

The yak drivers stop their small column and invite us to go with them. Why not? A yak carries our tent and utensils. This journey is over in two hours. The two drivers put up their small tent and put the yaks out to pasture. It is 3 p.m. so we have a lazy afternoon and slip away to bathe in an icy river.

The next morning we travel further with the caravan. After a while it turns off right down into the mountains, we take our leave and continue in the direction of the Nangpa La. We cross tender green meadows and climb higher.

Just under the Nangpa La we see some Sherpas approaching from the Nepalese side. I can hardly grasp the fact that I recognize their faces: these are old friends! We were together on Ama Dablam. They are on the way to Tingri where they want to exchange some belongings for salt.

The Sherpas, a Tibetan race which centuries ago travelled over the passes into Nepal and settled there in Solo Khumbu, have for years been allowed to carry on a small border traffic between Tibet and Nepal. Generally, they bring grain and take salt. Although they are still faithful Buddhists and hold the mountains to be the home of the gods, they have long since become the world's best high-altitude porters, without whose help most expeditions would still be unthinkable.

The Sherpas tell us that the Nangpa La, which leads over a glacier and at one time was well-used, has become passable only with difficulty and is rather dangerous. The stream of refugees which poured into Nepal after the religious prohibition of the 1950s has dried up.

After wandering on for a few more kilometres I sit for a long time on a moraine crest, from which I can see Cho Oyu in all its beauty. I let my thoughts roam while scanning the distant horizon to the north. I let them gush and flow with the glacier water, fly with the wind, amble irresolutely on the glittering snow slopes.

After a makeshift camp on the edge of the glacier we return to our base camp next evening.

Sherpas under the Nangpa La.

Cho Oyu from the north.

141

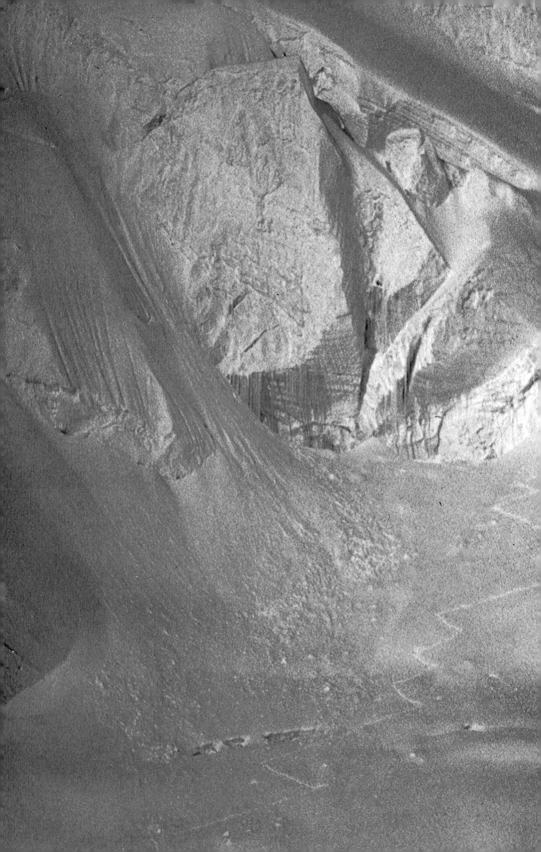

North Col –
Stuck in the
Monsoon Snow

*Leave victory and booty to others, take
sacrifice and defeat upon yourself.*

*Bsodnams Rgyamtso, third Gyalwa
Rimpoche*

North Col –
Stuck in the Monsoon Snow

East Rongbuk Glacier

By midday the sun has already disappeared behind a thick layer of cloud. A strong wind comes up which howls ever louder. Cheng fears a storm and fixes his tent with extra guy-ropes. I want to have a look round the hermitages in the vicinity of base camp. As Nena has no desire to come I go alone. Meanwhile she sits in the tent and writes in her diary:

When my emotions are churned up and I feel I wish to say something, Reinhold has either no time or he is not in a similar mood. Once again I am alone with my ego. The old persecution complex is there again. Sometimes I feel myself crushed by this man! But I know that that is exactly what I want: a strong man, an independent identity. It can be that in my uncertainty I seek an idea which I myself can hold fast to. But occasionally my ego becomes so affected that I can hardly bear it. Damn it! I trust his judgement but when he says 'you can't do that' or 'you will never climb up there', I think, damn this man! What does he know? If he could transfer himself to the innermost recesses of my heart, would he perhaps see how harmless it is when I say: 'Oh, it's possible that one day I shall climb the Matterhorn by the North Face.' Sure I know that's aiming a bit high. I have always worn my heart on my sleeve and know how difficult it is to turn dreams into deeds. But nevertheless I don't like people to say that to me before I have actually attempted it.

At times I am completely irrational. Reinhold makes me mad. I become towards him insulting and accuse him of insulting me. In my heart I know that I am wrong but it doesn't restrain me from being intolerable to him. In his way Reinhold is the most patient and most lenient man I have ever known; perhaps because he perceives how nasty he himself can be. While sitting here in camp, writing, I experience more than a small crisis. Women are universally more adroit at household affairs, and so Reinhold and I have divided our duties as at home. I concern myself with the cooking, the camp, the pharmacy; he is responsible for the organization, the mountain, the reconnaissance and the writing.

We have made the base camp as orderly as is possible with this constant wind. Tsao woke me the first night with a high fever, and I have sent him back to Shigatse. I cook, wash, tidy up. It leaves me no free time to sit out and read or write. I don't mind carrying out these jobs. But when I once ask for help and get as answer: 'leave me in peace, can't you see I'm reading?' I go through the roof.

Yesterday we came back from a five day tour. We have hiked at least 150 kilometres. By the end we had run out of food and now we both need a rest period. Since we arrived here yesterday Reinhold has read ceaselessly. 'Can't you understand that I must work?' he says, while he reads about people who make a boat trip or occupies himself with Marcel Proust. When he is studying maps and Everest material I can appreciate that. I would like to participate in it but he shuts me out.

11 July 1980. I regret that I did not undertake my excursion today alone as I originally intended. One never learns! As I was preparing our midday meal I was in such a good mood, full of energy. So while eating up the tinned chicken I proposed an excursion. No answer. Therefore, after clearing away I say: 'Then I'm going alone'. 'No', he says. It gives me much pleasure to go around alone, however. I gaze at Nature, muse, come to terms with myself. Reinhold has snuggled himself up comfortably in his sleeping-bag and says: 'Wait, until I have finished reading, then we'll go together.' I ask

how long that will be. An hour and a half, he thinks. So I suggest he finishes his reading after going for a walk. No answer. Just as I decide that I shan't get a better offer, he says: 'I'll come, in about twenty minutes'. So I make some coffee.

The twenty minutes are long since past. Reinhold says: 'It's raining.' 'Not really,' I retort, 'it's only a few drops.' Time passes by. Suddenly Reinhold sits up: 'Okay, I'm going now. But I must go at my own speed, you

see that Reinhold has set off. I run after him and attempt to catch him up. He goes along by the river, I take the mountain side which leads from base camp to the road. I go over the hill and try to meet him at the road. But he goes fast. As I arrive on the hill and look into the distance he is already on the next hill. I stand and stare at him. He turns round and looks towards me. Then he goes on. I can't believe it.

Clearly it makes no difference to him

Site of base camp.

know!' I reply that I do not want to convert my meditational stroll into a sprint, for that is Reinhold's speed. We get ready. Then suddenly Reinhold is standing quite ready in front of the tent saying: 'I'm off now!' By itself that is a harmless observation. But it makes me mad, and I yell: 'All right, you bastard, go then! But after I have waited an hour and a half for you, you could at least wait until I have put some other socks on.' 'Why?' 'Because these socks are too thin for my hiking boots.' I change my socks in less than a minute and

whether we go together or not. And I have no more desire to run after this man. So often I have tried to overtake him but somehow I am always behind him. I can understand that one keeps one's distance when making trail or on difficult terrain. But when people want to take a stroll together?

I am sad and go down to the river alone. After a while I cannot see Reinhold any more. In the big, wide river bed I jump from stone to stone. Why am I so concerned about this relationship? Why do I have him always in mind? Quickly I run further and try to banish him from my thoughts.

In a warm spot protected from the wind in front of a block of rock on the slope of the moraine I settle down. It is a place which I like. From here, stretched out like a lioness on the rock, I can overlook all that lies around me. I think of the wolf which recently ran across the moraine at Rongbuk. Suddenly everything seems to move. Stones turn into yaks and the man we are expecting from the last village appears now here now there. It is like an apparition. I scan down the scree slope above me and wish the wolf would come to me. I know that I should be frightened and consider how I can defend myself. Now, while writing, I see once more the eyes of the wolf, see them clearly before me, and I know that they are the eyes of Reinhold, when he is raging and furious. His eyes become piercing, with cold blue flashes. They are like a knife. Clouds come together, encircle me. I go back to the tent and feel better. I reflect on how argumentative I am, as I know Reinhold will ask me about it. But I am no longer sad because he went without me.

This afternoon I visited Everest. I kept studying its clear aesthetic lines. With its white monsoon snow cloak on its shoulders, on which the still, dark rock head of the summit pyramid sits, it looks like a wonderful bird with out-stretched wings. Now I understand the old wisdom of the lamas: 'Everest is a bird which no other bird can fly over.'

But real animals also meet me today, a few hares, and higher up some wild sheep. All the animals here have coats the colour of the moraines. If they don't move you cannot disting-uish them from the stones. Our inter-preter has returned, recovered, from Shigatse and has ordered yaks for the march to advanced base camp.

At last on 13 July we can set off with

Yaks near base camp.

three animals and two drivers. We cross the river bed and climb up the true right side of the valley. Above the main glacier we see on the moraine slopes earth pyramids up to 10 metres high which remind me of the Gaudi Cathedral in Barcelona.

It is a beautiful day. Chomolungma stands like a giant folding screen in the valley background. It always amu-ses me that I see it not as one but as two mountains. The Nepalese south side which I have climbed, a dark pyramid which is visually cut off for the most part by the Lhotse–Nuptse wall, has not the slightest similarity to, and a completely different aura compared with, the free, winged north side.

Although the Rongbuk Valley is narrow I do not feel myself hemmed in. Many times, up side valleys and over snow fields, I can glimpse the distant horizon. Once I can even see away over the barrier of the Himalaya far into Nepal to the south. Nowhere else have I ever had such a distant view from the floor of a valley.

147

The beginning of the East Rongbuk Valley.

These distant strips of horizon, translucent as frosted glass, have attracted me magically ever since my first mountain excursions as a child. Bright, transparent strips belong to my strongest childhood memories.

Cheng and Tsao at base camp.

Now I know that it is the horizon which I am captivated by in the mountains. I am reminded that during a tour as guide in the Dolomites a few weeks after my divorce I burst into tears at the sight of these strips of horizon. The horizon is my strongest experience when climbing; that was something I first recognized in Tibet.

The great moraine walls are unending; it is hard to comprehend the masses of stone and earth moved by this savage glacier.

In a hollow at the start of the East Rongbuk Glacier we erect our bivouac. The yaks are given some of the hay, which they have carried with them, our porters, tea, soup and some tinned food. Nena and I wash ourselves in a tiny deep-blue glacier pool. While I sit in our companions' yaks' wool tent Nena writes:

As we climbed higher following the East Rongbuk river we knew that we would find the camp sites of the previous Chinese and Japanese expeditions. The yaks were slow and often stopped for a rest. We moved light-heartedly along the glacier stream. We saw isolated green, bushy and strongly scented plants, and everywhere tiny herbs between the rocks. Wild birds fluttered away screaming. I was in the best of moods. The river, although fast and brown, looked like an icy geyser. It bubbled out from the moraine-covered glacier, created a great pool and ran in cascades towards the valley. We went round this pool, climbed over a moraine bank and stood in the biggest rubbish dump one can imagine. How can people who come to such an untouched country leave their waste lying around? Even the small blue pool was dirty. Once again I am disillusioned with humanity.

Next day our yaks climb like chamois farther along the edge of the glacier. A non-mountaineer cannot follow these nimble animals with their intelligence and assurance up there. In one place a mud-flow starts – the yaks hear it rumble – they shake their heads and will not go one step further. Our drivers – peasants to whom the yaks belong – want the animals to carry on. The yaks throw off their loads and run away. We lose a lot of time dragging the boxes up ourselves and have all the trouble of encouraging the nervous animals across this dangerous stretch. It is the only place in the world's mountains where yaks can climb to 6,500 metres. That is possible only because a mound of detritus winds between two mighty streams of ice as far as the ice face under the North Col.

We have planned to set up our mid-way camp at 6,000 metres as a depot for the descent. We take our time,

The yaks are loaded.

carefully levelling the ground before putting up the tent. Around us are dirty white séracs with vertical walls which tower high as houses above our tent. More bizarre the world cannot be!

On the third day after leaving base camp we continue on our way along the central moraine which has melted a trough between the walls of the

Tsering, one of the two yak drivers.

149

glacier. So we pass between icebergs, séracs, ice walls. In Tibet not only the clouds change in the wind, but also the mountains, the hills, the ice. I can literally see that this high plateau is alive like the sea, that it smells like hide, that it vibrates like a sea of lava. I know nothing of meteorology, little of geology, and I am no geographer, but what I see here, smell, feel, belongs to the most important things which give me strength and zest for life.

So on the gravel stream we approach advanced base camp under the northeast face of Mount Everest. The summit still lies far in the background and appears like an appendage. The yaks are tired, also they are feeling the altitude. Nena and I erect our tiny tent. On the same day the yaks return part of the way.

What already alarms me here on this first day are the avalanches which come thundering down everywhere, over the North-East Face, over the North Col. I had never envisaged it as bad as this. I was aware that the face leading to the North Col contains many dangers with its deep crevasses and avalanche slopes – it is the most dangerous section of my ascent – but I did not expect so many avalanches.

None of the solo climbers before me got beyond this North Col, the religious fanatic Wilson did not reach the top of it. But perhaps I am madder than Wilson. Are my chances in the monsoon nil? Each avalanche represents simultaneously question, doubt, loss of self-confidence. The Tibetans say that to approach the throne of the gods is to court disaster. Even the working of mineral deposits counts as pernicious because thereby the equilibrium of the material and spiritual world is disturbed. Whosoever clumps around on the stones gladdens the Devil who can then escape into the

Glacier trough.

Yaks on the East Rongbuk Glacier.

world. And I, I shall not only stumble about, I shall disturb the gods.

For hours on end during the following days I study the North Col through binoculars. The 7,000 metre-high col is my next objective. The detached giant blocks of ice at its foot certainly inspire little confidence. The ice slopes under the saddle ridge are furrowed by avalanche cones.

The snow is so soft that I sink in up to my tummy. Have my fantasies, my ambition enticed me into a trap?

Ten Long Days

We do not miss Cheng and Tsao, who are waiting down at base camp until we return. Tsao would have collapsed again at this height, and without him Cheng cannot stay with us.

I concentrate on the weather and the mountaineering obstacles. If the Indian weather statistics are correct, then the weather will follow a sixteen year cycle, and we shall find ourselves in a dry spell. In defiance of the statis-

tics it snows daily, accompanied by sudden falls of temperature.

I need at least four days of fine weather in a row to reach the summit from advanced base camp. At the moment it seems hopeless. On the

Advanced base camp and Everest.

151

Slopes leading to the North Col.

slopes of the North Col the soft snow still lies thigh-deep. It is extremely avalanche prone. Also, the yellow band under the first rock step appears to be unclimbable on account of a lot of powder snow. I begin to consider whether I would be able to get to the summit pyramid below the edge of the ridge. The area just under the summit doesn't look to be particularly difficult. On my preferred ascent line, 300 metres below the ridge and in the great couloir, dangerous snow is lying on the sloping slabs. Would the week-old monsoon snow offer a sure foundation? What disturbs me most about this idea is that I would deviate so far from Mallory's route. The hope of finding some trace of him is continually alive in me.

One fine morning as I sit with Nena on the pass at the foot of the North-East Ridge and gaze at the fluted snow furrows on the East Face of Mount Everest, I think about my belief that Mallory and Irvine can only lie on the north side. This is not a rational judgement, it is as if Mallory himself were speaking to me. The east side falls from the ridge along which Mallory and Irvine climbed in 1924 so precipitously that the two of them must have stayed well on the north side. Moreover, they would have run the risk of being hurled down the holdless East Face by a sudden gust of wind if they had stuck to the ridge crest.

At the spot where we are now sitting,

Lieut.-Col. Howard-Bury saw, during a reconnaissance in 1921, some remarkable footprints in the snow, which gave new support to an old legend. At the turn of the century a Himalayan traveller had talked of a wild anthropoid high in the mountains. He had taken it to be the yeti, the fabulous snow creature about which the Tibetans and Sherpas had related the most remarkable stories for centuries. The talk about the yeti amuses me, for we too can see tracks in the snow which look like giant

Furrowed snow on Lhotse.

View from Rapiu La towards Makalu.

measurements are lacking. According to how fast I can climb to altitude, whether it gives me a headache or not, I know if I am well acclimatised or still need time to become so. I content myself with these palpable results, observe the speed and effect of the adjustment, without asking myself how it comes about.

One thing is certain; altitude makes me irritable and nervous. But it does not affect my will-power.

footprints. They are spots, made bigger by the sun, on which birds have squatted or where dust particles carried up here by the storm have lain. The possibility that big mammals live up here is absurd.

Meanwhile Nena and I are really well acclimatised. I have concerned myself for years with physiological investigations, but I have only subjective answers to the question of adaptability to altitude. Exact

Mount Everest from the east.

153

The unclimbed East Face of Everest.

On the first clear day I climb to the foot of the Chang La face to examine the conditions. I can see far to the east, as far as the Kangchenjunga group. The distant, glistening mountain chain looks like lines of clouds. The horizon dissolves. Today I want to go further but I know that I am still too tense, too uncertain. Fear is like a clenched fist. Only an open hand needs no energy. At present I lack the inner harmony. I need so much strength to thrust aside all the possible dangers of a solo ascent which fill my mind.

Only when the stream of these fears· dries up can I set out! Naturally it is easy to upbraid oneself to master these fears and not to be ruled by them. But to completely switch off, to eliminate all thoughts, is so difficult! To let oneself go and at the same time be as alert as a cat, that is the art. Perhaps I need only block out the climb to the summit from the start in order to be able to live in harmony? Does that not already lie behind me – proofs, recognition, conquest of self? Not the flags on the summit, the document – I don't mean these proofs. They are only superficial. What stops me from enjoying life is the compulsion to prove to myself, to everyone, that Mount Everest can be climbed alone.

I am a fool who with his longing for love and tenderness runs up cold mountains.

But I still have the excuse that the weather is too warm, the weather too bad! While Nena writes or cooks, I stare steadfastly at the topmost point of Everest.

Nena feels what is going on within me:

A supposed yeti footprint.

The past days at 6,500 metres have been hard for me. I had a headache and was as crotchety as an old witch. I know that altitude brings on depression and aggression. From time to time I felt so weak and nauseous that I thought Reinhold would never take me with him again. He is very sympathetic. But he has his problems too.

Between Rapiu La and North Col.

155

His unbelievable abilities, his creative will, his desire for self-expression are so great that they could kill him.

Who was the First?

With the possibility of climbing on the north side of the highest mountain in the world a puzzle revives. A few days ago I read something up here in the tent which lends wings to my Everest plan. In 1974 on the way to the summit a Chinese climber sighted a body. We was a severe blow for the Victorian-minded British expedition hero worshippers. For half a century they have puzzled over whether Mallory and Irvine did perhaps reach the summit before they were overwhelmed. An ice axe belonging to the pair, which was found in 1933 below the North-East Ridge – perhaps the scene of their fatal plunge – was held by some people to be an indication of success. The two could have reached the summit and in their

Monsoon above advanced base camp.

in the West heard of that for the first time in autumn 1979. It is quite possible that it had something to do with Mallory or Irvine.

The disappearance of the pair – as likewise the death of Captain Scott at the South Pole twelve years earlier – tiredness slipped during descent. And now I know additionally that the Chinese Wang Hung-boa found a dried-up corpse, directly under the place where the ice axe was found. Wang reported that the clothing had been 'in part in fragments and blown away by the wind,' that the dead man had been an 'Englishman'. Wang first related all that in 1979 during a Japanese expedition, on which he had been a porter. The following day, before the Japanese could be told further particulars, Wang was caught up in an avalanche, catapulted into a crevasse and killed. In olden days one would have said there was a curse on this affair. More than ever I want to track down the answer.

The answer to the question whether Mount Everest was climbed in 1924 is probably to be found with the dead man. Mallory had a Kodak folding camera with him and Irvine too carried a camera. If the men reached the summit, then they would also have photographed it. Even if they turned back shortly before the top they would have certainly taken a picture of the highest point reached. At Eastman/Kodak in Rochester they are of the opinion – provided the camera case remained intact – that the film would not have been ruined by the extreme cold up there. Whosoever finds one of the two cameras, therefore, can prove whether Mallory and Irvine got to the top before Hillary and Tenzing. The question of who was first on the summit has raged for many years and has led already to the most dreadful arguments. Less so amongst climbers than with the general public, who have a sort of Olympic medal mentality about it. When Hillary and Tenzing returned to Kathmandu after their undoubted ascent in 1953 they were made to feel that special crassness. The world argued over the question: which of the two was the first on top? Hillary, said some. Tensing, at once

The mystery-enshrouded summit pyramid of Everest from the east.

protested Indians and Nepalese. Mallory and Irvine, opined the veterans. The discussion lasted many days and nights. On his arrival in the city Tenzing had signed a document in which he stated that he had been on the top five minutes before Hillary. When a journalist asked him how he could have done such a thing he only raised his hands.

'On all sides people were talking at me. I didn't know actually what I signed . . . We got to the top at almost the same time.'

Now Hillary was pressed. He said only:

'I led the final metres. Tenzing belayed. I find it quite immaterial who was first up. Neither could have done it without the other.'

When an Indian journalist wrote that Hillary had been the first, he was reviled by Nepalese colleagues as

Sir Edmund Hillary in 1974.

'greaser and agent for the Anglo-American block'. I know why I find heroism to the glory of nations idiotic and detest all 'victories' on mountains.

Avalanche Snow

The tiny advanced base camp in which Nena and I have been for the past few days is the Camp III of the 1920s expeditions. Usually we crawl out at about 9 a.m. on to the rickety stone slabs on the slope on which the tent is erected. Nena cooks, I refill the aluminium pots with snow once more. It is unbelievable how much snow one needs to get a bit of water. Not before late morning at the earliest does the little stream between the glacier and the moraine thaw. Then we lie in the tent again and wait until we have hot

water. That all sounds very pleasant but is very strenuous at a height of 6,500 metres. Up here, eating also requires willpower. Solid food often sickens me, I can only take liquid in any amount. It is now time either to climb to the North Col or to return again to base camp proper.

Night falls on this world of stone and ice. High above us I see the tip of Everest in cold shadow. For three days now I have been waiting for a fine morning, ready to venture a reconnaissance ascent to the North Col. I want to set up a small depot up there and pin down the final ascent route. What will the weather be tomorrow?

I sleep restlessly, often peer out into the night. At 2 a.m. it is starry clear. At 8 a.m. I am ready to start. Too late? At altitude getting up early is much more difficult than lower down. Half an hour later I am standing at the foot of the face leading to the North Col. In spite of the soft masses of snow I continue. I have no illusions. No more hesitation. Once again a proof that an active life is the answer to all the world's doubts. The activity does me good after all the sitting around in camp. The monsoon doesn't worry me any more, indeed I see fresh signs in the sky, but I shall get to the North Col.

On the glacier floor my boots sink in no more than a few centimetres and I am hopeful that the wall will consist of hard, frozen snow. This 22nd of July must be a good day for me. The foot of the wall lies at 6,600 metres. I gain height continuously, if somewhat slowly. After I have climbed over the marginal crevasse I stick fast in the snow up to the hips. My God, that didn't hold me! I don't want to turn back now. So I wallow slowly, quite slowly, metre by metre higher, always concentrating on not setting off a snow slide. The damp snow penetrates through my leggings, into the plastic boots which soon give out a squelching noise. In spite of my caution small snow slides often start under me. Some 200 metres below the col I stick fast. Laboriously I manage to free myself from the cramped embrace of this down-left. Here I hope to find a place where it will be possible to cross the huge transverse crevasse in the wall above me. But when I get there I see that I have no chance. Doggedly I plod to and fro until I find a snow bridge much further to the right. I don't know whether I can trust it. With a long bridging stride I can perhaps reach the wall on the other side. I search on it with the ice axe for a hold – done! To my disappointment the snow is also soft and

Ascent of the Chang La face.

right vicious water snow. Under such conditions getting to the summit is quite hopeless. Why do I want to reach the North Col at any price in circumstances like this? But each time after I have struggled a little bit further, I rest, breathe and am again full of new energy. I want to get up there today!

In the last flat trough I turn sharp difficult here. The wall is 'very steep. But I don't want to give up now. I must stand at least once on this North Col which I have stared at perpetually, or else I know I shall give up.

I reach a ramp which leads obliquely right towards the col. While I am studying it I realise how tired I am. Step by step I traverse upwards along

Telephoto of ascent to North Col.

not the slightest sign of another expedition. The blue sky lies like a great unending roof above the mountains. And again this distant view awakens memories of childhood . . .

When a child like me has lived for ten years in the bottom of a narrow valley, hemmed in by steep forests and craggy limestone cliffs, the day must come when he sees a broad sky above, and this becomes a decisive factor in his life. Long before I could leave the narrow valley I often experienced this limitless horizon from above. The overpowering impression while ascending – that the rock walls were much bigger than I remembered them from the village square – was surpassed by the immensity which assailed me, which opened up like a dream landscape. Then for the first time I could see that behind the furthest mountain range lay another mountain range and behind that yet another. The world expanded.

It moves me very much that this expedition time and again becomes a journey into childhood. I sit there and am composed only of memory, childhood, experience. Everything which I have heard, read or seen belongs to me just like my hands, my eyes and this horizon of glass, which has stamped my life more than anything else. My father showed it to me and my mother let me set out. Until this expedition I had not realized where my life was leading me.

And the summit? At present it is impossible. I need at least two bivouacs above the North Col. The weather is too uncertain and the avalanche danger too great. Certainly I have the most difficult part of the

the ramp. It is endless. Because I know, from all of my expeditions, this deceptive feeling of being on top only then to have the next rise before me, I no longer look upwards but push myself on relentlessly. And then suddenly I am there!

As I look around I make out that I am not only on the col but a bit higher, for to the left of me the ridge falls in the direction of the North Face. I am blinded by the light. While I gaze up towards the North Face it seems to grow before my eyes. It is not its steepness which impresses me, it is its enormous white surface.

I squat down and look for a while towards the west where I discern some much-loved peaks: Pumori, Cho Oyu, Gyachung Kang. Also, I look down on the west side of Everest. It is deserted, mountain already behind me. I am more than 7,000 metres high. I have plodded for hours, have pushed and hacked in order to make a relatively safe track. Sitting in the sun I enjoy the view and my own tiredness. Sliding and tumbling – tent and sleeping-bag left behind, twice I go down on my backside when a lump of snow breaks off – I descend towards the valley.

Nena waits for me in camp with some hot soup. We don't want to stay up here any longer. The spot no longer pleases me. The stones are mostly covered with snow, the drinking water must be melted from snow, it will soon snow again for sure. I have burrowed in deep snow the whole day. Enough! In spite of the privations Nena is still very strong. She would be able to hold out here for a time. But who knows if she may break down mentally and bodily at any moment? At this height anything is possible and we have lived here for over a week; it is time to go down.

During the descent it begins to snow. Across the wind-scoured glacier we stumble towards the intermediate camp and on towards base camp. When we arrive it is evening. Cheng and Tsao cook us a meal.

We must bide our time. But because I have made it to the North Col I know that I shall get further. Already I know Everest in the monsoon a little better.

Crevasses and séracs at the foot of the Chang La face.

The team at base camp.

Under the North Face

The restlessness in this man is unbelievable. He reminds me so often of Elton John's 'Single Man': 'I've got everything a man could need but it still ain't quite enough.' He appears to me like an unanswered question, a puzzle that waits to be solved. Where does this driving force come from, this compulsion to press on? The phenomenon of Reinhold Messner lies also in the fact that he challenges himself, again and again, although he cannot be said to be in any way neurotic. I can only wonder at the strength he has, but sometimes when I too would like to participate, a feeling of helplessness overwhelms me. He expects me to do everything with him and I like that. He obliges me to be the strong person which I gladly would be. But it is hard, sometimes impossible. Luckily I am a fast walker but here at great height and in difficult country everything is different. 'You are so slow,' he says. I am not as fast as he, it is true. He always seems to be in a hurry. He wants to be everywhere but when we have hiked many kilometres over ice and rock and finally stand on a breathtaking summit, we must immediately hurry down again.

I am no beginner as regards mountaineering, and I know that speed can sometimes decide between life and death. That is not what I mean. There is a driving force within him which has nothing to do with the mountains. One cannot separate it from him. It makes him what he is. It drives him to 8,000 metres on his own, it drives him whether he is at home, in Shigatse, in Lhasa, or on the way to back to Europe. It determines his life. It carries him to the sky and destroys him at the same time.

From this fragmentary insight into his life and through our relationship I have the impression that Reinhold combines two completely different personalities. Is he schizophrenic? He moves fast and dexterously like no other and yet wishes to laze about. He does many things at the same time, yet takes in everything. He shouts and rails, he understands and accepts. Sometimes he has great tenderness for me, and sometimes he flies into a terrible rage. He consists of so many characters that he must tear himself apart.

After four days' recovery at base camp we made a new trip. The last night Reinhold and I bivouacked just under the Lho La, a pass which leads to Nepal and which is 6,000 metres high. It snowed. Today we hiked for four hours, sometimes together, sometimes each alone with himself. In the early evening light we cleared some big stones from the ice and laid our thin mattresses on the cold ground. Between some bigger rocks there was a narrow place for sleeping. The plastic sheet which Reinhold had brought from base camp served us as a roof. It kept the snow off, no more. The whole night, water dripped on Reinhold's head. He didn't complain, didn't curse, slept well. In the morning I was completely washed out, wanted nothing but to descend. Reinhold got up, climbed a few hundred metres higher and studied the North

vidual climber could have all the pitons and rope in the world at his disposal but during the monsoon he would never get anywhere in the fall line or even in the vicinity of the summit. The Japanese made their ascent to the right, in the long snow couloir; the route looks steep and difficult, but logical. Once I thought of climbing high to the left up the big couloir but, as Everest rises from the Central Rongbuk Glacier to a height of 7,500 metres, so too this route is too

Nena during the ascent to the Lho La.

Face of Mount Everest from this new viewpoint. He knew that all his bivouacs would be higher up and still harder. That did not disturb him. Something drives him aloft.

The great North Face rises like a mighty pyramid above me, a sheer, invincible ice and rock wall. An indi-

dangerous during the monsoon. The end of the Rongbuk Glacier is covered with new snow, also on the face itself there is an awful amount of snow. I had hoped that the North Face was too steep to be able to hold so much snow. I deceived myself.

Now a thin white streamer of cloud,

163

the famous Everest 'feather', sits on the summit ridge. Hopefully the wind will sweep the snow from the ridges and the summit!

As part of my route investigations, I also take a look at the approach to the North Col from the main Rongbuk Glacier. Against the gap I can still make out a shattered glacier which rises in steep and avalanche-prone snow slopes under the pass. This way seems to me to be even more dangerous than the one I have already reconnoitred on the opposite side.

The climb to the height of the Lho La through thigh-deep snow lets me forget these thoughts at last. We turn round and go back to base camp. A soft high-summer glacier fills the bottom of the valley. The ice reefs further down, which were yesterday still dim and grey, light up in the reflection of a vibrant blue sky. It is not the pale soft fine weather sky, it is a stark glassy monsoon sky, thundery. White, tattered clouds glide across the fathomless blue of the sky.

All tiredness and melancholy has left me. Just as the landscape seems to be resolving itself, so too my own mind becomes clear. I feel confident even though everything militates against success.

It is decidedly cold. An icy wind blasts us in the face as we march valleywards through the narrow corridor between the pillars of Changtse and some six-thousanders. Descending from the ice world into the brown grey of the foothills I experience the other side of the Himalaya, Tibet, as a world of other moods. The colours here have, so it seems, another spectrum. Everything is earth-coloured, with a patina, even the rainbow. Only through fine tints do the individual

The broad North Face of Everest.

March to the Lho La.

shades distinguish themselves from one another. The valley floor to the north-west must be Rongbuk, the black shadows there have something of blue; the chains of hills farther north gleam reddish.

Often, valley troughs are only to be distinguished from high ridges by a

On the moraine of the Central Rongbuk Glacier.

North peak from the East Rongbuk Glacier.

soft gradation from light to dark, similar to crevasses on shallow snow slopes. Where a ray of sun streaks the grey-green moraine landscape below us, I surmise there must be a stream. I cannot see the floor of the glacier, I notice only gloomy colours.

Nena and I descend to the spot, and in a labyrinth of séracs actually find water in a strip of moraine which leads directly down into the valley. With a lively following wind we go towards the sunbeams which break through the strips of cloud like searchlights. The shadowy grey of the North Face behind us, the cloudy grey of the moraine embankments around us and the white-grey of the glacier stream beneath us, those are the appointed colours. The sky is now ash-grey.

Occasionally I leap from rock block to rock block, balancing, dancing from edge to edge, and am full of anticipated joy. The ascent to the summit worries me no more, I am confident.

At the first monsoon break, as meteorologists call this pause, or at the end of the great rain-wind, I shall be able to count on good conditions. The stream which comes from the East Rongbuk Glacier is so swollen that we cannot cross it. So we go round over the main Rongbuk Glacier. It gets late. In the light-as-day sky the moon rises. The Tibetan plateau in the evening now lies like a sea of brown earth far to the north. It reeks of a silence of decades. All the moraine ridges look like paths, with big stone blocks as landmarks. I find Mount Everest far beyond to be a symbol of my resolve, which now has no substance. It has condensed itself into this mountain – a concept.

During the following days we rest in base camp. Nena writes a letter to her parents:

29 July 1980

Dear Parents,
I have no idea when this letter will reach you as there is no postal connection before we get back to Peking. So this is not so much a letter as an attempt to talk to you.

Trying to cross the East Rongbuk stream.

Somehow everything is different this time – we are so far away from any inhabited place. This time we know we can get no mail, but we don't miss it. It is now exactly a month since we arrived here on the Rongbuk Glacier and set up our camp. It is a wonderful, peaceful and free spot. Yaks from the lower lying villages, and nomads, sometimes go along the scree slopes. The raging glacier river which storms by the camp gets more swollen day by day. At the upper end of the valley stands Chomolungma. This is what the Tibetans call Mount Everest; the

Nepalese call it Sagarmatha. It dominates this region, it dominates our present life.

We have now set up three different camps. This one, where we rest and recuperate, is the lowest and biggest. We call it Rongbuk Main Camp. This is where Tsao, our interpreter, who we heartlessly but with some reason call 'Brainless', and Cheng our liaison officer, a nice man, stay. Neither of them has so far accompanied us to the higher camps, Tsao, because he is not accustomed to mountain going and glaciers: Cheng, who is

a good mountaineer, must remain below because Tsao is frightened if left alone in base camp. It is understandable. He comes from the city, and here wolves, wild sheep and yaks roam around free.

Our next camp consists of a small two-man tent at a height of 6,000 metres. It stands at the place on the East Rongbuk Glacier which the Chinese and Japanese climbers used for their second camp during the last big expeditions. We call the tent which is equipped with provisions, medical supplies and cooking utensils, Intermediate Camp. It

lies on the way to Advanced Base Camp.

The highest camp is exactly at the same place where the third camp of the last expedition stood, 6,500 metres high, exactly under the steep, glacier-riven slopes which lead to the North Col. This spot at the foot of the steep North-East Face of Everest is marvellous too. We brought food and equipment for a month up here on yaks.

The minute the weather clears up and the temperature falls – hopefully soon – Reinhold and I will return to our high camp at 6,500 metres. What we need are hot days and cold nights so that the upper snow slopes become hard. Reinhold must climb very carefully, for he is alone and the slope under the North Col is rather dangerous – avalanches, big crevasses, vertical stretches.

It frightens me every time I sit below and watch him climb higher and higher, grow tiny in the deep snow between the crevasses. Nevertheless I trust his judgement and his climbing skill. Since I saw with what speed he went up that 500 metres to the North Col I have been calmer.

Reinhold would like to reach the summit in three, maximum four days from advanced base camp. That is the sole tactic which will bring him success. He must not spend too long at great height, especially not without oxygen, because otherwise the body deteriorates rapidly.

Be that as it may, he is now fit and as well-balanced as a guru. We hope only for the right conditions and a break of several days in the monsoon weather.

It is now 9.30 p.m. and we are going to sleep. I am very tired. Now here where we have dispensed with all material comforts our human relationship shows itself hard and clear. Nothing is lacking. I feel myself rich, relaxed and sure at Reinhold's side. I love you with all my heart, Nena.

Nena at the Rongbuk camp.

Bizarre ice towers on the Rongbuk glacier.

*Rongbuk –
In the Wake of the
Cultural Revolution*

It is the spontaneous presence of one's own consciousness,
What use to me is a homeland,
That is filled with delusions of passion and hatred?

Tulshig Dharmamati, Tulshig Rimpoche

Rongbuk –
In the Wake of the
Cultural Revolution

Westwards

Meanwhile I am accustomed to silence and loneliness. Since I have been living with Nena in the mountains a sense of security, that grows out of the silence, begins to calm me. Nena too has learned not to let her emotions always take over, to enjoy the silence.

At the beginning of the expedition I was running around like wound-up clockwork. The hectic period of planning – drumming up support, assembling equipment, raising a budget of 80,000 DM, mostly by my own efforts – lies far behind me, is forgotten. That abortive question: 'Is it worthwhile?' that, too, has gone. Here, in the presence of the mountain, it does not bother me.

The desolate Rongbuk valley shows its spring colours, a weak glimmering. The July sun is hot. I wait for my chance as the hermits in the surrounding caves waited for enlightenment.

The idea of leaving base camp once more and travelling westwards comes to me suddenly. One morning I awake with this resolve. We have permission to reconnoitre Shisha Pangma for a future expedition, and because at the moment there is nothing to do on Everest, we can start the necessary observations there.

We send Tsao down the valley to order a jeep and wait for three days at Rongbuk Monastery. The ruins are sad and deserted but the idea that the CMA want to build a mountaineers' hotel here makes me sick. We Europeans have allowed our most beautiful areas to be completely disfigured by tourism, but when people get the same idea about one of our exotic vanishing beauty spots we are incensed. That is part of the schizophrenia of our world scene. I know also that in the last analysis I too contribute to this development. All tourism begins with the reports of enthusiastic pathfinders from the land of one's dreams.

At last the jeep arrives. We travel first to Tingri where the valley broadens into a wide plain. Here in earlier times, year in year out, trade was carried on. Here the caravans to Nepal camped and bought salt which had been brought here from the Tibetan highlands. Nowadays Tingri looks empty. Near the 100 houses which make a picturesque nest on a slope lie new Chinese metal-roofed barracks with walls and barbed wire. More than anywhere else we see remains of walls and other signs of repeated destruction. On the opposite slope communist slogans are written in stone. 'We shall not rest until the upstarts are exterminated,' it says, or: 'Whosoever is for the Dalai Lama, is against President Mao'. Everywhere on our journey westwards people are working in the fields. The Tibetans irrigate the soil, plough with their shaggy yak teams or pull weeds. Now and then I espy at the edge of a field a small altar made of clay. The dampness of the monsoon has roused the soil from sleep. Hundreds of head of yak leave their winter quarters at the edges of the villages and move to higher grazing grounds.

Tingri.

Our liaison officer wants us to reach Shisha Pangma in one day. Our route lies in shade, nevertheless it is hot. After about 100 kilometres we turn off to the west, cross some streams and reach a broad plateau. It stretches to infinity. To the right and left rise ranges of hills, their bluish-brown colour distinguishing them sharply from the olive of the plain. Small rivers flow through the plain like silver lightning. Their clear geometric form, a zigzag that is far removed from any romantic meandering, fascinates me. Again and again the broad plain is broken up by the black dots of grazing yak herds. In the high blue sky move clouds the like of which are only to be found in Tibet. Underneath they are broad and smooth like the plain, on top they pile up into the most wonderful animal forms. Dragons, tigers, carp and lotus blooms sail across the infinity of the highlands. Their thick, white cloud shapes cast islands of shadow on the steppe grass like mammoth parasols. On the horizon a sole rider emerges, crosses the plain and disappears. Here loneliness has a dignity which I have never seen in it before. Abruptly I comprehend the metaphor 'hidden in the cosmos'.

Some black tents are scattered here and there, inviolable. Amongst the stones small bunches of yellow flowers, blue forget-me-nots, scarlet-red primulas.

To the left, squashed up against the hill, the 'Four Dragon Village', beautiful Tibetan houses, earthy and plain, whitewashed, brushwood on the roofs for the winter. Above the dark wooden doors yak horns, paintings in blue and red. Opposite, a kilometre distant, a turquoise-blue lake like a Fata Morgana. Behind that a peak thrusts its steep ice face into the sky. On the ground a white cloud of sheep. Crystal-

Tibetan yak caravan.

clear air, a landscape in which one can see the distance of a day's journey. A Tibetan who carries this scenery in his heart can never be lost. I know all at once that ideologies can bounce off landscapes, that there are impregnable people and strengths.

Cloud formation above a ruined caravanserai.

175

Nomads in Tibet.

Shisha Pangma

The sun is already low and casting long shadows, the air is soft. Our jeep travels past limestone cliffs, at the foot of which nomads are encamped. Juniper trees, clematis, broom. We turn left, cross a river. Suddenly there it stands before us – above gigantic walls of moraine, Shisha Pangma. 'Ridge above the Meadows' its name means; that image is perfect. In white clarity it is the culminating point of an aesthetic harmony the like of which I have never seen before.

Here on the northern side of the watershed we are enjoying splendid weather. The clouds boiling up behind the chain of the Himalaya enliven the evening landscape. After the long journey Nena and I are craving for exercise. We climb up the shallow valley. Then the way goes across sheets of detritus which were poured across the plain by primaeval glacier flows. Mighty bank moraines wind like monstrous snakes towards Shisha Pangma. In front of us lie ice-falls, above that a striking deep face, the North Face of Shisha Pangma. We frequently hear the call of the white grouse which is almost invisible between the stones, and which runs away screaming if we come too close. The grey-white stone, the famous bright granite of Shisha Pangma, seems to shine in the light of the setting sun. All around us glaciers, ice walls, rock peaks and snow ridges rise out of a sea of clouds that stretches endlessly as far as India.

Slowly it becomes night, the moon shows a conspicuous halo, and a complete silence reigns which is broken or accented only by the distant rushing of the wind. Far to the south we see lightning.

Hours have passed since we left the jeep back at 5,300 metres. The sky becomes livid in all directions; at the same time it drives forth a few pale stars. During the night we stumble back to the tent. Nena is very fit and has, above all, a tenacious will.

During the night the weather seems to become settled. For hours on end I listen, half awake, until morning comes. As I open my eyes the sky is coloured violet. We take down the tent, load our vehicle and begin the return journey. I am glad now that I am not alone, that I can talk over everything with Nena.

'You climbed up Nanga Parbat alone and said that was, in a word, your alpinistic dream. Do you also want to climb Shisha Pangma alone? Won't Everest do?' she asks me.

'After my solo ascent of Nanga Parbat I saw the possibility that Everest too could be climbed alone. And it is the biggest mountain in the world. So the thought is quite logical. The fact that I have been up there once already doesn't count, for I want to attempt it alone. I used always to say to myself, one eight-thousander solo will suffice. I needed that to dot the *i's* and cross the *t's* of my mountaineering, following which I could stop climbing. I can't. After I had done Nanga Parbat the Everest plan ripened. I am not only a lone wolf, I am a sort of Sisyphus who never really reaches the summit. I am Sisyphus and the stone which I push up the mountain is my own psyche.'

'And Shisha Pangma?'

Shisha Pangma from the north.

At the foot of Shisha Pangma.

'That is a mountain which is imprinted on my mind, no more and no less. The way in which I shall climb it, with friends or alone, doesn't interest me at the moment.'

'If you go alone won't you miss having a friend with whom you can share your experiences and also the privations?'

'If I am not alone I see the tiredness which is also in my partner's eyes. He becomes my mirror.'

'Can Nature comfort you?'

'Yes, very much so. The first light of morning, for example, has often given me a great inner peace. I would not like to call this feeling happiness. It is peace.'

'Why are you afraid of the word happiness in this connection? I believe that a human being cannot experience anything more blessed than to feel part of the world and to draw strength from this knowledge.'

'The word happiness I just find so horribly hackneyed.'

Meanwhile our jeep has covered a good 100 kilometres. Formerly journeys in this region were not only dangerous but also adventurous. I have read that the wind alone has swept whole caravans to their deaths. In those days it could take days, weeks even, to get from one safe resting place to another. However we travel safely – and much too fast – with our attendants on relatively good roads. This uneasiness is reduced but we have traded it for a different sort. We experience now an extinct Tibet. The other, the old Tibet remains largely a closed book to us. This is the other land that I wanted to see, and there are moments in which I see, smell and feel the old Tibet.

After the outbreak of the Cultural Revolution and during the systematic destruction of the 'Four Ancients' – the old culture, the old practices, the old customs and the old mentality – old Tibet did not die. At that time it withdrew into a sort of Sleeping Beauty state, to await the times when it could live again. And it seems to me that these times have already announced themselves.

The Tibet which we are allowed to see lies on the new roads and our Chinese companions never fail to point out the improvements since the 'liberation' by the Chinese: irrigation canals, schools, hospitals and not least the roads on which we travel. Certainly the peasants are no longer exploited by the monasteries and large landowners: today they starve for the People's Republic. In order to be able to judge whether things are 'better' for a people, one must first find out how well off these people are for 'essentials', what their independent quality of life amounts to.

In a country in which people are convinced on the grounds of their belief that they influence their own *karma*, reason should not rule alone. In past lives Tibetans have determined their fate through their good or bad behaviour. They must bear life's blows with equanimity, in order to approach enlightenment, which alone can redeem them from the wheel of eternal rebirth. In such a country five-year plans and ideological co-ordination are not 'essential'. Essential here is an inviolable inner world. In a country in which for centuries there has been

Sparse vegetation on the sterile Tibetan plateau.

A ruined temple construction.

prayer and meditation, only a superficial change can be carried out through technocratic intellect, and these changes are now presented to us.

This 1,500 year old Buddhism of the Tibetans, Lamaism, arouses in me the longing to take part. It is mixed with pantheistic conceptions and the ancient Tibetan Bon religion, in which the four elements are full of good and terrible demons. Nowhere has the shabby ridiculousness of technological progress, which makes up our own culture, become more obvious to me than here. But at the same time I know that I, as a child of the West, am not at all capable of being absorbed into the mystery of the East.

Outside, the scenery passes by. The wide spaces breathe freedom. In the distance the play of the colours changes. The weather is friendly, and even on sandy areas plants are alive.

179

The countryside is never without life. As we stop in a valley which makes a giant U-turn, it is entirely still. And this stillness is music.

Two hours from Kathmandu

On the way to Shisha Pangma the still-intact beauty of the 'Four Dragon Village' struck me. Now on the way back we take a closer look at it. On the wall of one of the houses sits a young man combing his black hair, which reaches down far over his shoulders. In his ears he wears small corals and turquoises on cords, he is dressed in a greasy wool shirt and sheepskin trousers. His dark skin is almost chocolate brown from sun and soot. Through the wooden door in the wall comes an old man with short white stubbly hair. 'Tashi delek', we say, for that is the most beautiful Tibetan greeting which we have learned. 'Luck be with you.'

The old man laughs and invites us into the house. Behind the wall is a forecourt with several low, walled pens for the animals. In one of the squares stands a small, narrow-chested horse, whose mane and tail are woven with bands into little plaits. An ancient, shaggy dog gives a few hoarse barks and then goes back to his corner. We step into an inner courtyard in which an old woman sits at a wooden loom. She weaves striped material for a woollen apron. She has long grey plaits and round her neck a long chain made out of enormous amber beads, corals and silver. On a covered wooden floor carpets and hides lie airing. The old man takes us with him into the closed part of the dwelling. It is dark, the only light coming in through the fire hole in the roof. Under this chimney stands a dwarf-sized iron hearth which has no oven. The floor is of stamped earth. Parts of the wall are hung with newspapers. By the walls stand wooden sleeping places with carpets, covers and pillows. We are allowed to sit down. Then, in silver embossed wooden bowls, we receive chang, barley beer. A young woman comes out of a nearby room. All look at us in friendly fashion, our conversation consists of smiles and curiosity. Scarcely have we drunk a few sips than we are topped up from a dirty white plastic container. With a few broken words, 'Shisha Pangma', 'Chomolungma' and signs we tell of our journey. Friendly nods. I leave behind my pocket knife as a guest gift. Later Tsao tells me that these people are semi-nomads who travel across the highlands fronting the glaciers of Shisha Pangma, occasionally taking tents, but always returning again to their houses.

At the branch where we turn on to the road from Lhasa to Kathmandu I ask Cheng if it is forbidden to go as far as the border. 'No,' he says. 'So let's go', I cry, and we turn off to the right. We cross a pass and descend into a deep valley. From here have come the bamboo-decorated lorries which we meet all the time. The gorge becomes ever narrower and deeper. Often the rock rises 100 metres vertically above us, above that is another flight which vanishes into the clouds. Gradually we enter the semi-tropical forest. It is raining. By the roadside are huge trees, bamboo and ferns. Birds bustle about in the tree-tops. We see colourful butterflies. Waterfalls rush exuberantly.

We overnight in Nyalam. Next

Tibetan semi-nomads.

morning we set out for the Nepalese border, which is two hours' journey from Kathmandu.

Suddenly we are in the midst of the rich lushness of the southern Himalayan valleys. My eyes, which have become accustomed to the soft, broad horizons and fragile colours of the Tibetan plateau, become all at once hungry for this voluptuous greenery. My skin is moist, my ear filled with the rushing of the waterfalls, with the song of the birds. The air is heavy, the colours are so deep that they almost crush me. We have dipped into a completely new world and now see the Himalaya with different eyes.

Millions of years ago Tibet lay on the shores of a sea, one supposes. The Himalayan range originated when the landmasses of India and China drifted towards each other. The Tibetan plateau was thrown up behind. One can still find fossilized sea shells on the high peaks. Tibet's lakes are the remains of the sea and that is why they are still salty. The collision of the two continents has not finished, and the Himalaya are still growing. Perhaps one day Mount Everest will be a nine-thousander. Overpowered by the overflowing and colourful hothouse abundance on the mountain slopes and in the savage gorge, we travel out of the valley. In the whole of Tibet one sees Chinese soldiers, technicians, civil servants. Here in the villages near the border there are especially a great

181

many. It makes me think of South Tyrol: of people who only live near each other and not with each other, an Italian and a German, who don't understand each other and don't like each other. In South Tyrol too an ethnic minority has become disunited through enforced foreign infiltration.

The weather is fairly good. Rain falls only at night. However, clouds fill Tibet once more. As the sun sinks, scenery and colours change; the deep green of the tropical forests becomes a shadowy grey.

During a rest on the main road to Lhasa former fugitives come past. They relate terrible stories about the activities of the communists, the destruction. Our liaison officer translates only hesitatingly and certainly by no

On the southern slopes of the Himalaya.

the gorge almost completely. We are in a prohibited valley and wonder that no one has barred our way.

After this two day trip through the forests north of Kathmandu we set out again on the return journey, leaving the Himalaya for the open vastness of means all that they say. Nevertheless they are now returning from Nepal to the homeland. They have heard that the mechanism of suppression has been dismantled, that one can again be Tibetan and Buddhist. They have dependents in Tibet – and in a strange land they are half-dying of homesickness. Now they are on their way, determined to return to Lhasa.

By midday we are in Tingri. After a rest in the barracks we travel in the direction of Shekar in order to refuel there before we set out on the return journey to base camp.

Between Tingri and Shekar it strikes us that the mountains are more clearly visible than a week before. The clouds are now isolated and lost in the sky. It must have become colder up there. Is this the beginning of the monsoon break I have been waiting for so eagerly?

In Shekar I urge haste. We buy some tinned fruit, search the market for vegetables, find some onions and travel back.

It is already late afternoon when we get to the Rongbuk river. The water is so high that we cannot cross until next morning, for during the night the melt-water diminishes on account of the cold. Therefore we prepare to camp for the night. During the evening there is a brief thunderstorm. It starts in the north and from there travels towards the south. The inhabitants of the village have come and stand in groups in front of the tent. Left of me squats a woman observing my every move with interest. She wears a one-piece cloak-like dress that reaches down as far as the ankles and is indescribably filthy. On her calm face, on the cheekbones and temples, are stuck dirty white strips of sticking plaster. They are symmetrically arranged. One sees the same thing on the faces of many women and girls, and it was a long time before I grasped that they are popular beauty spots.

In the border village between Tibet and Nepal.

The woman is very friendly and gives me a handful of tsampa flour. Then she goes to fetch a few tiny eggs. I buy them off her. Everyone now tries to catch a glimpse of us. Laughing, men, women and children press around the tent until I think it will cave in. While I try to ward off the people, Nena writes:

8 August 1980. This is something one can scarcely describe. I feel like a monkey in the zoo. Cheng, the jeep driver, Reinhold and I are sitting in a tent at the edge of the village opposite the river. When I want to prepare the evening meal it is like a circus. Every time I open a can they tumble all over me and want to see what's inside. Then I made a big mistake, namely gave out a few chocolates. At once we were afraid of being squashed in the tent. From then on the people begged. I can hardly open a paper bag without a hundred arms pressing around me. All

Returning Tibetan refugees.

around everybody is screaming at the same time.

When we arrived, a drunken young man in front of the tent begged rather vehemently for some bread. Cheng said something very brusque to him that I could not understand. The man ran away furiously. None of the other village dwellers begged until I got that dumb idea with the sweets. Now all the people come and ask for something edible. In their eyes we are unimaginably rich, and they cannot understand that we must budget and keep house with our allotted rations. After this turbulent and finally extremely uncomfortable interlude I am pleased with the peacefulness of the Rongbuk camp, for the noise of the river which sends us to sleep at night, and for the barren moraine slopes.

10 August 1980. We are again in Rongbuk camp. Today is new moon. The weather doesn't seem to change. Reinhold's altimeter which we use as a barometer rises and falls alternately. We both have stomach disorders. I proposed we fast for a day like Maurice Wilson but when we woke up we had become so hungry that we quickly forgot this idea. We also have diarrhoea. Perhaps we shall be better tomorrow.

11 August 1980. For me it is an exciting game to climb around on the big lumps of rock near the monastery. I am as thrilled as a kid on there. Some of these boulders are so difficult that I could only get up when Reinhold gave me a top-rope. When I have done a difficult bit and stand on the block I am quite beside myself. I don't give up, and train over. If then I succeed in finding a good rhythm, I am pleased. For Reinhold these blocks present

no difficulties; his grip appears light and a matter of course. He began climbing at the age of five and slowly forgot his fear in the course of innumerable climbing trips.

12 August 1980. I am feeling better, but Reinhold is still weak; the diarrhoea gives him a hard time. I wish I could do something for him. His mood is depressed, he is sensitive and irritable. He knows that it is time for the summit assault and for that reason he cannot take any antibiotics, as the body would be additionally weakened by them. Reinhold is convinced that the slightest diarrhoea or a little stomach problem would suffice to turn the solo ascent of Everest into a deadly risk. This is no fancy. He knows how severely diarrhoea dehydrates a person. Altitude complicates the problem of human water retention, so that an additional risk can not be entered into.

13 August 1980. I am very sad that the marmots have gone. Earlier I had fun watching them when they crawled out of their holes, climbed on to the rocks and lay in the sun. Occasionally they stood upright and peered around. It was so peaceful to have them around us. However, Tsao put an end to them all with his damned gun. He spent whole days shooting into each single hole. I believe that only a sick person with sick thoughts can act like that.

The wind has come imperceptibly during the night. With each gust it becomes colder. At last! At this thought Nena beside me gives a deep sigh. She stares at a solitary star in the sky which shines down on us fixedly. My diarrhoea has diminished during the day; I feel better. We sit for a time on the moraine hillock above the tent and discuss the plan for the next ascent.

It appears that the monsoon stream from the Bay of Bengal has finally come up against the monsoon from the Arabian Sea, this well-known inter-

An inquisitive Tibetan.

Just below Rongbuk camp.

ruption in which two cloud fronts stand face to face so to speak, waiting. The promised break, my chance!

It is a clear evening, and the formerly restless wind from the Rongbuk glacier has dropped. No showers, no squalls, a fresh high sky summer evening.

Tomorrow or the day after I must set off. Now is when the best conditions are up above. Who knows how long this interruption in the monsoon will last? It would be lovely if I could enjoy all these impressions and moods without having to think about my climb. But with the resolve, the old fears and doubts also arise again. The North Face of Everest rises in stern whiteness above the Rongbuk camp, as we crawl into our small sleeping tent.

Throughout the long night, I am afraid. A two year cherished, thousand

Life on the high steppe.

186

times dreamed of wish is about to fulfil itself. Feverishly slopes and camps run through my head. Old pictures appear before my inner eye, as if Chomolungma stood behind my forehead, between my eyes. But at the same time hope and fear; it could not be otherwise.

*Chomolungma –
Ascent and Descent*

So I think about this world flowing by:
A star in the twilight, a whirlpool in the
stream;
The lightning of a thunderstorm out of the
summer cloud,
a flickering lamp, a phantom,
a dream.

from 'The Diamond Sutra;
Vajrachchedikaprajnaparamita Sutra'

Chomolungma – Ascent and Descent

Monsoon Break

It is as if the sky were made of cloth. The azure blue over Everest is so intense that it looks heavy; but not oppressive. The long drawn-out striae wind like scoria in a viscous mass. The distance to Mount Everest shrinks.

For hours on end I can watch the sparring, pushing and idling of the breezes above the Rongbuk valley. There are no storms, no mist, the monsoon is suspended. But this vacuum is full of energy; as if two fundamental forces were met together, a strip of blue-white cloud between them. With the colours of the firmament the landscape also has become more alive. There is a hint of green on the slopes and even the stones radiate energy. I can see them, feel them as if by touch. I want to start. I must.

I am now well acclimatized. I no longer have the feeling of being short of breath when I exert myself. After seven weeks at an altitude of more than 5,000 metres I run around in base camp as if I were at home. Once again I have established the fact that you accustom swiftly to the rarefied air if you have already often been at great heights. For newcomers, it is harder. During my later expeditions I have had less trouble than on my first. Then, from 1969 to 1970, there was a feeling of paralysis, of insecurity; those deep moments of despair when suddenly you have no more strength. The body seems to become inured not only through frequent repetitions – it also develops a sort of memory for it, adapting itself more easily. But even that takes three or four weeks and is progressive. Without first making these adjustments, reaching the summit of Everest would be unthinkable, even if you had previously climbed all the eight-thousanders. This adjustment to altitude is fundamental to the ascent. But I don't see it as a preparation. Just as I have waited for good weather, so I wait for the best bodily state. Human nature and the cosmos control my bio-rhythms. For the rest I can anticipate nothing and everything. My planned solo climb is like life, a mystery – unpredictable, risky, often dependent on chance and thereby illogical. An attempt to pre-plan it would be madness. An Everest solo climb is not an arithmetical exercise. Luckily for me I believe in human instincts. If in nature a man confronts

View from base camp towards Everest.

only two possibilities – death or survival – he does the right thing. Only I cannot rehearse it – there is only the real thing. Nena, too, stages no dress rehearsal for the decisive attempt. Her confidence is great. Or does she keep her worries to herself? Is her diary a consolation?

15 August 1980. We are about to set off. How I have waited for this! We want to climb up to the East Rongbuk Glacier, further, higher. This is not just romancing, I really enjoy it, being nearer the summit, nearer the sky. Just as the air up there becomes clearer, so too will my understanding. You are closer to yourself in the mountains. And everything seems to come together – comes from the soul. Perhaps many perceptions condense, perhaps there is just less distraction. At all events up there there is intensity, something like second sight. Everyone feels these effects. This strikes me especially in my personal relationship with Reinhold. Here he shows himself as a man whose South Tyrol upbringing becomes ever more crystal clear. I begin to understand why he sometimes seems so unfriendly. He is not hampered, he is a free thinker. But the conservatism of the small village in the Dolomites in which Reinhold grew up has stamped its impression upon him, never leaves him. Even if he wanted it, there is no escape. Sometimes he is reserved, sometimes coarse, mostly suspicious. For weeks I have seen through Reinhold like glass, unmasked. It is lovely to go to the mountain with him. Up here he shows more of himself; besides his compulsions he has more freedom in himself. He is so sensitive behind the rough shell; the 30 years of mountaineering, the people who envy him, South Tyrol – all these have made him armour himself. And since when is armour transparent?

Today I don't feel too good. It's a long way but it will be easy as this time I don't have to carry anything. The headaches which I had at the beginning of our travels have gone; also I am well acclimatized. And I love to

Nena, Cheng and Tsao at base camp.

climb with Reinhold, to be travelling with him. We each go our own pace and yet we are never far apart. We have space to think our own thoughts.

The packing ritual doesn't last long this time. Everything is at advanced base camp: provisions for four weeks, fuel, equipment for the ascent to the summit. There are the small items which must not be forgotten – films, pocket knife, a spare pair of sunglasses. In my mind I go through an endless list. I picture the ascent to myself and go over it step by step, bivouac by bivouac, what I shall need above the camp at 6,500 metres. As little as possible but double supplies of the essentials of life, that is my motto.

As I put the altimeter in the top flap of the rucksack it strikes me that the barometric pressure has gone up more. So another monsoon break! I repeat for my own comfort the predictions of the peasants in the valley below and the findings of modern meteorology: 'In the monsoon summer there are one or two periods of fine weather of from four to ten days'. It is striking how often the weather lore of the local people, reduced to instinct, corresponds with the observations of the weather researchers.

I read something about the monsoon in a scientific work by Helmut Kraus about the weather in the Himalaya before I left. This information, added to the testimony of the Tibetans and my own observations, tells me that I must go now.

The summer monsoon which brings with it great amounts of precipitation does not begin suddenly. During the

Nena during ascent to advanced base camp.

pre-monsoon convective and frequently thunderstorm-laden precipitation, there is a gradual change from the dry time of year in the winter to the summer monsoon.'

This change was six weeks ago. It was only during the first few days in base camp that the full fury of the monsoon was not apparent. But what exactly is this monsoon? In Kraus I read:

'By monsoon one means a wind system with a marked annual change of prevailing wind direction. The physical causes of the monsoon winds are the annual movements of planetary pressure and wind belts and the varying warming of land and sea. Mountains and high land also have an influence,

as the air above them becomes warmer in summer and cools down in winter more than at comparable heights in the neighbouring atmosphere. In the widest sense, it is not only the wind system of the monsoon that is significant. Many other facts are included, such as meteorological phenomena and atmospheric effects which are bound up with certain prevailing wind directions. Thus the Indian south-west monsoon (June to September) is marked by decreasing air temperature and frequent precipitation, the Indian north-east monsoon (in winter) by dry, cloud-free weather.'

The weather in July and August is above all of interest to me.

'There is a temperature reduction in July above north-west India at a height of 1·5 kilometres, on the south side of which west winds prevail, forming part of the equatorial west wind belt. To the north-east of this low pressure are south-east winds over the Ganges plain. At a height of 3 kilometres at 20°N is the ITC; at a height of 6 kilometres this is shifted still further towards the equator, and without exception there are east winds between it and two high pressure regions, one of which lies over Tibet (a semi-permanent warm anticyclone produced by the warming of the air over the high-lying heated surface) and the other over Iran and Afghanistan. These east winds are constituent parts of the tropical east current of the trade wind. At a height of 9 kilometres east winds blow over the whole fore-Indian zone southwards from 30°N; their speed in the Nepal Himalaya amounts on average

to about 20 km/hour. This description characterizes the general circulation during the summer monsoon.'

As a layman I find all that rather complicated, and look for information about breaks in the monsoon:

'The summer monsoon is a rain-giver of extraordinary importance for the agriculture of India and Nepal. The nourishment of the population depends upon the length and intensity of the precipitation. So the practical importance of the winter monsoon recedes far behind that of the summer monsoon. That is why in these countries they frequently speak only of 'the Monsoon' and mean thereby the summer monsoon, with its entire meteorological character. Because of this great practical importance for the nourishment of the country, Indian meteorologists have occupied themselves above all, for a long time past, with monsoon problems. Questions about the start of the monsoon, monsoon breaks, retreat of the monsoon and the precipitation pattern, distribution and intensity play a special part in this.'

What is said here agrees with my own observations of past years. These factual bases lend wings to my intentions. I must not hesitate another day. If I do not utilize the present situation I may have to wait until the beginning of October for another chance.

'Monsoon depressions form in the north of the Bay of Bengal and move west-north-west along the ITC (Monsoon trough) then combine with the temperature depression over north-

Monsoon clouds in Tibet.

west India and Pakistan or break up on the Himalaya mountains. According to L.A. Ramdas these monsoon depressions occur on average at intervals of 7–10 days. Their frequency during the year (June to September) fluctuates somewhere between 6 and 14. If the monsoon trough occasionally shifts further to the north, as compared with its normal position, the east winds of the lower atmosphere over the Ganges plain and over the southern slope of the Himalaya are replaced by west winds. The northerly shift of the ITC implies an interruption of the precipitation on the Ganges plain and in the central parts of India. That is why one speaks of a break in the monsoon or an interruption of the monsoon, which can last up to two weeks. It is clear that in the mountainous parts of the country, if they lie far from the monsoon trough, precipitation can occur daily even during the break period.'

'There is no doubt', I say to Nena when we have reached the first moraine ridge just above base camp, 'we are in a monsoon break'. Never have I seen the great mountain look so overwhelming. But I have no fear. Mount Everest with its white snow surfaces blends into the background like a distant mirror. On the left ridge hangs a snow streamer. The sky is like frosted glass. It is fresh, a little windy, and everything seems unearthly to me. Nevertheless I am warm. The track lies firstly in waves and curves, always easily uphill, on the true right side of the valley. I know each stone and that increases my expectation. We must be just about there, or there. Our distance

from the mountain cannot be estimated by the eye. Since the beginning of the monsoon break it has become smaller day by day. For the first time it becomes noticeable how mists form in the tunnel between mountain and me. The summit withdraws, the face beneath takes shape; the white, featureless surfaces in the background begin to come alive.

At so great a distance it is always difficult to estimate the steepness of a face, but I am certain that the North Face of Mount Everest is flatter than it appears to be. Am I trying to comfort myself or do the historical facts make the mountain seem harmless to me? Almost 60 years ago the English pioneers made the ascent to over 8,000 metres, with equipment which today strikes one as downright antediluvian. Therefore the North-East Ridge cannot be steep. To be sure, I have only a fraction of what the English lugged up, my climbing aids are light, tested a hundredfold, the best of the best: ice axe and twelve-pointed crampons made of titanium, Gore-Tex tunnel tent; mat and sleeping-bag. A boyish feeling of 'nothing can stop me' dominates me as I blink in the sun.

Now or Never
How quickly a piece of country can be memorised. This is the fourth time that I have covered these first 6 kilometres of the approach route, I have come to know it step by step. Already somehow it belongs to me. Moreover I have built three cairns, rigged up a well out of two stone slabs by a small rill and sat down each time on a stone by the violet-yellow bell-flowers, to see them nod in the breeze. In a trough

The ascent to intermediate camp.

between the old and the new moraines they lie embedded as in a giant hollow hand. It smells here of grass and damp stones.

It is perhaps for that reason that the nomads love their homeland more than stationary citizens, because they must be forever discovering it anew. Or do most citizens understand by 'home' primarily only possessions, friends, ideologies – things that wind and time decay like autumn leaves? My roots lie deeper, in the stones. The distance between the standing camp and the high camp is divided into two parts, but not of equal lengths. It takes six hours to reach a height of 6,000 metres. This

tent is situated directly to the north of the North Col at the foot of Changtse, the fore-peak of Mount Everest. From there it is another four hours to advanced base camp on a moraine.

We want to over-night in the camp at 6,000 metres. That sounds as if we had booked a room. And in fact I have the feeling of finding more than just protection up there. In a simple tent, 1·80 metres by 1·20 metres, tunnel-shaped, barely a metre high, I can rest, cook and sleep. The knowledge that I can survive a snowstorm in this tiny half-ball fills me with confidence. Not pride – 'I can do that' – only a feeling of being secure.

197

We cross the East Rongbuk Valley at the place where the icy stream rises. From between stones, ice dubs and the tongue of the glacier water bubbles up vigorously. I am in good form, excellently acclimatized, and yet the up and down on this moraine debris is still an exertion. If the stones under my feet suddenly slide away my steps become frantic, irregular, agonizing. I have to stop and stand. Breathe. Rest. We make 900 metres of height this first day, but actually we climb much more than that. Each metre downwards must be compensated by a tiring step upwards. For a while we follow the stony left bank of the glacier, then the conspicuous central moraine. Here the climbing is even and the ground firm. Beyond a dip we reach the wide bay of the small intermediate camp. To our surprise the tent is standing just as we left it three weeks before. Nena cooks, I fetch water from a nearby ice stream. From the glacier tunnel through which it disappears comes a gurgling and rushing; at intervals the ice crackles. All these noises remind me of synthesized music. The glacier groans, snorts and squeaks. The tent flap stands open, to let in the fresh air. Lying with my head against the tent door I look out at the weather over and over again. All the signs are favourable, the few clouds are compact. The sky is high, pale blue; a turquoise gleam enlivens it in the twilight. In the evening there are many quivering stars in the black firmament. I am finally at ease. It is as if the monsoon

Taking a rest on the East Rongbuk Glacier.

Departure from intermediate camp.

break has also interrupted my inner restlessness.

The high-altitude climber is even more dependent on the prevailing conditions on the mountain than on his own ability, his condition. The weather plays the most important part. I judge it now more or less by my feeling and am convinced that it will stay fine. My decision to descend to the Rongbuk camp was right. The ten days at a height of 6,500 metres left their mark on us, but in the main camp we recovered quickly. The desire to eat and sleep have returned. The three weeks at 5,000 metres have completely restored us to health.

I can observe this especially distinctly in Nena. Now she climbs smoothly, has no sort of trouble any more. She sleeps deeply despite the height. I, on the other hand, sleep very little tonight and pack my rucksack in the morning, while Nena writes up her diary. She has more energy than I.

My God, Reinhold is in a bad mood! So today he has a sort of rest day. It is not a long climb from this tent to our high camp. We wait until the sun is higher. Otherwise there are no problems. Reinhold had a miserable night. We lay together in one sleeping-bag. It was cold, with the usual problems: tugs on the down bag, grumbles, exaggerated moving away from each other. The atmosphere is full of unpleasant vibrations. Reinhold is nervous. Naturally I am to blame for his sleeping so badly. Who else's fault could it be?

Subconciously the stress of the solo climb has been growing in me and all

199

my new-found poise has disappeared. I can blame no one, am completely at my own mercy. How unjust I can be at such times! As tense as that I could scarcely sleep under ideal conditions. How, then, am I to find peace on a finger-thick foam rubber mat? The fist-sized stones on which our tent stands stuck in me, I froze, and restlessly anticipated the coming days in a half-waking condition. Partly with curiosity, partly in fear I waited for the dawn. I know the dangers that await me up there: crevasses, avalanches, mist and storm. I know above all of my own weaknesses: exhaustion, fear, loneliness. With inactivity my self-understanding, my self-confidence shrinks too. Perhaps that is the reason why I so wonder at the hermits – because through meditation they can survive loneliness. It is hardest to endure the desert in idleness.

The tent is left standing. Impatiently – Nena is once again not ready to start – I pick up the rucksack and climb up 100 metres over the dry central moraine. I feel as if I would be missing something while waiting for Nena. My compulsion to move is animal-like, the pressure of the self-imposed solo climb so great, the spiritual burden so deep, that I can only endure them in activity.

We round the corner of the North Peak. The steep avalanche slopes of its eastern spurs look rutted. The snow holds. The route continues upwards. How calming this regular plodding is! As if the rhythm of my breathing determined not only paces and heartbeat, but also the flow of feelings through my head. The air here is low on oxygen but all the richer in other

forms of energy. In spite of the slightly low pressure, of the deathly hush of nothingness, up here is something like life to me. Something like spiritual strength. Without being able to hear it, without seeing it, without measuring it, I know it is there. Sometimes when the thunder of an avalanche releases my senses again, I am re-energized, as if this sudden explosion which comes from nowhere like a shock wave is absorbing the vacuum. I am becoming crazy. From whence comes the explosion and implosion of life that pulses without physical existence?

At this height I do not have to go slowly. I put one foot a little in front of the other and climb using the firm stones in the debris, although I would not have the strength to balance from rock block to rock block. Nena is somewhere behind me and keeps her own pace. Climbing together would throw us both out of our individual stride so that we would quickly tire. No two people can climb at the same rhythm at over 6,000 metres without mutually disturbing the energy flow. So, is man born to go alone?! To go alone, yes, but not to be alone. How quickly I shut myself off from others! But as I am incapable of sharing expectation and accomplishments, much preferring to climb alone, this argument is only partly valid.

I still cannot see the higher tent. A glacier hump completely hides it. The steeper the path, the shorter my steps become. But what could be called the path here? The gravel moraine on which we stand runs like a dark stripe between the glaciers, but is no road. Crevasses and scree force me to climb in an irregular zigzag. Each time my

The last stretch to advanced base camp.

foot is placed on firm ground I concentrate totally on finding the next stable footstep amongst the ice, water and rock blocks. In between, a glance across the glacier in order not to lose the general direction. In front and behind, our road of detritus vanishes in perspective to a black thread between glistening ice; optical proof of our progress. I have a misgiving as to how far it still is. There are no comparisons which can explain exertion at this height, and the optical impression is deceiving. In the thin air the distance to the next fixed point seems to be shorter than it really is. Thus there is the danger of despair with the summit actually in sight; constant deception saps the strongest will.

Here below things are not quite so bad. As long as one makes 200 metres height per hour the feeling of making progress prevails and also produces energy. As long as this return flow of energy continues, mountaineering is like cycling and running. The moment it exceeds that it becomes a torment beyond human measure, it becomes the work of Sisyphus. The 'sport of suffering' is then only bearable because with the loss of a sense of time, other senses also fall apart – above, below, here, there. Making headway becomes an animal compulsion. Just as the real Sisyphus had to resist despair at his repeated exertions, yet at the same time could not go up or down, so the high altitude climber runs the risk of exceeding his limitations. The goal of the summit releases him momentarily from the train of suffering, but gives him at the same time the energy to begin the tragic cycle afresh.

The sun has melted the ice between the stones. A trickling and gurgling sets in. Intense heat builds up. It is like spring. We climb over the steep, loose scree to the flat bay of the Upper Rongbuk Glacier. The tent platform lies on the scree of these slopes, out of range of stonefall. A shallow trough separates us from the glacier.

In good weather we get a lot of sun here. The first rays of the morning – to the east lies a broad snow basin with relatively low peaks in the background – strike full on the tent. Only in the evening does it fall into shade early. An hour of sun is sufficient to thaw the water course nearby for several hours. It is the best place I have ever found at such a height. While we re-anchor the tent I look again and again at the Rapiu La, the flat saddle to the east of the snow basin at the foot of the North-East Ridge of Everest. So long as no mist wells up there, the weather is settled.

In spring – the end of April to May – high storms can be so fierce that climbers cannot leave their tents for days on end. It is dreaded. Now the wind is my salvation; above all the west wind. It would be ideal if it held. Were it to strengthen for a while there would be fairly favourable and safe conditions on the mountain: firm snow, ridges blown free of snow, scarcely any avalanche danger.

In spite of the fine weather, striking changes can occur in the mountains within a few hours. Often, they seem literally to disintegrate. The spikes of the seracs which hem in the edge of the glacier like the giant teeth of a crocodile are beginning to crumble, even to collapse here and there. Stones crash from the moraine, and small snow glides plunge noisily from the North-East Face of Mount Everest. I observe with satisfaction how each avalanche leaves behind dark narrow stripes. I am in luck again. My God, these snow conditions! The landscape is bathed in clear blue air: the blue of Everest's snow, the deep blue of the sky, graphically overstated like peep-show pictures. Thick white clouds sail across apparently infinite space. Now and then they condense into mist which envelops everything around us within minutes, wiped out, damp and grey. Then a half-hour later it is swept away and the shining clarity of a summer's day takes its place.

As I watch this springing up and fading away I grasp a little better the lively attitude of Buddhists towards death. Again I think of Mallory, of his mysterious death on Mount Everest. I feel once more that he died there in order to live again. Nothing in life has brought me closer to enlightenment than landscapes. They have stamped me and are my mentors. But for the first time here on this trek it becomes so clear to me that I can contemplate objectively the interplay of impression and reflection. For short, redeeming moments I am able to step outside myself.

It is said that a long, unbroken stay at a height of 6,000 metres and above makes people gradually deteriorate. I know that is right and must therefore act quickly. I want to carry my rucksack up to just below the North Col from this upper base camp tomorrow, 17 August. It doesn't weigh too much, 18 kilos perhaps, and contains all the essentials for a solo climb: food and fuel for a week, a bivouac tent, sleeping-bag, mat and camera. If I deposit this rucksack 500 metres higher I can save strength and time on the actual ascent. Whether the equipment which I left up there weeks ago is still to be found I don't know. I have one more of everything with me; for all eventualities.

The ascent to the North Col is the most dangerous part of my solo climb. The Chang La face, almost 500 metres high, is similar to the ice-fall on the south side of Mount Everest, shattered and threatened by seracs, but above all avalanche prone. In 1922 during the first assault on Mount Everest a whole team was swept away there by an avalanche, and seven Sherpas died as a result. Miraculously Mallory and his comrades were able to save themselves. As a solo climber I must not only beware of avalanche fracture lines, I must also cross the crevasses safely without a rope. To find a safe route of ascent amongst seracs and crevasses requires long years of practice and a definite instinct for it. I have no radio with me; I quite consciously want no contact with 'down below'. Apart from the fact that Nena could not help me I decline to have other people risk their lives because I enter into a deliberate risk and thereby endanger myself. The solo ascent of Everest is really only a solo if there is no bridge between 'up there' and 'down there', no safety link with a watchful ground crew.

How fast I climb this time! In light climbing boots I clamber light-footedly up the 400 metres of height. I stop just to the right of the wide angle where the faces of the Chang La and

The rucksack in the ice.

Mount Everest meet. The snow is so hard that only the treads of my soles penetrate, leaving behind a dainty pattern in the snow surface. This is not climbing with hands and feet, I climb evenly, using the ski sticks as balance aids like a second pair of feet. An enormous quantity of new snow has fallen during the past weeks. But now it is consolidated and firm. For the first time, where after a left-hand bend the slope becomes steeper, I rest after each fifty paces. I alter the adjustable ski sticks, make them a bit shorter. How precisely my body is programmed! It is always this same number of paces that I take without a rest. Plus or minus one. Higher up it will be the same, proof that I am fully adapted to

altitude. A rest pause suffices to compensate the oxygen deficiency in the blood; the freshly fuelled reserves run out in about 50 paces. In between, a feeling of energy, security, almost high spirits surges through me. While resting there is a comfortable tiredness in the mind: only my lungs heave.

The sun is still not hot. Although it stands high above the cloud streamers in the east and hits the 45° inclined snow slope almost vertically the air remains fresh. If it holds thus tomorrow I shall do it.

Just under the North Col, about 80 metres below the knife edge, I deposit my rucksack in a tiny ice hollow and tie it fast to an ice screw. I cast a look back, then turn round and make a note of the spot. I must find it again in the early morning, perhaps even in half light. Now I want to get down quickly again to the upper base camp. I must relax, sleep, drink a great deal. I must also prepare myself spiritually for the decisive days.

Nena has watched me the whole time through the telephoto lens of her camera.

17 August 1980. I am surprised how fast Reinhold climbs in his hiking boots towards the North Col. When he left with his rucksack at 8.15 a.m. to test the snow and deposit the equipment, I didn't realize that he was not just testing the route. In spirit he is already on the way to the summit. I had the impression he would go up only a little way and immediately come back again. I turned over and tried to go back to sleep. But an hour later when I peeped through the tent flap I saw that he was already half-way to the col and was going on. Suddenly I was wide awake. When he goes up to this col I always feel cold shivers up and down my spine. Each time it is a great risk and I marvel to myself how he finds the way between the gaping crevasses.

Half an hour later I am again in the tent with Nena. Already absent in spirit I prepare my body for the days of utmost exertion. I drink and eat, and sleep in between. In the tent the temperature is pleasant. The ventilation flap and entrance are open.

This time I have myself under control. I give fear no chance from the outset. The most dangerous part of the route, the ascent to the North Col, I know already, and as far as that is concerned I could only get stuck in the snow or lose myself in the mist, but not perish. The weather is fine, there will be no mist! My self-control costs

energy. I sense how keyed-up my whole body is. Even during the night I have to force myself to lie quietly. Only twice do I look out at the weather. It is fine but the air is too warm. In the blue of the night Mount Everest stands over me like a magic mountain. No pondering, no asking why, I prepare myself with every fibre of my being for the big effort.

When it is time to get up I pick up socks, boots, breeches and top clothes like a sleep-walker. Each movement is quick and sure as if I had practised them a hundred times. No wasted movement.

In front of the tent I stretch myself, sniff the night air. Then I continue my ascent of the previous day. I am soon well up. Nena has remained down below. I reach the ice hollow and pick up the rucksack.

18 August 1980. Yes, he has gone! A tender kiss on the lips was all. Just once. When Reinhold kisses me it is full of meaning. I call after him: 'I shall be thinking of you!' He didn't hear me properly or didn't want to hear me. His voice sounded absent-minded, as he asked back: 'What?' He was a bit disturbed because the night had been warmer than usual. He was much afraid that the snow would have become too soft. So what I called after him in the still morning must for him have been irrelevant. So as not to hold him up any more I said simply: 'Bye, bye'. And back comes his answer: 'Bye, bye!' Empty words hanging in the air. What experiences will he have? What sort of change will take place in him, in me?

1,300 Metres Higher

The snow suddenly gives way under me and my headlamp goes out. Despairingly I try to cling on in the snow, but in vain. The initial reaction

Rucksack depot under the North Col.

passes. Although it is pitch-dark I believe I can see everything: at first snow crystals, then blue-green ice. It occurs to me that I am not wearing crampons. I know what is happening but nevertheless remain quite calm. I am falling into the depths and experience the fall in slow-motion, strike the walls of the widening crevasse once with my chest, once with the rucksack. My sense of time is interrupted, also my perception of the depth of the drop. Have I been falling only split seconds or is it minutes? I am completely weightless, a torrent of warmth surges through my body.

Suddenly I have support under my feet again. At the same time I know that I am caught, perhaps trapped for ever in this crevasse. Cold sweat beads my forehead. Now I am frightened. 'If only I had a radio with me' is my first thought. I could call Nena. Perhaps she would hear me. But whether she could climb the 500 metres up to me and let a rope down to me in the crevasse is more than questionable. I have consciously committed myself to this solo ascent without a radio, and discussed it many times before starting.

I finger my headlamp and suddenly everything is bright. It's working! I breathe deeply, trying not to move at all. Also, the snow surface on which I am standing is not firm. Like a thin, transparent bridge it hangs fragile between both walls of the crevasse. I put my head back and see some eight metres above the tree trunk sized hole through which I have fallen. From the bit of black sky above a few far, far distant stars twinkle down at me. The sweat of fear breaks from all my pores, covers my body with a touch which is

as icy as the iridescent blue-green ice walls between which I am imprisoned. Because they converge obliquely above me I have no chance of climbing up them. With my headlamp I try to light up the bottom of the crevasse; but there is no end to be seen. Just a black hole to the left and right of me. The snow bridge which has stopped my fall is only one square metre large.

I have goose-pimples and shiver all over. The reactions of my body, however, are in stark contrast to the calm in my mind: there is no fear at the prospect of a new plunge into the bottomless depths, only a presentiment of dissolving, of evaporation. At the same time my mind says, that was lucky! For the first time I experience fear as a bodily reflex without psychological pain in the chest. My only problem is how to get out again. Mount Everest has become irrelevant. I seem to myself like an innocent prisoner. I don't reproach myself, don't swear. This pure, innocent feeling is inexplicable. What determines my life at this moment I do not know. I promise to myself I will descend, I will give up, if I come out of this unhurt. No more solo eight-thousanders!

My sweaty fear freezes in my hair and beard. The anxiety in my bones disappears the moment I set my body in motion, as I try to get my crampons out of the rucksack. But at each movement the feeling of falling again comes over me, a feeling of plunging into the abyss, as if the ground were slowly giving way.

Then I discover a ramp running along the crevasse wall on the valley side, a ledge the width of two feet in the ice which leads obliquely upwards and is full of snow. That is the way out! Carefully I let myself fall forward, arms outstretched, to the adjoining crevasse wall. For a long moment my body makes an arch between the wedged snow block and the slightly overhanging wall above me. Carefully I straddle across with the right foot, make a foothold in the snow which has frozen on the ledge on this crevasse wall on the downhill side. I transfer weight to the step. It holds. The insecure spot I am standing on is thus relieved. Each of these movements I instinctively make as exactly as in a rehearsed ballet. I try to make myself lighter. Breathing deeply my whole body identifies itself with the new position, I am for a moment, a long, life-determining moment, weightless. I have pushed myself off from the snow bridge with the left foot, my arms keep me in balance, my right leg supports my body. The left foot can get a grip. Relieved deep-breathing. Very carefully I move – face to the wall – to the right. The right foot gropes for a new hold in the snow, the left boot is placed precisely in the footstep which the right has vacated a few seconds before. The ledge becomes broader, leads obliquely upwards to the outside. I am saved!

In a few minutes I am on the surface – still on the valley side to be sure – but safe. I am a different person, standing there rucksack on my shoulders, ice axe in my hand as if nothing had happened. I hesitate for a moment longer, consider what I did wrong. How did this fall happen? Perhaps my left foot, placed two centimetres above the underlying edge of the crevasse, broke through as I tried to find a hold with the right on the opposite wall.

Down below in the crevasse I had decided to turn round, give up, if I got out unharmed. Now that I am standing on top I continue my ascent without thinking, unconsciously, as if I were computer-programmed.

The first glimmer of dawn illuminates Everest's North Col. I look at the time – shortly before seven. How long was I down there? I don't know. The fall into the crevasse is already wiped from my mind. The vow to descend could not have been fundamentally serious. I don't ask myself how I came to deceive myself thus. Determinedly I go back along the lower edge of the crevasse, my mind totally fixed on the summit, as if this perilous incident had only shaken my body, but not that identification which has for weeks constituted my being – my identification with Everest. The fall into the crevasse has put me into a far greater state of alertness than normal. I know this is the only place where I can cross the crevasse which runs right across this 500 metres-high ice wall below the North Col. During my reconnaissance ascent four weeks ago I discovered the snow bridge, just 2 metres wide, which today proved almost my undoing. Then it had borne my weight. It may hold up now as well, if I only put weight on the outside edges.

On my solo climb I have no aluminium ladder and no rope, which larger expeditions would use to overcome hindrances of this sort. Two ski sticks and the titanium ice axe are my sole aids. Trance-like, I turn back to the hole I fell through. I shine my light down. Black as night. This time I must watch like hell so as not to make any mistake. On the other side of the crevasse is a steep snow wall. Soon decided, I bend forward and thrust the ski sticks – handles foremost – into the snow up to the discs. High up on the wall above me they now make two firm anchor points, artificial holds. I must cross the hole with a big straddling step and find a hold up there on the other side of the crevasse with the ice axe and ski sticks. Even though I know that on my descent I must find another route, I am immersed in the ascent as if there were nothing more to follow. With a powerful move I swing myself up, make a few quick steps and feel safe again. All these movements are fast but not hurried.

Slowly it becomes day. Far to the east stands the Kangchenjunga massif. Otherwise there is not much to be seen of this world. Up above a grey-blue sea of mist spreads a firmament which changes with infinite variations from blue to red.

The weather is fine, the air biting cold. What a good thing that I broke off the attempt in July. The snow softened by the monsoon then seemed bottomless, and the avalanche danger was great. It is not without danger now – more than once I have lost the route on the slopes leading to the North Col – but today, 18 August, the snow is so firmly frozen that I leave only a light track behind me.

The highest slope is very steep but the previous bad snow has consolidated. What I am climbing on is not iron-hard névé like lower down; shallow crust predominates here. Frequently I break through the splintering surface and sink in up to the ankles. As I step on to the top of the pass, I quite

suddenly feel a strong west wind in my face. It takes my breath away, makes my eyes water. I stop briefly. Look, breathe more quickly and intermittently. Then a regular rhythm sets in again. The wind does not penetrate my thick clothes, but occasionally makes me stagger. Instinctively I stoop, thrust firmly on to my ski sticks. I follow the old route exactly, along the north rib, the English route. For the first 500 metres this ridge looks like a steep ski slope. Its rises are slightly undulating and perhaps 30° inclined. Endless masses of névé overhang to the east. An intense dawn seems to enliven the cornices. The shadow colours the snow blue, in the soft light of the rising sun outlines blur. In between on the blunt knife-edge snow crystals flash like diamonds. Now the sun touches the pinnacle of Pumori, the broad flank of Cho Oyu. The nearby North Peak stands like a gigantic wedge between day and night. Also, above the summit of Mount Everest lies a rosy dawn. The mountain appears so clearly against the deep blue sky that I can recognize each separate rock tower on the North-East Ridge. Up there in 1924 George Mallory and Andrew Irvine were seen for the last time on their bold summit push . . .

The distance as the crow flies from myself to the 'first step' now amounts to perhaps 2 kilometres – a distance at which one would not be able to recognize a person's limbs. Odell, who had stood much higher, said that he was able to see the two climbers for five minutes. He had not spotted them through moving swathes of mist, rather through a sudden clearing of the air, such an air as now lies above me. He saw them on the 'first step' and did not mistake rocks for men as has often been put to him. I exclude the possibility of an optical illusion, although I too, as I now stand and stare at the 'first step', for moments succumb to the illusion of seeing black points in motion. Mallory did not climb the 'second step', he attempted the ascent, but gave up. That I know for certain as I stand and stare.

Where does the ability to look back more than 50 years come from? Or can I no longer distinguish between reality and fantasy because I have read so much? Does this attempt of 8 June 1924 continue to play itself out up here, visible only in a heightened state of consciousness? This is no optical illusion, the sensation of human energy surrounds my body like the wind, like the sunbeams.

As I continue climbing the tiny figures disappear. I place one foot at a time so firmly in the snow that my whole being becomes this step. Leaning on my ski sticks I climb as evenly as possible – 50 paces, rest, 50 paces. When I have rested I cast a glance upward to orientate myself approximately. Thus I never have the feeling of being alone on this slope. As intensely as I now gaze upwards I am observed by Nena from below:

View of the North Peak from north rib.

I carry on with the daily tasks which occur in camp at 6,500 metres and watch him as he climbs higher and higher. In many respects I envy him. I would love to look down here from up there, to see the summit from up there. But more than anything else I would like to climb with him. 'One day perhaps', I tell myself . . . He becomes smaller and smaller in my field of vision, and the further he is from me the stronger becomes my love.

Nena does not know that the most dangerous moment of my expedition lies behind me. She did not see the fall into the crevasse. It was still dark then. Now she follows my route and photographs it. The sun floods the slopes to the North Col. Through the telephoto lens Nena can make out my tracks which look like a pearl neck-

lace. The hole through which I fell won't strike her, as the chain of pearls runs across the crevasse. I am climbing smoothly now and am at a height of more than 7,200 metres. The air quickly warms up. The sun beats full on Cho Oyu to the west and on the North Peak of Mount Everest. Its shadow spans the glistening valleys like a giant black hole. I can allow myself time.

I have already made 700 metres height this morning. Never before in my life have I climbed so easily at over 7,000 metres. It is not only the ideal snow conditions which urge me on. It is my mood.

Nevertheless I must not over-strain myself. I always rest before total tiredness goes to my legs like a numbing pain. I must allow myself time, apportion my strength.

211

Telephoto of the North Ridge from advanced base camp.

Frequently while sitting down I trace the route up the North-East Ridge. I want to get to just under the shoulder and then across the shallow ridge to the second step. The views which I have during my rest stops impress themselves like pictures on my mind. When I seat myself on the tightly filled rucksack, back to the slope, facing the valley, I photograph, so to speak, with my brain. Only occasionally do I take the camera out of the rucksack, and then I take more snaps than I can really use. Photographing myself – screw camera to the ice axe with the shaft stuck in the snow, set delayed action release, walk a dozen paces, wait for the click, rest, return and dismantle the whole thing – I find, as always, comical and an unnecessary waste of strength. Once, I spot my shadow in the view-finder of the reflex camera. Involuntarily I have to laugh, as one laughs when one recognizes the clown in one's friend. Now I find the climbing soothing. It is almost like the rhythm of my very fibres, clearly audible music. Leaning on the two ski sticks I can also rest while standing. On the move and in uneven snow they help me to balance. With pitiful equipment by today's standards – normally I would not even climb the Matterhorn with it – on this ridge nearly 60 years ago Mallory and his friends Norton and Somervell crossed the 8,000 metre barrier for the first time in the history of mountaineering. George Leigh Mallory, that fiery spirit, recognized then that, even after thorough preparation and a six-week acclimatization, Mount Everest would have to be stormed in six days from Rongbuk base camp. This early realiz-ation seems to me like a vision. Since I reached base camp via Lhasa and Shigatse, more than seven weeks have elapsed. I have been on the move for four days, I require two more days to reach the summit if all goes well and the weather holds.

Now I am 7,220 metres high. Again I squat down to rest. Haste at this altitude produces exhaustion, and I have most of my day's work already behind me. However, I want to go on as long as I have the strength for it. Far below is the valley end of the Rongbuk Glacier. The view to the west is still clear. To the left under the sky lies Nepal, in front of that a tip of the west shoulder of Everest. In the distance great ranges of mountains fade away. The bright light of the morning dissolves mountains and valleys. The rock bastion of Changtse, also known as the North Peak, falling abruptly to the Rongbuk Glacier, is now a most impressive view. The beautiful pyramid of Pumori looks supernatural and uncanny. Here and only here is God able to manifest himself. To the right the Tibetan plateau loses itself in infinity. The few clouds there, distributed like spiders' webs, are motionless. Up here, too, no wind. Snow only whirls through the air far below on the North Col; it seems to me as if this col is a funnel for all the winds in Tibet. Orographically speaking, looking down, the broad North Flank of Mount Everest is slightly sunken and wind protected on the left. Likewise the north-east surface to the right is hollowed out. The ground plunges steeply down on each side.

The rock slopes on the north side are deeply snowed up, everything looks

213

gentle and flatter than it really is. Up here everything seems peaceful. Now I have to rest at shorter intervals but each time my breathing quickly returns to its former rhythm, and I feel myself recover. This change between going on and stopping, exhaustion and returning energy determines my speed. With each metre of ascent this rhythm becomes shorter phased, more constrained. Higher up above, I know from experience, it will be only will-power that forces the body from complete lethargy for another step. This sort of snail's pace compels me to rest now for some minutes every 30 paces, with longer rests sitting down every 2 hours. As the air up here contains only a third of the usual quantity of oxygen I climb as the Sherpas do. I climb and rest, rest and climb. I know that I shall feel comparatively well as soon as I sit down but put off this compelling feeling minute by minute. I must be careful to avoid any harsh irritation of the respiratory tracts. The bronchial tubes and throat are my weakest points. I know it. And already I sense some hoarseness. So I am doubly glad that on this windy mountain hardly a breeze is blowing today. A steep rise now costs me more energy than I thought. From below, going over it by eye, I supposed it would require 5 rest stops. Meanwhile it has become 8 or 9 and I am still not on top. There, where it becomes flatter, something like deliverance awaits me. I don't want to sit down until I am over the rounded top.

Now and then small snow crystals swirl in the air above me, a glittering and glistening enlivening the space. A whistling and singing comes and goes. Still 80 paces?

While climbing I watch only the foot making the step. Otherwise there is nothing. The air tastes empty, not stale, just empty and rough. My throat hurts. While resting I let myself droop, ski sticks and legs take the weight of my upper body. Lungs heave. For a time I forget everything. Breathing is so strenuous that no power to think remains. Noises from within me drown out all external sounds. Slowly with the throbbing in my throat will-power returns.

Onwards. Another 30 paces. How this ridge fools me! Or is it my eyes? Everything seems so close, and is then so far. After a standing rest stop I am over the top. I turn round, let myself drop on the snow. From up here I gaze again and again at the scenery, at the almost endless distance. In the pastel shades of the ranges lies something mystical. It strengthens the impression of distance, the unattainable, as if I had only dreamed of this Tibet, as if I had never been here. But where I am now, I have been already, that much I know. I stare at the plateau, think I can recognize a village. Tingri perhaps? In spirit I see before me the whitewashed mud houses with the black window holes. Red scarves wave beside Tibetan prayer flags. I see blunt-featured faces. The people in Tibet do not laugh as merrily as the people in the mountains of Nepal. All that goes through my mind as if I were standing at the edge of this village; it is no memory, it is the present. The altimeter shows 7,360 metres and it is about 9 a.m. I did the stretch to the North Col in two hours. By this ploy I have spared myself a bivouac. Now I am climbing slowly, consciously slowly.

View to the north-west.

Now and then the snow gives way up to the ankles, and snowdrifts cost strength. Mostly, however, I can go round the spots of crusted snow. Each avoidance feels like a personal triumph. I must not waste my energy. This impulse determines my thoughts and feelings more and more. Tomorrow and the day after it will be more strenuous. The two adjustable ski sticks really are a wonderful help here. I can distribute my weight to legs

time being I stay on the blunt North Ridge. That is not only the safest route, the wind has also blown away a lot of snow. In spite of all that, there is no trace of my predecessors. Everything is buried under a thick cloak of snow. Only once, at about 7,500 metres, do I see a red rope in the snow. I go over, touch it. The rope seems fairly new and is anchored to a rock outcrop. That must have been done by the Japanese, I think. In customary

View across the Lho La to the west.

and arms. I balance myself from up top, not on my legs.

The North Flank to the right of me is a gigantic snow slope. Only a few rock islands lie scattered darkly across this vertical ice desert. Avalanche lines are distinctly recognizable. For the

expedition style and team work they had set up a chain of high camps in May. On steep sections they anchored fixed ropes, on which they could descend to base camp when the weather became bad, and on which they could pull themselves up in order

The North Peak.

to continue the preparation of the route. Step by step they pushed forward to the summit with the support of Chinese high altitude porters. With exactly these tactics I climbed Mount Everest myself in 1978 by the southern route. On that occasion there were eleven of us climbers employing two dozen Sherpas as high altitude porters and taking turns with building camp. Only for the last 900 metres did Peter Habeler and I climb on without support – as far as the top.

This time there is no one to help carry; no one to prepare my bivouac; no comrade to help me break trail in deep snow and no Sherpa to carry my equipment. Nobody. How much easier it is to climb as a pair. The knowledge that someone is standing behind you brings comfort. Not only is solo climbing far more strenuous and dangerous, above all the psychological burden is more than doubled. Everything that lies ahead of me, including the descent – while resting this is all often blown up out of all proportion – weighs me down. Like a snail which carries its home on its back I carry my tent in my rucksack. I shall erect it, sleep in it and take it with me for the next night. I am equipped like a nomad. I can survive for a week. Nevertheless I have scarcely any reserves. After seven days I must be back, nothing can be allowed to go wrong. A second tent would be too heavy, to say nothing of oxygen apparatus which would double my load again. My 18 kilos weighs so heavily at this height that I now stop and stand after every two dozen steps, struggle for breath and forget everything around me.

The stretches between the rest stops

The upper North Ridge, with the summit of Everest behind.

become shorter and shorter. Often, very often, I sit down to have a breather. Each time it takes great will-power to stand up again. The knowledge that I have completed my self-inflicted day's stint helps me now. It is as if thinking of that releases energy. 'Still a bit more, you can do it', I say to myself softly by way of encouragement. 'What you climb today, you won't have to climb tomorrow.'

Soloing doesn't feel like isolation now. Only occasionally does a feeling of impotence strike me with the thought of the awful endless exertion which still lies before me. If a friend, a partner, were there we could alternate with breaking trail. Physically I am carrying the exertion alone. Psychologically helpers appear sporadically. There is again someone behind me! Is it my separated ego or some other human energy which compensates for a partner? Thus am I accompanied up to a height of 7,800 metres.

The first bivouac spot which I tread down on the snow does not please me. I must camp on a rock and anchor the tent securely. The wind increases. A few metres above me I see the ideal camping place. Once more I hesitate before I make a platform. It is as if it did not smell like a campsite. Several metres lower perhaps. Finally, I feel within myself I have found the correct place. At first strength to unpack the rucksack and put up the tent fails me. I stand there and gaze down at advanced base camp. It must have been warm down there, there is less snow on the mountains.

sees me too. No longing, only the knowledge that she is below, waiting.

Down below the heat is generally worse to bear than the cold, although the thermometer there at night sinks below minus 10°C, and up here perhaps to minus 20°C. The sun and the dry air parch me. I remember that

Resting on the North Ridge.

It is after 3 o'clock, I must cook. Below I recognize a tiny red speck. Nena has placed the sleeping bag on the roof of the tent to protect it from the heat. Or is it a signal for me? I hope that she

I have with me a tiny bottle of Japanese medicinal herb oil, and put two drops of it on my tongue. For a while that brings relief and opens the air ways. Apart from aspirin this herbal remedy is the only medication I carry on the mountain.

The thin air works like a grater on my throat. Each breath leaves a pain in the throat and a feeling of stickiness in the mouth. I take my time setting up the bivouac.

I am tired and glad that I have finally decided to stop. Already the consciousness that no further effort is required works wonders. Was it not myself, but a power from without which drove me on? I feel it to be so. My will returns to normal and I begin to think clearly again. I can perceive again, not merely see. I enjoy a magnificent view to the glacier below me, towards the snow world to the east. Far below is the gloomy form of the North Peak which looks as if it had turned its head round. Behind it swim soft and wavy ranges of mountains; there, behind the Tibetan plateau, are people. For a long time I search in vain for the ice pyramid of Pumori, over 7,000 metres high, in the sea of summits to the west. It has dwindled to an unimportant hump of snow by the bank of the Rongbuk Glacier. Meanwhile I have unpacked the tent. I fix the rucksack in the snow above the camp site so that it cannot move and roll away. I remain standing between the handles of the ski sticks and peer upward. Still a short rise, then comes the gigantic dip before the ridge. The conviction, a hunch condensed almost to certainty, that I shall reach the summit in a further two days makes me light-hearted. There don't seem to be any serious hindrances in the way. The 'second step', the only section which could frighten me, has been secured with ropes and pitons for years

now. What a good thing that I know that. Above me I divine a yellow band of rock below the snow; some rock outcrops betray the horizontal stratification of the mountain.

Before starting I had already reckoned that there should be no problem if I made 1,200 metres height the first day. I have done at least 1,300 metres. During the solo ascent of Nanga Parbat in 1978, which is the psychological support for this solo trip on Everest, I was actually able to climb 1,600 metres on the first day, but on that occasion I started from 4,800 metres, and there is a vast difference between climbing at 6,000 and 7,000 metres above sea-level. Here, just under 8,000 metres, each action becomes a triumph, an ordeal.

My tiny tent, not 2 kilos in weight and constructed so that it can withstand storms up to 100 kilometres per hour, does not need much space. It is just big enough for me to lie with my knees bent. Nevertheless I require a long time to flatten out a site for it. I push the snow backwards and forwards with my boots, stamp it down. I have no shovel. The tent must not be sloping. I have trouble putting it up. Again and again a gust of wind comes and lifts it. Not until I have the tent wall stretched on the light metal tubes do I feel all right. With my ski sticks, ice axe and the only rock piton I have with me I anchor the bivouac cover. Then I lay a thin foam rubber mat on the floor, and, pushing the full rucksack from behind, crawl inside. For a time I just lie there. I listen to the wind hurling ice crystals against the tent wall. It comes in waves, ebbs to and fro and its rhythm keeps me awake. The

221

wind is blowing from the north-west, that is a good sign. I ought to cook, I must. Again a command that absorbs everything in me and about me. But more tired than before from the many small jobs, from the erection of the bivouac, I cannot brace myself to it. For the last time I go outside the tent, fetch snow in my little aluminium pot and peer down into the valley, as if to dodge the all-important work of cooking. It becomes terribly cold. For a time I sit on the knob of rock which I picked out from below as an 'ideal resting place'.

Far to the north I see the Tibetan hill country, still further northwards the grey-brown stone cone of Shekar and right at the back a chain of white mountains. Clouds fill the valleys to the south. The wind becomes stronger. If Wilson had managed to get up here, I think suddenly, would he have reached the summit? Wilson was tougher than I am, uncompromising and capable of enduring loneliness. The stretch above me seems to be really easy, so Wilson would have been able to climb it, at least as far as the North-East Ridge. Do I understand this madman so well because I am mad myself? Or do I take comfort in the constancy of this man in my delusion to prove something? I don't know exactly what it is, at least not rationally; I can still look at myself objectively, but I behave like one possessed, who uses himself to express himself.

I know of no mountain, no other region from which there is such an

Tibetan women praying.

Preparing for the first bivouac.

infinite view as from Mount Everest across the Tibetan plateau. With this impression I crawl back into the constriction of the tent. The space about me shrinks to a cubic metre, and I quickly forget where the tent is standing. Feet in sleeping-bag I begin to cook on my small gas burner. Taking off the rucksack, levelling the camp site, fixing the tent, all that was a hard piece of work after more than ten hours of climbing. Now follow six hours of chores, and these chores are as strenuous as the climbing was before. I eat cheese in small crumbs and nibble a piece of coarse South Tyrolean brown bread. At intervals I fall asleep. When I wake up again the first pot is full of warm water. The soup tastes insipid. The snow has taken ages to melt.

I am surrounded by so much peace and at the same time so powerfully aroused that I could embrace anyone. Although I have eaten nothing since this morning I am not hungry. Also I must force myself to drink. The feeling of thirst is less than the fluid requirement of my body. I must drink at least four litres; this is a fundamental standard which I have set myself, like the course of the route and weather studies. Again I think of Maurice Wilson who in his fanaticism had ventured a solo ascent of Everest, although he was certainly no mountaineer. He knew little about altitude. Even after terrible snowstorms and several falls Wilson had not given up. I lack nothing, the forthcoming climbing problems are well within my capabilities, and yet I must force myself to

223

believe in success. I know that I can do it. Nevertheless I try to talk myself into not giving up. So long as Wilson was able to remain on his legs he climbed upwards like one possessed, borne aloft by belief and by God. I need so much energy just to fight against fear and inertia. In this I pursue a goal which not only climbers can understand. When shall I finally be able to live without a goal? Why do I myself stand in the way with my ambition, with my fanaticism? 'Fai la cucina' says someone near me, 'get on with the cooking'. I think again of cooking. Half aloud I talk to myself. The strong feeling I have had for several hours past, of being with an invisible companion, has apparently encouraged me to think that someone else is doing the cooking. I ask myself too how we shall find space to sleep in this tiny tent. I divide the piece of dried meat which I take out of the rucksack into two equal portions. Only when I turn round do I realize that I am alone. Now I am speaking Italian although for me the mother tongue is South Tyrol German and for three months I have been speaking English with Nena.

I know I can prepare warm water simply from snow with the heat of the sun. Basically it works on the hothouse principle. I have brought especially for this purpose a plain black plastic bag to fill with snow which is connected by a tube to a transparent plastic bag. But it is too windy, and now in the afternoon the sun is veiled. I therefore cook in the tent on the tiny gas flame. Half outstretched, changing position from time to time, I lie there. The mat is as hard as stone. The wind has become so strong that the

The bivouac tent at 7,800 metres.

tent flutters and is constantly blowing out the flame on my gas burner whenever I open the tent flap a few inches in order to shovel snow with the lid of the cooking pot. It will be a bad night I think. But at the same time the wind is a good sign, so it also comforts me. I need a lot of snow before I have melted a litre of water. Once more I make tomato soup, then two pots of Tibetan salt tea. I learned how to make it from the nomads. A handful of herbs to a litre of water, plus two pinches of salt. I must drink a lot, if I am not to become dehydrated. My blood could thicken up too much if I do not take enough fluid, so I force myself to melt more snow to drink. The cooking lasts several hours. I just lie there, holding the cooking pot and occasionally pushing a piece of dried meat or Parmesan cheese into my mouth. I have no desire to leave the tent. The storm outside gets up even more. Now grains of ice beat like hail against the tent wall. The poles sing. That is good, for the wind will clear snow from the ridge and drive off the monsoon clouds which were advancing during late afternoon. There is no question of going to sleep. Terrible buffets beat at the tent. Or does my over-wakeful sense only deceive me? Tent floor and sleeping-bag are lifted up time and again. If the storm becomes stronger it will hurl me together with my lodgings into the depths. I must hold the tent fast. Snow powder forces itself through the cracks. Cooking has now become impossible. I lie down, arms in sleeping-bag, and wait. I would like to keep my eyes closed but every time a solid gust of wind comes I open them again involuntarily. Am I still here?

This lying here tensely itself takes energy. The tent walls flutter, the storm whistles, howls, presses. Whirling snow beats on the tent like spray on the bow of a ship.

Once when I look out through the tent flap a torrent of ice crystals beats against me. Nevertheless, no panic wells up. My surroundings are completely hidden, extinguished. The black rock outcrops above me appear ghostly. This storm really threatens to catapult me and the tent into the depths. The fine ice dust in the tent, the fingers which stick to metal, all that makes me shiver continually. Nevertheless I manage to remain fairly warm. Whenever the wind allows I put both arms deep into the sleeping-bag and hold it down from within. Only my face remains free. Once I fall asleep briefly.

The night is tolerable. The storm has abated. In the sleepless intervals endless thoughts go round and round in my mind. I feel this thinking as something tangible. From the back of my mind springs one fragment of thought after another, to and fro, like points of condensed energy, finding no way out, with a life of their own. As if there were an energy in my field of force which is independent of me. Indeed it belongs to me, but exists without my so much as lifting a finger, without impulse. Even in sleep.

It comes and goes against my will. So it is also with this almost tangible power around me. A spirit breathes regularly in and out, which originates from nothingness and which condenses to nothingness. Only somewhere between these extreme forms do I perceive it, even with my senses.

There is also my plan for tomorrow. Is it possible in 'x' hours to climb 'y' metres? Over and over again, this question. I answer it irrationally, I answer it emotionally – a game, like the counting of petals – she loves me, she loves me not. 600 metres of ascent perhaps? 700? As far as the 'second step'? Then the weather penetrates my half-wakeful consciousness. The wind has not entirely calmed down; nevertheless I feel its decrease as something like peace. The quiet before the storm? The moon shines but still the night is warm. I am no longer freezing. Is the monsoon break over? Is it still ice crystals the wind hurls against the tent or is it snowing already? If it snows suddenly, and a lot, I shall be able to go neither up nor down. Then I shall be trapped. In my inertia I don't know which I prefer, good weather or snow. What should I do in the case of avalanche danger? How long could I survive here? These questions, to which my imagination knows no answer, and also wants to give no answer, pursue me into my dreams. Again chains of thought without conclusion, independent streams of energy in my mind. Certainly the avalanche danger is slight higher up but this grainy new snow is like a morass, it not only holds one back, it also saps one. Once exhausted I am lost for ever.

As the morning dawns sluggishly I notice that the wind is dropping again. That lends me wings. I manoeuvre the gas burner into the sleeping-bag to warm it up. An hour later I am drinking luke-warm coffee. With that I chew the hard, coarse brown bread from South Tyrol again. All the small chores in the constriction and cold of the tent add up to a bodily ordeal. I work with numb fingers; uninterruptedly, hoar-frost trickles from the canvas. To be able to stretch out fully, or to stand up to adjust my clothes is a luxury which I cannot perform in here. Such a tent would weigh at least three times as much as my special construction. Once more I force myself to cook. The dry lumps of snow produce an unpleasant noise between my fingers. It is an eternity before my fist-sized pot is full of water.

For an hour I lie still with my clothes on in the sleeping-bag, drink and doze off. I don't want to look at the time. When I open my eyes I often don't know whether it is morning or evening.

I feel a driving unrest in my innermost being. It is not fear which suddenly seizes me like a big all-embracing hand. It is all the experiences of my mountaineering life which spread out in me and press for activity. The exertion of 30 years of climbing; avalanches, which I have been through, states of exhaustion which have condensed over the decades to a feeling of deep helplessness. You must go on! Time won is energy saved. I know what can happen to me during the next few days, and I know how great the grind will become below the summit. This knowledge is now only endurable in activity.

I must go, and yet each smallest chore is an effort. Up here life is brutally racked between exhaustion and will-power; self-conquest becomes a compulsion. Why don't I go down? There is no occasion to. I cannot simply give up without reason. I wanted to make the climb, I still want to. Curiosity (where is Mallory?), the game (man versus Mount Everest), ambition (I want to be the first) – all these superficial incentives have vanished, gone. Whatever it is that drives me is planted much deeper than I or the magnifying glass of the psychologists can detect. Day by day, hour by hour, minute by minute, step by step I force myself to do something against which my body rebels. At the same time this condition is only bearable in activity. Only a bad omen or the slightest illness would be a strong enough excuse for me to descend.

As the sun strikes my tent and slowly absorbs the hoar-frost from the inner wall I pack up everything again. Bit by bit, in the reverse order to which I must unpack again in the evening. Only two tins of sardines, a gas cartridge as well as half the soup and tea, do I leave behind in a tiny depot, to make my rucksack lighter. I must make do with the remainder of the provisions. It is almost 9 o'clock.

The weather is fine. Tomorrow I shall be on the summit! The moment I crawl out of the tent my confidence is back once more. As if I am breathing cosmic energy. Or is it only the summit with which I identify? The air above me seems to be thin, of that soft blue that looks transparent. The mountains below me I see only as wavy surfaces, a relief in black and white. Take down the tent, fold it up! I command myself. But now these impulses no longer come from the mind, they come again from the gut.

Each drawing of breath fills my lungs with air, fills my being with self-realization. There can be no doubt. I

The north-east shoulder from the first bivouac site.

set out on my way. The first 50 metres I go very slowly, then I find my rhythm again. I make good progress. At an avalanche fracture I hesitate. I climb somewhat to the right of the North Ridge; the ground becomes steeper. There is more snow here than down below.

Suddenly the weather worsens. Like massive wedges, grey white cloud formations force themselves over the passes from the south into Tibet. Already the valley bottoms are filled with monsoon mist. Instinctively I keep further to the right. The weather on Everest is often not what it seems. Is it the monsoon or a sudden fall in temperature? Is a storm coming on?

You must have experienced the wind in the region of the summit to know that it can easily sweep people away. Now streaks swim in the sky; this battle with the mountain air makes me nervous. The halts for rest between climbing become longer. Hesitation. Uncertainty. The slopes are not steep, an average 40° perhaps. But above 7,900 metres all terrain is strenuous. Around me the morning air is still clear. Over the Rongbuk Valley, strands of cloud form constantly, shunt as far as the eastern horizon and evaporate.

Sisyphus on Everest

As always at great height I need a long time today to get the life-giving energy circulating again. It is as if the harmony had been disturbed. Through movement – right foot placed, weighted, released, dragged, left foot . . . – a field of energy develops in my body. After the initial kick-off the sluices open, guy-ropes slacken. With the reduction of anxiety, currents concentrate throughout my body – immeasurable, intangible forms of energy.

On this morning of 19 August I climb for a long time – much longer than normal – with this power dammed up. It is as if something were blocked, not so much to do with the height but with me, so that I scarcely make headway.

Yesterday it was so easy. Now each step is an ordeal. Why am I so slow? The rucksack weighs more heavily, although it has become lighter. I feel myself lost, vulnerable. However, I cannot make myself believe that there is a God who governs this world, who concerns himself with each single one of us. There is no creator outside of me, outside of the cosmos. I don't know when this faith was lost to me, I only know that since then it is more difficult not to feel myself alone and forsaken in this world. The snow lies deeper here. When my boots sink in an odd noise results: it is as if someone were behind me.

At last I must accept being alone, inevitably alone. In the long stops for breathing something like homesickness comes over me. My need for security overcomes me, and with that I know that all hopes that someone waits for me down below are, like the anxiety before my solo climb, impeding, paralysing. Only when moving, seeking and seeing does it become possible for me to accept this loneliness.

When I think, the energy at my disposal is quickly used up. With willpower alone I can get no further now but when I disengage my brain I am open to a power from without. I am like a hollow hand and experience a regeneration. The balled fist or outstretched fingers contribute with exhaustion to helplessness. Only when I am like a hollow hand does an invisible part of my being regenerate, not only in sleep, but also in climbing.

The rhythm of climbing – rest is determined by energy, and this energy determines my rhythm. The stops between climbing are already longer than the 15 paces I make now each time. This is my measure of time, step by step. Time and space are one.

It is so difficult to cope, to take upon oneself all responsibility, not only for one's actions, but also for being here at all, especially if the whole body is desperate through exertion. In spite of the risk freely entered into I cannot, like Wilson, entrust myself wholly to a God. To what, then? During the ascent I am like a walking corpse. What holds me upright is the world around me: air, sky, earth, the clouds which press in from the west. The experience of proceeding one step at a time. The sense of one's will as something tangible prior to the last two paces before resting. The terrain is easy. Nevertheless it demands my whole attention. That I can stand, that I can proceed, gives me energy to think ahead, to want to get ahead. At least as important as success is joy at one's own skill. It is astonishing how often I have overlooked this part of the pleasure of climbing and have talked solely of loads carried to the summit. High altitude climbing requires a whole range of proficiencies, knowledge and inventiveness. The higher you go, the more man himself becomes the problem. Ability also to solve problems of

this sort is what makes a good climber. I see the usefulness of climbing not in the further development of technique, rather in the development of the instinct and proficiency of man to extend himself. Learning about his limitations is just as important as his claim to be able to do anything.

With my snail-like advance I have lost the ability to estimate distance. Also sense of time. Am I about to break down? As I once said, the development of the self is part of my motive, yet what constitutes development when comparisons cannot be made? If I am frequently said to have a compulsion to succeed, this is characteristic of the people of today, for whom experience of an effort, and not the learning process itself, is what counts. He who only perceives his body as a vehicle for success cannot understand me, can not follow my thoughts. I carry on – without calculating or anticipating how far I have got. This climbing, resting, breathing has become a condition which completely absorbs me. It is merely movement along a fixed line. The forward-thrusting impulse in climbing is often referred to as aggression; I prefer to call it curiosity or passion. Now all that has gone. My advance has its own dynamic force, 15 paces, breathe, propped on the ski sticks which are inwardly and upwardly adjusted. With the knowledge that God is the solution. I confess that in moments of real danger something acts as a defense mechanism; it aids survival, but evaporates as soon as the threat is past. I am not at this moment under threat. It is all so peaceful here around me. I am not in any hurry. I cannot go any faster. I submit to this realization as to a law of Nature.

My altimeter shows 7,900 metres. But altimeters have the capacity to become inaccurate up high. Generally they show less than the actual height. It is also possible that the air pressure has altered during the night. I no longer take the altimeter seriously.

The weather is still fine, and I want to go on. Retreat no longer comes to mind. About 100 metres above the camp site I decide that climbing up the ridge is becoming too dangerous. Also too strenuous, for there the snow lies partially knee-deep. All the hollows are filled in. And above me a single giant-sized trough. Not only the avalanche danger, but the exertion above deters me. A feeling of hopelessness grips me as I poke the right ski stick into the floury mess. Snow slab danger! The topmost layer is firm but gives way with a crack when I step on it. Underneath the snow is grainy. On my own, under these conditions, I would quickly tire myself out.

Then I see that on the North Face the snow slabs have gone. What luck! There the foundation is hard. Yes, that's the way! Without thinking much I begin to cross the North Face. Instinctively, as if pre-programmed, I want to get to the Norton couloir and to climb it tomorrow to the summit. The traverse of the North Face extends a long way, and gains little height, but is good going in the firm monsoon snow. I don't need the ice axe; leaning on the ski sticks I cross the slope. The rucksack with the tent, which I have tied on outside so that it can dry, is still heavy. At almost 8,000 metres even standing with this ruck-sack on my back is an exertion. Without the ski sticks I would stagger, collapse. I rest like a four-legged creature; in this way the weight of the ruck-sack does not constrict my breathing.

When I continue again, I do it likewise, largely bending forward, having also shortened the ski stick in my left hand which is on the uphill side. I have completely given up counting my steps; I have not the inclination or strength to take any pictures. Rhythmically – go – rest – I progress like a snail. And out of this progress energy flows to me; it suffices exactly to maintain this rhythm.

The terrain is inclined and rolling. The stretch as far as the great snow couloir seems short. Without asking myself how many dips must lie between me and my planned bivouac spot I climb unhesitatingly upwards. My confidence grows. I no longer feel the loneliness as isolation, much more as detachment. The bridge of wife and friends, the embodiment in a community – supports which I need – I experience now for what they are: aids to endure the awareness of loneliness.

I am now directly under the 'first step'. Above me projects a blunt flat-topped buttress shaped like a sickle. It is snowed up, and to the right of it stands an unfriendly steep wall, dark; snow lies only on some of its ledges. The rock outcrops in the monsoon snow increase. With that my perception grows of already having been here before – do I know this route?

What disquiets me is the weather. No wind. The sun burns. Clouds press in from the south. Like wedges they push their grey white masses north-wards. Yes, there is no doubt; the monsoon storms are sending out their scouts.

Nevertheless I climb on determinedly. Always upwards to the right. I stop in exact line with the summit; or what I take to be the summit – the final point up there is presumably invisible – makes no overpowering impression on me. I stand close under the North-East Ridge and the route appears flattened.

The view too is restricted: on one side by the mass of the mountain, on the other by the rising cloud ceiling. The North Peak appears now flat and small; it separates the mist welling up from the valley. Only after longer rest stops am I capable of such observations. Between the North Ridge and the Norton couloir I am standing on a mountain side which has no equal in the Alps. A slanting trapezium, 2½ kilometres high and almost a kilometre wide.

I progress so slowly! How long my pauses to breathe are each time I don't know. With the ski sticks I succeed in going 15 paces, then I must rest for several minutes. All strength seems to depend on the lungs. If my lungs are pumped out I must stop. I breathe in through my mouth and expel the air through mouth and nose. And while standing I must use all my will-power to force my lungs to work. Only when they pump regularly does the pain disappear, and I experience something like energy. Now my legs have strength again.

I took the spontaneous decision to follow the North Flank of Mount Everest even though I wanted to be on the look-out for signs of Mallory and Irvine. But I do not resent my change of plan, not only because there is so much snow, but also because I know of their failure. I am on the best route to the summit. The going is at times tiring, at times agony, it all depends on the snow conditions. The downward-sloping slabs luckily lie buried beneath a layer of névé and up to now I have been able to go round all the rock outcrops. I can see the North-East Ridge above me, but know that at the moment nothing of the pioneers can be found there. Mallory and Irvine climbed along this ridge, exactly on its edge. That is no guess. I am convinced that Odell saw them on the 'first step', on that knob which rises out of the line of the ridge. I know now that they failed on the 'second step'. In the deep trough above me Mallory and Irvine lie buried in the monsoon snow. This hunch absorbs me like an old fairytale and I can think about it without dread.

It is as if I saw now the origin of a legend, as if I have perceived the truth. The observations of the Chinese climber Wang in 1974, who told the Japanese Hasegawa of his discovery five years later before an avalanche killed him below the North Col, appear now just as struck from my memory as the contradictory descriptions of the two steps. 'First' and 'second step' now lie above me. There Mallory and Irvine live on. The fate of the pair is now free from all speculation and hopes. It is alive in me. I cannot tell whether I see it as on a stage or in my mind's eye. At all events it is happening in my life – as if it belonged to it.

Close up, the 'second step' appears to

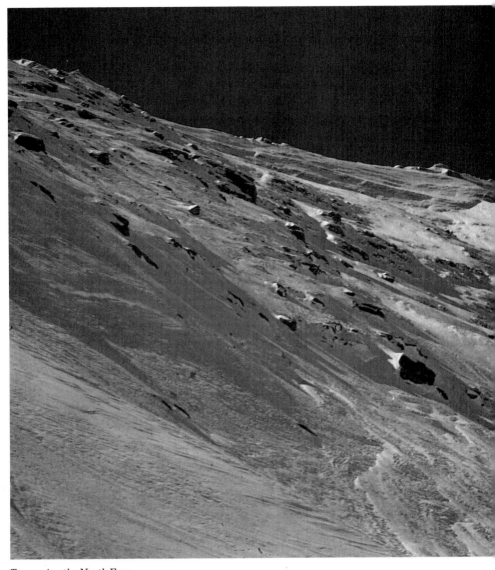

Traversing the North Face.

overhang. Only a little snow adheres to it. No, without pitons and ladders like the Chinese installed it is literally impossible to climb over it. Likewise today. A few months back the Japanese climber Kato also used the climbing aids left behind by the Chinese.

Between the two steps, therefore, Mallory and Irvine are presumed dead, without previously having

234

reached the summit. I don't ask myself how they died, I only see them turn back. Mallory and Irvine, decades-long legends, live for me forever up there, and not just in Odell's words.

Disappointed and exhausted they turn round below the 'second step'. In the failing daylight the difficulties increase. The two force themselves to make the laborious descent. They get slower and slower. Night falls. Only energy from success could have saved them. The vision fades. How the pair died can not be answered until someone finds Mallory's body or the camera which Somervell had lent him. Perhaps it can never be answered conclusively. That the two of them did not reach the summit is for me, however, beyond doubt.

After a longer rest my breathing is quiet and regular. Is that someone talking nearby? Is somebody there? Again I hear only my heart and my breathing. And yet there they are again. In this silence each sound, each atmosphere-drowning noise sounds like a spoken word. I jump frequently because I believe I hear voices. Perhaps it is Mallory and Irvine? With my knowledge of the circumstances surrounding their disappearance, which has occupied me many years, now each noise brings a vision alive in me. At any rate I believe sometimes that it is their calls which a breath of wind carries to me or takes away. But I do not recognize their voices for I have never tried to imagine them. So, do Mallory and Irvine really live on? Yes, their spirit is still there – I sense it distinctly.

I gaze at the 'second step' and already two beings fill my imagination, release phantoms; in the driving mist everything seems so near, ghostly. In spite of my tiredness I stare up again and again at the knife-edge above me. The 'second step' rears closer. A relatively easy snow gully leads to a steep groove. Quite distinctly I perceive a barrier at the top. At this moment I do not know that in May 1980 Yasuo Kato and Susumi Maka-mura took 40 minutes over the 'second step'. I see the real proof that Mallory and Irvine, with their comparatively primitive equipment, failed there in 1924.

Because the swelling mist envelops everything and because I am exhausted by the climbing, everything around me disappears. With my eyes hurrying on ahead a few metres, I look for the way to go. Brightness pierces me when the sun breaks through the clouds: flashing snow crystals move past me like water from a spring.

In spite of the gloomy snowy waste around me which ebbs and flows with the pulsating clouds, I feel no panic. I know the route. And the track behind me is still there. True, it is snowing lightly, but it is warm. I approach the Norton couloir over enormous, gentle waves – I have two behind me already. I can't see it, I only sense it. Nevertheless I am not for a moment afraid of being too high. Is it the tiredness which makes me indifferent, or is it this feeling of knowing the way that gives me the assurance of a sleepwalker? – I am convinced that all is well.

Every time I cross a rib there are more lumps of rock. In a row above and below me they make a sort of border. Far above and far below they disappear into the mist. These are the rock islands which show me the way. Like cairns they all have a definite form and each dark speck has a meaning, each gives support to my eyes and to me.

Meanwhile the mists around me have become so dense that the sun only now and then breaks through. Direction-finding becomes more difficult. Sometimes the breathless silence after resting fills me for a few moments with terror. Have I already gone too far? When the silence becomes unbearable I have to continue climbing. Always obliquely upwards. The pounding in my body and the gasping for breath after each ten paces lets me forget the emptiness about me. For a pain-filled eternity there is nothing at all. I exist only as a mind above a body. While resting I literally let myself fall: with my upper body leaning on the ski sticks, the rucksack tipped on to the nape of my neck, I go through a period of only breathing out and breathing in. Then I perk up again, and with the first step experience the exertion of the next section. Onward!

Sometimes I feel as if I am stuck in the snow. Nevertheless, I don't let myself get discouraged. I move continually to the right up the North Face. The whole face is like a single avalanche zone. New snow trickles down from above and it is sleeting. I tell myself that it is only a temporary disturbance; the snow will consolidate itself. 'It will hold for two days yet', I say to myself.

The ascending traverse continues endlessly with many but regular pauses. Because of the exertion and concentration I have not noticed that the weather has become so bad that I ought to turn back. All around everything is covered in mist. I squat and rest. Perhaps I should put up the tent. The spot seems too insecure to me. I must bivouac on a ridge. If it snows any more that means avalanche danger. These are not rational thoughts, but come from the instincts which lie

deep within me. For at least another hour I force myself on still further. On a blunt elevation which runs across the face like a giant rib I squat down again. For a while I feel only heaviness, indifference, numbness. Then the clouds tear themselves apart. The valley appears: grey, lightly covered in snow, soon masked again by mists. Not only do the mountains seem flattened, also the slopes beneath me and the snow shield in the big couloir. I see all that with the feeling of no longer belonging to the world below. When I notice it is 3 o'clock in the afternoon, it sinks in: I am still about 200 metres to the east of the Norton couloir. When I then peer at the altimeter it shows 8,220 metres. I am disappointed. It's more than that surely! It's not only that I would be delighted to have got as far as 8,400 metres, but that I have exerted myself much more than yesterday. It is misty and snows lightly. I can't go any further today. And yet that is an evasion: I do not know whether there is a bivouac place higher up.

I am dead tired. Conscious of this I scarcely make it to the next rocks. Earlier than planned I erect my tent. On a rock bollard, safe from avalanches – snow slides would branch off to the left and right of it – I find a 2 by 2 metre big, almost flat surface. While I make the snow firm I remain standing up. I ask myself how I shall find my way back if the weather stays like this. This doubt and the knowledge of all that can happen condenses into fear. Only when I work am I inwardly at peace. The quite light snowfall, the stationary clouds, the warmth, all that is sinister to me. Is it the monsoon or only anxiety? A fall in temperature is on the way, it seems to me. If I cannot get back for days my reserves will be soon used up. The avalanche danger on the North Face and below the North Col grows with every hour.

An hour later my tent is standing on the rock outcrop. Once again I anchor it with ice axe and ski sticks. I can camp here protected from the wind. Also, if there is a storm there is scarcely any danger. I place the open rucksack in front of the tent flap, and push the mat in. Lumps of snow for cooking lie ready to hand. All is prepared for the long night. A feeling of relief comes over me.

I take only two pictures then abandon photography again. It takes too much energy to take the camera out of the rucksack, walk away ten paces, rest, press the self-release. Then I must go back. And for what? Documentary proof, reports, all that has become meaningless. It seems to me much more important that I make myself something to drink.

Tonight I keep my clumsy, double-layered plastic boots near all my clothing; they must not be allowed to become cold. I sense my clothes as something alien. The layers between skin and outer covering feel like unpleasant stuffy air: hence the feeling of being in a strait-jacket. While I lie in the tent – too tired to sleep, too weak to cook – I try to imagine advanced base camp. Nena will now be making tea. Or is she looking straight up here? Has it cleared up meanwhile? Perhaps the weather is improving. Time passes too fast and too slowly. Only when I manage to switch off completely does it cease to exist.

On the evening of this 19 August Nena writes in her diary:

It is 8 p.m. and twilight invades the narrow glacier valley. The snow began suddenly and still continues to fall. I could not see Reinhold the whole day. But I know that he is up there, perhaps somewhere in the vicinity of the 'second step'. Tomorrow, he will go to the summit. Hopefully the weather will improve again. The heavy black clouds came from nowhere, towering up, spitting snow and sleet. What does it mean? I can do nothing but think of him constantly. If this flurrying doesn't stop he is lost. How much snow has fallen? How dangerous are the avalanches up there? How difficult is the descent in new snow? How long will it take him back to the North Col? Somehow I am sure that Reinhold will do only what is right.

But there is something incalculable in this man. His whole being is possessed, is energy, action. I am anxious, but I don't mind. Above all I am vexed because the weather is playing him such a dirty trick. That's unfair. I sit in the empty tent and force myself to eat and drink. I try to read about medicine and inflammation of the lungs. But my thoughts are up there in the whirling snow. I am madly excited and sad, both at once. I keep repeating the traditional Tibetan prayer 'Om mani padme hum', over and over again.

When it gets dark I put on something warm and venture outside. Didn't I just know it? The 7,000 metre peaks are clearing, the clouds melting away. The wind is coming up. It drives the new snow off the ridges. I shout and scream. He does not hear me, cannot hear me. Nevertheless I speak to him: 'I am with you!'

How does one live at this height? I am no longer living, I am only vegetating. When one must do everything alone each manipulation takes a lot of will-power. With each job I notice the effect of the thin air. Speed of thought is greatly diminished and I can make clear decisions only very slowly. They are influenced by my tiredness and breathing difficulties. My windpipe feels as if it were made of wood, and I am aware of a slight irritation of my bronchial tubes.

Although I have not been able to prepare any really hot drinks, because water boils at a lower temperature on account of the height, I still keep on melting snow. Pot after pot. I drink soup and salt tea. It is still too little. I am not very hungry. I must force myself to eat. Also I don't know what to eat without making myself sick. Should I open this tin of sardines now or something else? The slightest effort requires time, energy and attention. All movements are slow and cumbersome. I decide on cheese and bread, chicken in curry sauce, a freeze-dried ready to serve meal which I mix with lukewarm water. I stick the empty packet under the top of my sleeping bag. I shall need it during the night to pee in. It takes me more than half an hour to choke down the insipid pap. Outside it gets darker. The many small tasks in the bivouac take as much energy as hours of regular climbing. The difference between arriving at a prepared camp, to be cared for by Sherpas or comrades, and evening after evening having to make camp and cook for oneself is tremendous. Perhaps it is the essential distinction between the classic big expedition and the modern small expedition. Going to sleep is by itself a big exertion. Up here I cannot simply get into bed, stick my head under the covers and fall asleep.

Once more I sit up in my sleeping-bag. First I loosen my boots. Tomorrow morning I want to have warm feet and boots not frozen stiff. So I first change my socks, then pull my boots on again. Once more I push feet and boots right back into the sleeping bag. I throw away the damp socks. Then, out-stretched, propped up on my arms, I stick the rucksack under the mat as a pillow. I arrange the cooking equipment so that I can get at it next morning from the sleeping-bag. Constantly I have to shift my body a little and keep my head up, not in order to sleep well, but only to be able to endure the night.

These movements in the narrow tent make me breathless. I am forced to breathe deeply. In between, I pant again. I have had numb fingers for hours. In spite of the occasional slumber of exhaustion – an inadvertent dozing – I cannot fall asleep properly during the night. I am endless like the night.

In the morning I am just as tired as the evening before, and stiff as well. I ask myself whether I really want to go on. I must! Then I use the little strength I have to move my body. I know well enough from experience that I can still carry on for a time, but I try to push everything aside – to think of nothing, to prolong a deliberate state which allowed me to endure the whole night.

I have only to get going and keep moving in order to have some energy again. The will to make the first decisive move still fails me. When I open the tent flap this morning, it is already day outside. A golden red glow bathes the summit pyramid; to the east, fields of clouds stretch away into the distance. Automatically I remember the monsoon. It is an eternity before I hold the first pot of warm water between my hands. There is ice lying in the tent. I can't eat anything.

While I fish lumps of snow into the tent I peer up into the Norton Couloir. Fairly steep. Smoky grey clouds cling to the mountain sides. The air is glassy, as if it were full of moisture. I feel a bit chilly in spite of the favourable temperature. Ice by the rocks and tent! However, cold is no problem on Mount Everest during the monsoon period. I am sure that it thaws in high summer when it is windless and misty, even on the summit. My three layers of clothing – silk, pile suit, thin down suit – are sufficient when almost undone.

Two years ago in May 1978 I endured up to minus 40°C. at night. Now it is minus 15°C. maximum, perhaps only minus 10°C. Nevertheless I must not be careless. As long as the sun is not shining I wear gloves, fasten my boots loosely. At this height a few degrees below zero can cause frostbite. I think only of going on. As if retreat, failure, had never crossed my mind. But what if the mist becomes thicker? Ought I to wait a bit? No, that is senseless. In any case I am already very late. I must get outside. At this height there is no recovering. By tomorrow I could be so weak that there would not be enough left for a summit bid. It's now or never. Either–or. I must either go up or go down. There is no other choice.

Twice whilst melting snow I take my pulse. Way above 100 beats per minute. I feel all in. No more trains of thought. Only commands in the mind. The night was one long ordeal. Painful joints, mucous in my throat. Morning is depressing. On this 20 August I leave everything behind: tent, ski sticks, mat, sleeping-bag. The rucksack too stays in the tent. I take only the camera with me. So just as I am I crawl out of the tent, draw my hood over my head and with bare fingers buckle crampons on to my boots. I retrieve only the titanium axe from the snow. Have I got everything? It must be after 8 o'clock already. Without the load on my back things are easier. But I miss the ski sticks as balancing poles. With the short ice axe in my right hand I feel secure, certainly, but for traversing it is a poor substitute.

Only when I climb directly upwards do my gloved left hand and the ice axe fumble about in the snow beneath my head. I proceed on all fours. While resting I distribute my whole weight so that the upper part of my body remains free. I kneel in the snow, lay my arms on the rammed-in ice axe and put my head on this cushion. I can still survey the steep rise above me, orientate myself, weigh up difficulties. Fortunately an uninterrupted snow gully runs up the Norton Couloir. So long as I can see and plod I am confident.

Once, before I reach the bottom of the broad trough, I look out for a longer rest possibility. The tent, a yellow speck, appears as through a weak magnifying glass. Is that only the light mist or are all my senses fooled? I remember the place and then climb up the rise above me to the right. Pace by pace. Step by step. Already after a short while I miss the rucksack like a true friend. It has let me down. For two days it has been my partner in conversation, has encouraged me to go on

Second bivouac.

when I have been completely exhausted. Now I talk to the ice axe. But a friend is little enough in this state of exposure. Nevertheless, the voices in the air are there again. I don't ask myself where they come from. I accept them as real. Lack of oxygen and insufficient supply of blood to the brain are bound up with it, are certainly the cause of these irrational experiences which I got to know two years ago during my solo ascent of Nanga Parbat. Up here in 1933 Frank Smythe shared his biscuits with an imaginary partner.

The rucksack has indeed been my companion. But without it things go easier, much easier even. If I had to carry something now I would not make any progress. I decided to make the ascent because I knew that on this last day I could leave everything behind. In the driving clouds, following my instinct more than my eyes I look for the route step-by-step. Again the distant memory of this couloir. I live in a sort of half-darkness of mist, clouds, snow drifts and recognition of individual sections. I was here once before! A feeling that even lengthy reflection cannot dispel.

An hour above camp I come up against a steep step about 100 metres high. Or is it 200 metres towering up in front of me?

The climbing is made easy by the snow. My whole foot always finds a hold without the crampons hitting the rocks. For hours repeatedly expending oneself, dying, bracing oneself, exerting one's will, letting oneself fall, collecting oneself. The rock islands to left and right of the great gully are yellowish with brighter streaks here and there. Often I see everything double and am uncertain where I should go. I keep more to the right. The slope is now so steep that I rest in the climbing position.

I literally creep along now. Only seldom do I manage to do ten paces without stopping to gasp for air. The view disappoints me. Yesterday morning it was still impressive. Now when I look down on the long glacier with the moraine ridges everything appears flat. The landscape is blunted, deadened by the new snow. Despite the swelling mist I lose all feeling of distance.

Light powder snow on a semi-firm base here. The rock slabs underneath, lying one on another like roof tiles, are approximately as steep as a church roof, and are almost completely snow covered. I leave the gully where it becomes wider and forms a pear-shaped bay. I take bearings on a blunt ridge up to the right. The going must be easier there.

It is getting steeper. When I move I no longer pound like a locomotive, I feel my way ahead hesitatingly. Jerkily I gain height. This climbing is not difficult but downright unpleasant. Often I can find no hold in the snow and must make out the steps by touch. I cannot afford to slip here. For the first time during this solo ascent I feel in danger of falling, like increased gravity. This climbing carefully with great concentration increases my exhaustion. Besides, the mist interferes more and more. All I see is a piece of snow in front of me, now and then a prospect of blue sky above the ridge. Everything goes very slowly. In spite of the enormous strain which each step upwards requires, I am still convinced that I shall get to the top, which I experience now in a sort of anticipation, like a deliverance.

The knowledge of being half-way there in itself soothes me, gives me strength, drives me on. Often I am near the end of my tether. After a dozen paces everything in me screams to stop, sit, breathe. But after a short rest I can go on. Worrying about the bad weather has cost me additional energy. And the ever-recurring question of the descent. But simultaneously in the thickening mist I experience an inspiring hope, something like curiosity outside of time and space. Not the demoralising despair which a visible and unendingly distant summit often triggers. It is now all about the struggle against my own limitations. This becomes obvious with each step; with each breath it resolves itself. The decision to climb up or down no longer bothers me. It is the irregular rhythm, the weakness in the knees. I go on like a robot. Against all bodily remonstrances I force myself upwards. It must be! I don't think much, I converse with myself, cheer myself up. Where is my rucksack? My second friend the ice axe is still here. We call a halt.

The way up the Norton Couloir is logical and not so difficult as I expected. I shall find my way back. When I reach the blunt rib above I should be able to see the summit. If the cloud breaks. Up there it seems to be flatter.

The fancy to have climbed here once already constantly helps me to find the right route. The steep step shot through with brightly coloured rock lies beneath me. I still keep to my right

– not so long ago an avalanche went down here. The snow bears. Under the blunt ridge it becomes deeper, my speed accordingly slower. On hands and knees I climb up, completely apathetic. My boots armed with crampons are like anchors in the snow. They hold me.

As I stand on the rib I hear the wind amongst the stones. Far below this rock rib continues as a buttress. For a short while the mist is so thick that I can no longer orientate myself visually. I continue somewhat further along the rib, where the least of the snow lies. For an hour. Until a dark vertical rock wall bars the way above me. Something in me draws me to the left, I pass the obstacle, and continue still keeping to the right. How long? My only adversary is the slope, time no longer exists. I consist of tiredness and exertion.

I guess myself to be near the top but the knife edge goes on for ever. During the next three hours I am aware of myself no more. I am one with space and time. Nevertheless I keep moving. Every time the blue sky shows through the thick clouds I believe I see the summit, am there. But still there are snow and stones above me. The few rocks which rise out of the snow are greeny-grey, shot through here and there with brighter streaks. Ghostlike they stir in the wispy clouds. For a long time I traverse upwards, keeping to the right. A steep rock barrier bars the way to the ridge. Only if I can pass the wall to the right shall I get any higher.

Arriving on the crest of the North-East Ridge I sense the cornices, stand still. Then I lie down on the snow. Now

I am there. The ridge is flat. Where is the summit? Groaning I stand up again, stamp the snow down. With ice axe, arms and upper body burrowing in the snow, I creep on, keeping to the right. Ever upwards.

When I rest I feel utterly lifeless except that my throat burns when I draw breath. Suddenly it becomes brighter. I turn round and can see down into the valley. Right to the bottom where the glacier flows. Breathtaking! Automatically I take a few photographs. Then everything is all grey again. Completely windless.

Once more I must pull myself together. I can scarcely go on. No despair, no happiness, no anxiety. I have not lost the mastery of my feelings, there are actually no more feelings. I consist only of will. After each few metres this too fizzles out in an unending tiredness. Then I think nothing, feel nothing. I let myself fall, just lie there. For an indefinite time I remain completely irresolute. Then I make a few steps again.

At most it can only be another 10 metres up to the top! To the left below me project enormous cornices. For a few moments I spy through a hole in the clouds the North Peak far below me. Then the sky opens out above me too. Oncoming shreds of cloud float past nearby in the light wind. I see the grey of the clouds, the black of the sky and the shining white of the snow surface as one. They belong together like the stripes of a flag. I must be there!

Above me nothing but sky. I sense it, although in the mist I see as little of it as the world beneath me. To the right the ridge still goes on up. But perhaps that only seems so, perhaps I deceive myself. No sign of my predecessors.

It is odd that I cannot see the Chinese aluminium survey tripod that has stood on the summit since 1975. Suddenly I am standing in front of it. I take hold of it, grasp it like a friend. It is as if I embrace my opposing force, something that absolves and electrifies at the same time. At this moment I breathe deeply.

In the mist, in the driving of the clouds I cannot see at first whether I am really standing on the highest point. It seems almost as if the mountain continues on up to the right. This tripod, which rises now scarcely knee-high out of the snow, triggers off no sort of euphoria in me. It is just there. Because of the great amount of snow on the summit it is much smaller than when I saw it in 1978; pasted over with snow and unreal.

In 1975 the Chinese anchored it on the highest point, ostensibly to carry out exact measurements. Since then they state the height of their Chomolungma as 8,848.12 metres. I don't think of all that up here. This artificial summit erection doesn't seem at all odd. I have arrived, that's all that matters! It's gone 3 o'clock.

Like a zombie, obeying an inner command, I take some photographs. A piece of blue sky flies past in the background. Away to the south snow cornices pile up, which seem to me to be higher than my position. I squat down, feeling hard as stone. I want only to rest a while, forget everything. At first there is no relief. I am leached, completely empty. In this emptiness nevertheless something like energy accumulates. I am charging myself up.

The last few metres.

For many hours I have only used up energy. I have climbed myself to a standstill, now I am experiencing regeneration, a return flow of energy.

A bleached shred of material wrapped round the top of the tripod by the wind is scarcely frozen. Absentmindedly I run my fingers over it. I undo it from the metal. Ice and snow remain sticking to it. I should take some more pictures but I cannot brace myself to it. Also I must get back down. Half an hour too late means the end of me. At the moment I am not at all disappointed that once again I have no view. I am standing on the highest point on earth for the second time and again can see nothing. That is because it is now completely windless. The light snowflakes dance and all around me the clouds swell as if the earth were pulsating underneath. I still don't know how I have made it but I know that I can't do any more. In my tiredness I am not only as heavy as a corpse, I am incapable of taking anything in. I cannot distinguish above and below.

Again a shred of blue sky goes by with individual ice crystals shining in the sun. The mountains appear far below and quite flat, between the black-white of the valleys. This time I am too late with the camera. Then clouds, mist again; now their primary colour is violet.

Is night coming on already? No, it is 4 p.m. I must be away. No feeling of sublimity. I am too tired for that. And although I don't at this moment feel particularly special or happy, I have a hunch that in retrospect it will be comforting, a sort of conclusion. Perhaps a recognition that I too shall have to roll that mythical stone all my life without ever reaching the summit; perhaps I myself am this summit. I am Sisyphus.

After three-quarters of an hour I have the strength to stand up, to stand up for the descent. It has become a bit

The North-East Ridge, near the summit.

246

brighter. I can still see my track. That is comforting. How much easier is the descent of this great mountain! It takes only a fraction of the effort and will-power compared with coming up.

My whole energy is now concentrated in my senses. I find the smell of the snow, the colour of the rocks more intense than in previous days, jump at the occasional sheet lightning out of the clouds far to the west. I want only to get down. Climbing down – once

facing inwards – as if I were in flight, I don't ask myself why I undertook all the strain of getting to the summit. I would rather be down already. This long way is a burden.

What disturbs me most is my coughing. It makes my life hell. Even gentle coughing tears at my stomach. Besides, I have not eaten for many hours. I must get to base camp as quickly as possible. Just before the onset of darkness I find my way back to my tent and rucksack.

This night I scarcely sleep at all. Also I cannot bring myself to cook properly. I drink a little snow water. Again I eat nothing. The warm flame of the gas burner which buzzes near my face is perhaps only to comfort me. I don't switch it off although I don't manage to sit up in my sleeping-bag and fetch in snow. Each activity costs now so much energy! Energy which I have derived from climbing, also the stimulus of reaching the summit. Now it fails me. I lie in the tent as if dead. Only the success keeps me alive. I obey the law of inertia. Between waking and sleeping, surrounded by the living dead, the hours slip away. Without any thoughts. I am not safe yet. Suddenly terror seizes me. Is Nena still there? She still does not know where I am, that I shall be down tomorrow. She too cannot sleep. For the first time she writes in her diary at night:

20 August 1980. Now I have accustomed myself to the fact that the snow and the clouds come and go; but I have not accustomed myself to sleeping here alone. I can do nothing else but worry about you, knowing that you are somewhere above 8,000 metres. I hope that you are not suffering. Even here at 6,500 metres life is an ordeal, what must it be like up there?! It snows more and more – 9 p.m.

My thinking weaves uninterruptedly further, always at the limit of consciousness. In the early hours I rouse myself with the feeling of having come to a decision, but cannot concentrate. Have I gone mad? Has this emptiness sent me mad? Am I altitude sick? When morning comes I am once again in flight. Without drinking anything I abandon camp. Tent, sleeping-bag, everything except the rucksack stays behind. Only the ski sticks do I tear out of the snow. Traversing east I climb diagonally downwards. To the east I look down into the snow basin of the Rongbuk Glacier as I reach the blunt ridge a little above the North Col. No tent stands there. Or is it just snowed up? The new snow is powdery and dry. It flies about when I step on it. It is bitterly cold today.

Not only during the ascent but also during the descent my will-power is dulled. The longer I climb the less important the goal seems to me, the more indifferent I become to myself. My attention has diminished, my memory is weakened. My mental fatigue is now greater than the bodily. It is so pleasant to sit doing nothing – and therefore so dangerous. Death through exhaustion is – like death through freezing – a pleasant one. As I traverse the undulating ridge above the North Col I feel as if I am returning from a shadow world.

I make myself carry on through my tiredness, using the knowledge that I have been on the summit. I offer no more resistance, let myself fall at each step. Only I may not remain sitting. Day after day I have endured the loneliness of the undulating snow surface of the North Face; hour after hour against the wind, the sharp ice grains which swirl with it; for an eternity through the mist which deluded me into thinking each block of rock was a friend. Each breath up there was an ordeal and still I took it as a gift.

Now a feeling attacks me of 'having survived', of 'having been saved'. Little by little I step into something which could be called 'place of fulfillment', a 'saving haven'. Like the pilgrims at the sight of the place of pilgrimage, I forget all the ordeals of the journey.

Nena does not know that I shall soon be at the North Col. She too has been uncertain these past days; being alone didn't agree with her, so she fills her diary with imaginary conversations:

21 August 1980. Good morning, River. Thank you for being here and keeping me company. 'Hi', croaks the big black raven. For the tenth time I try to look through my telephoto lens. For an hour I have done nothing else. Since sun-up. But my eyes ache terribly. I have tried telling myself not to look for a while. I can't stop. The telephoto is like a mania. Then even the rocks begin to move. Sometimes I see several people descending the North Ridge. Either he is just climbing down, or . . . I won't think further.

It is a glorious warm day. I wash my face in icy water by the glacier. Reinhold, please, come down. I don't feel too good, soon I must descend. If only I knew where you were! Later I fetch water from the stream between ice and moraine. As I stroll away from the river I catch a fleeting glimpse in the bright midday light of a point, a dark moving point on the ridge crest of the North Col. I am suddenly completely wild with excitement. Evidently Reinhold is not climbing with his usual surefootedness; it seems as if a drunken man is descending from the col, not the same man who went away four days ago.

I burst into tears. It is Reinhold, it must be! I run around like a madwoman. I shout up to him that I am coming. I know that he can't hear me but nevertheless it helps. I must speak with him. Quickly I put on my top clothes, prepare myself to go to meet Reinhold on the glacier.

A High Price

Bright swathes of mist rush over the North Col. The seething sea of clouds over Solo Khumbu is blindingly white and the curved line of the North-East Ridge stands like a wall between the clear weather in the east and the monsoon in the south. With the certainty of a sleep-walker I descend. But the snow does not please me. It is jellified and makes no firm bond with the firn base. It slides down the smooth ice slabs when I step on it. Presumably I am now also less awake because I expect no serious difficulties in the descent from the North Col. Thus I face them unprepared. Still in a trance, I slip for the first time and immediately lose the ground under my feet. I try to brake, but cannot control the plunge. With the increasing speed of the fall new strengths appear; as always, real danger rouses my abilities. And that to a degree that I ask myself from whence I derive so much skill, stamina and energy so quickly.

I stand up again quickly, ram the ice axe firmer and climb down a steep snow wall facing inwards. My carefulness is an instinct: no reflex flinching, no more sudden terror if the snow gives way; only a slow complaisance in my body. In my leaden tiredness there is no sort of hampering nervousness, much more a sleep-walking-like

249

knowledge. This sort of feeling of security is directly bound up with tiredness and danger.

The big transverse crevasse into which I fell four days ago during the ascent I by-pass to the right and now stand at the upper edge of a steep slope. Avalanche danger! The morning sun has softened the snow. I experience these alarm signals now as searing pains in my body, not as thoughts in my head.

The precipice drops 400 metres beneath me. Down below, the ice slope runs out into the glacier bottom like the splayed-out feet of the Eiffel Tower. Only brighter or darker shadings indicate crevasses, hollows and domes.

I don't hesitate for long, then continue the descent. Soon I have such numb fingers and such tired legs that I sit down in the snow and slide on my backside. I am dehydrated, want to drink. Even the snow sticks like dust in my mouth. I remain sitting. As I rouse myself for a last exertion of strength I move without thinking to the right. A wide open crevasse forces me to dodge. Too late I notice that I should have gone to the left. I can't go back. I can only keep on descending. Suddenly I slip down again unexpectedly, break the motion with the ice axe and, as my arms refuse to work, slide down the middle of the avalanche cone to the foot of the wall. I lie there for a while. Then come to on the flat glacier bottom. I kneel, lie down again in the snow, gather myself up again. Groaning I stagger forwards, lose the ground under my feet, fall once more. Once I throw everything away from me, roll my face in the snow, shake myself. I am down. I am happy and at the same time despairing. Then Nena comes over the glacier ridge. She stands there, then comes on. Yes, it is her. I can no longer shout. Everything goes black in front of my eyes. Slowly, very slowly I let myself dissolve. With each further step downwards, with the marker poles in front of me, the first moraines in sight, the whole world

The last bivouac.

Lhotse from the north.

stands revealed within me. I see my whole being from without. 'Here' is now somewhere else. I am transparent, made of glass, borne up by the world.

Nena says not a word. Or do I not hear her? Involuntarily I hold my breath, stand still. I have trouble staying in balance. I want to take hold of Nena and just stay there, laugh and cry, to rest myself on her and remain lying on the glacier. Immobile, without a word I stand there, as fragile as a light bulb. A single word would suffice to destroy this glassy delicacy, this strange envelope which is all that is left of me. I can see through all my layers and know that I am also transparent for Nena. Leaning on the ski sticks I stare at her a while. Then I break down. All my reserve is gone. I weep. It is as if all horizons, all boundaries were broken. Everything is revealed, all emotions are released. How far must I go before I finally

break in two? I myself am now the open book. The more I let myself go the more it forces me to my knees.

Nena remains calm and from now on takes charge of me for the hours and days which follow. Now she makes the plans, she brings me to safety, she leads the expedition and keeps her diary.

Men always talk of the conquest of the mountains. And here he comes across the glacier, looks up only once, very slowly. He glances at me, comes on with sunken head, is no longer consciously there. Going up to him I say: 'Reinhold, how are you?' A few sobs are the answer. At the same time I can sense all his feelings. This moment I shall hold fast to for ever – without doubt the most profound feeling of union that I have shared at any time. For a moment I hold him quite tight then as he lies there bend down to him and say: 'Everything's O.K., Reinhold. You are alright. The camp is over here.' 'Where are all my friends?' is his first question. 'I'm your friend, I'm here, Reinhold. Don't worry,

251

we're going to our camp now,' I reassure him. 'Yes, where is the camp actually?' He looks at me with tears in his eyes. His face is yellow, his lips are split and chapped. Probably he is suffering from heat-stroke. I ask myself whether it is really he who has returned or only a part of him. Or more? I have to struggle to hold back my tears. When he can stand up again I take his rucksack, give him a ski stick. He staggers forward across the glacier. I have compassion for this man. He has so expended himself that only reaching the summit could have given him the strength to survive, to return. Here he is, the strongest person I know totally at an end, leached even to the soul.

When we get to camp and are safe Reinhold collapses once more on the stones in front of me. Yes, he was on the summit and people will say once again that he has conquered the mightiest mountain in the world. He has been successful, has attained his goal – but still more successful was the mountain. It has exacted its price from this man.

I know that Reinhold too sees the mountain thus. For him it is a giving and a taking in equal quantities, a sharing between the mountain and him.

22 August 1980. A different man lies beside me in the tent. Reinhold dozes and drinks the whole day. He has not the strength to stand up. Often I feel I can see right through him.

23 August 1980. It is lovely to know that someone is waiting, someone is helping you. We need to carry our heavy rucksacks the whole day down to base camp. Using the rocks to take a rest we count the hours and kilometres before us. It is such a joy to meet people below in the camp. Cheng and Tsao make countless cups of hot milk for us, serve a proper meal with chicken and rice. A bottle of French champagne emerges from our secret stores. The alcohol goes at once to our heads. We have marched a whole day without anything to eat after days at altitude. 'That was a damned good idea – that champagne,' says Reinhold on going to sleep. Slowly he regains his strength. I notice it also by his gruffness.

26 August 1980. In June, in Lhasa, Reinhold and I had a bad time with each other; we were rude and irritable. I felt crushed and no longer tried to follow Reinhold in his arguments. It was hopeless; we were mean to each other. The more Reinhold tried to be free of me the more I clung to him. Now I know that I must let this man go his own way. His urge to be alone is just as big as his urge to find love. Reinhold is in all things extreme.

28 August 1980. We have packed up everything and are waiting for the promised jeep in order to be able to set out on the return journey. Reinhold begins to get cross over the delay. In spite of everything we have time to fool about. But it depresses me that Reinhold is satisfied to be with me one minute, while the next it doesn't suit him at all. Up at 6,500 metres after the descent from Chomolungma I was a real comrade for him. He could have had no better company. And now, in base camp, he says quite distinctly that he is indifferent as to who waited for him in the high camp. Nevertheless I fool myself that I am as important to him as he is to me.

29 August 1980. To leave base camp at sundown on a tractor was not foreseen by us. It all happened so quickly that we had no time to say goodbye to the stream, to the grasses and the stones. As the dying sun casts an orange-coloured light on Mount Everest we are already on our way down the valley. Despite everything it is lovely to travel away. Nuptse disappears steely blue in the twilight.

When we finally arrive at the first village below Rongbuk we look for quarters by the light of two dim torches. All the inhabitants of the village come out to stare at us. Reinhold cannot bear noisy crowds of people and it makes him mad when they all mill around us and our things. I try to calm him down.

Rather abruptly he bellows at Cheng, the liaison officer: 'Why is nothing organized, what are we paying these vast sums for?' The CMA has pledged itself to send a jeep, to take care of accommodation. None of that has been taken care of. For Reinhold it would be an easy thing to arrange on his own account with the Tibetan population but that is forbidden us.

When at last we lie down for the night under the open starry sky and the people disappear into their houses, Reinhold calms down. He is relaxed and sleeps deeply. I lie awake for hours, pondering, until the stars fall from heaven one after another.

30 August 1980. Once more Reinhold has grounds to fly into a rage. A whole week we waited in vain in base camp for the jeep which was already paid for months ago, before this lousy tractor fetched us. Then they promise us that the jeep is waiting on the other bank of the river. When we get over there – no jeep far and wide. We feel left in the lurch. Reinhold reacts angrily once again.

While the tractor trundles along the bumpy road the Chinese driver stops a few kilometres on to buy butter and tea for himself. In vain Tsao tells him to make haste. Finally he hurries but only to revenge himself on us. On a long muddy piece of road the dirt sprays in great arcs on the trailer in which we are sitting. Faster and faster the driver pushes his vehicle. We are covered with mud from head to toe. The Chinese grins.

Enraged, Reinhold jumps from the moving tractor. I can no longer stop him. 'I'll kill him,' he yells as he crashes on the driving seat ready to tear the man off. 'Are you mad or what?' Reinhold spits at him. I really can't tell whether his behaviour is for real or whether he is playing games. But I have the feeling that he wants to drown all three men who are sitting on the tractor in the river. The driver is chalk white in the face, stammers an apology. Leisurely our vehicle then jolts over the bad field paths. Reinhold is again friendly and obliging and laughs with the people. This is the only time he goes so berserk.

I needed a week to recover, a week to really come to. Now we are on the way to Lhasa. We make a stop at a straggly village. It is snowing. The Tibetans who regard the powers of Nature as gods, peer shyly from their houses. The Chinese, often voluntary soldiers like our driver, have only taken the herds and monasteries away from these people, not the faith. Snow and wind, hail and rain, aridity and heat determine life now as before in these endless wastes.

It is freezing this morning sitting behind the tractor, and I am shivering with cold. An icy wind blows down from the mountains and even though the sun slowly breaks through the thick clouds it stays unpleasant. Two hours later we meet the jeep designated for us. Now the journey becomes somewhat more pleasant. The weather has changed too: the monsoon with its changing moods is here again. Heavy clouds hang low over the hills. The sky brightens in the west and darkens in the east. I immerse myself in the narrow space between heaven and earth.

Since the descent I have been infinitely melancholy. Inwardly assuaged by the emotional release certainly, but at the same time depressed like the valleys under the monsoon clouds. I sense that this heaviness is now fading little by little. With the inner easing, serenity returns, a little strength, yes even bodily well-being. By itself the fact that I can now relax is something like happiness. Past an endless succession of desolate mountain ranges, stony deserts, endless sand dunes which ripple away under the eternal wind we travel eastwards. This bare landscape whose distances are plunged in soft wonderful colours is like my own reflected image. The setting of the sun in the west, the glistening backbone of the Himalaya in the south mean more than memory. It is unbelievable how multicoloured the scenery is here: yellow, ochre brown, red and blue streak the endless distances

253

in front of me; the mountain ridges behind are steel coloured. And everything is so bare, scarcely a blade of grass grows at this height. Different lichens and minerals make the veins of the earth's crust gleam; the colours range across the whole spectrum of the rainbow.

As far up as the 5,000 metre-high passes countless little white stars now sprout from the bushy green flower cushions. Bright granite blocks with everywhere in between cushions of plants. Butterflies too – swallowtail and apollo. The birds, marmots and hares seem to me luxurious and exotic after two months spent in snow and ice.

In the villages it smells of dust and decay. The old, mostly toothless men look at us aghast. I love this land now more than before the climb. It is September and the weather changes from hour to hour. This is the land of contrasts, of extremes. The summer has passed. Snow showers rush across the high ridges. The bare hills – for months past thrusting up to the white clouds, as the sun shone week long on the plateau – look now like wave mountains in the night. There is no forest which protects and no tree as anchor. The sea of the steppe has stiffened into a tossed-up primaeval landscape. Plateau, mountains and deserts are no longer friendly, the millenium-old law rules the wilderness. Nature becomes God. The Tibetans stare at us as if we were creatures of fable, spirits from the mountains, which may not be driven away. Their eyes ask for understanding, space, peace.

A mighty snow pennant hangs from the summit ridge of Mount Everest as I look at it for the last time. These material wreaths of wind and snow are my flags which have no other meaning. Now suddenly I realize that I lost my composure at the foot of the mountain and surrendered my innermost feelings. I am ashamed, want to take back my most intimate sensations. They are mine alone. It is easy enough to return to the summit, to re-enact the ascent in spirit; but it is impossible to reactivate these feelings. They died with me, I think now and then.

Death, the inevitability of death, has played no leading part in my sensations. And yet perhaps it is that too which determines my behaviour. Never have I come so near my limit, the limit between this side and that side, between self and other. Never has a mountain expedition influenced me so enduringly as this one. Perhaps I have crossed the Rubicon and made a leap which I have still to absorb.

Gánpéi, Gánpéi

The week-long struggle for survival in that hostile environment has altered me. The overwhelming landscape has made me still more of an individualist, detached from humanity, perhaps even morbidly absorbed in fantasy. Broad plains swim past outside in the morning light like a peaceful ocean. The scenery in these high valleys varies in impression between sea and earth. It changes also the smell of the air. Now there are strolling cloud shadows, which simulate islands, now steppe grass which flashes like golden lakes. The horizon is an eternity away. Here I experience the infinity of the elements. I am merged in them, no longer oppose them, swim.

We are driving to Shekar, eastwards, again towards Lhasa, once the 'holy city'. The further we get into the interior of the country, the more peaceful the clouds become. This morning I crawled out of my ice-encrusted sleeping-bag, having woken village. Children's sleepy faces stare from low doorways. We drive on to Shigatse. Often I fall asleep sitting, little by little forget the many brief impressions that I have experienced during the past weeks. Already this expedition begins to run in my mem-

Back in base camp.

up with hair wet with dew, stiff and chilly. Here in Shekar it is dry and hot. Two dark figures are driving a herd of sheep through the dusty lanes as we drive at walking speed through the ory like the brush strokes on a water colour. Many people hold it as self-evident that on such expeditions one should give an account of each day. On the mountains however, while on the go, time does not subdivide itself in the usual way. A day filled with countless impressions quickly passes, another is filled with unremarkable events. The 300 kilometre journey is like the ascent to the summit, an eternity and a nothingness at the same time. There are no time values running through a book of such adventures.

In Shigatse I visit once more the Tashi Lhunpo Monastery. The young monks radiate confidence. I ask myself how the government can succeed in introducing real Tibetan self-administration without the aid of the former ruling class now in exile. So I enquire of one of the local officials of the CMA why they are anxious to induce the Dalai Lama to return to Tibet. No answer. However, at a small banquet in the evening in the rest house the Chinese chairman of the local tourist organization explains to me that Tibet needs its religious leader as mediator; that is why they have been negotiating for his return. 'But how,' I ask, 'can the Dalai Lama help with the government of the country if he no longer has at his disposal his monks and monasteries?'

'The confidence of the population in the Dalai Lama is still unbroken, and it is this trust which can now be used positively.'

I grasp that this makes sense. The Dalai Lama himself put forward the concept that one could create a coexistence between Buddhism and Marxism. Buddhism is an atheistic philosophy, and also by its concept all are equal. Logically the Dalai Lama does not want to exclude the development of a communistic Buddhism or a Buddhist communism from the outset.

Hermitages.

These thoughts occupy me more on the return journey than all the celebrations and congratulations. The Chinese authorities have no intention of returning real power to the Dalai Lama. What will happen if he returns to the fairytale Potala, to his 100,000 golden statues? Is the restoration of lamaism in Tibet conceivable? How far can one trust the Chinese who always raise their glasses to me where ever I stop: 'Gánpéi Gánpéi!' and who always seem to me unfathomable?

In Lhasa, too, the authorities have prepared a hearty reception for us. But as I turn my narration from the mountain to the country they get excited and hasten to bring the evening to a close. The subject is a sore point, as some weeks before there had been a delegation from the Dalai Lama in the country. We both know that only a calm Tibet can be a protecting buffer for the People's Republic of China against aggressors from neighbouring countries and, together with Sinkiang, above all against Soviet Russia. Why not speak openly about it, talk about it as about my solo ascent and Chomolungma? Or shall I be condemned exclusively to climber's talk here too, as in Europe? To me the many believers in the country are now just as important as the question of where Mallory died and the fact that I have got to the top before Naomi Uemura.

No people in the world have stirred me so deeply in so short a time as the Tibetans. After the countless ruined monasteries which I have seen along the way, their persevering faith touches me more than ever. Instead of going to bed after the banquet I go along the dark road into the city. An hour's walk brings me to the Barkhor. I seem to be like a pilgrim, magically attracted by power, warmth and equanimity. It is almost midnight. A densely packed stream of pilgrims jostles clockwise as always around the Jokhang Temple, which the Tibetan king Songtsen Gampo had built 1,200 years ago, in order to prepare a worthy house for the magnificent Bodhisattva which his Chinese wife had brought with her from her homeland. I am dazed. The Barkhor, this inner street of pilgrimage, is the heart of the old city, here Lhasa lives day and night. The steady singsong of the praying fills the air between the houses. Overhead the starry night sky covers the land. Two girls from Kham giggle as I want to pass. Their mouths smile between flaming red cheeks. I smile back. One sticks out her tongue. Elaborately decorated prayer-wheels turn around me.

A nomad speaks to me and wants to buy my Xi-stone which I wear as an amulet between two cherry-sized corals around my neck. I give a sign of refusal, I wouldn't sell it for all the money in the world. I got it from a very old Tibetan in the neighbourhood of Tingri, and in it heaven and earth and my life are united. The nomad laughs for he knows it. He stays beside me a bit further. I play the game, murmur the 'Om Mani Padme Hum,' merge into the stream which revolves like a human prayer drum around the Jokhang Temple. Next morning I am unwell. I have slept too little, I have drunk too much. First motai with the Chinese, then chang with the Tibetans in the old city. I stay in bed with a frightful headache.

The Rongbuk chorten.

A village on the way to Lhasa.

Through the window of my hotel bungalow I see the Potala. Supernaturally it lifts itself out of the dusty valley bottom. Like a castle in the air it stands against the brown background of the mountains over which the black cloud shadows fly. The sky is so dense that it lies on the mountain peaks, a solid mass with the clouds. The Potala seems to be weightless. What will happen here? Today the local functionaries practise self-criticism. But why was my political conversation stifled yesterday? Sometimes I have the feeling that one is playing against marked cards here. The peasants and nomads are now allowed to offer their surplus products for sale openly. Why, then, am I forbidden to purchase in the bazaar? Are the concessions by the Chinese to the Tibetans only half-hearted? Time and again I have seen anxious faces. Many small liberties are spreading hope across this endless land of snows. Anxiety remains, however. And is it only anxiety at the thought of losing these small liberties again overnight?

A Single Night

In Peking, for the first time in two and a half months, I can have a bath again with the door shut behind me. Every day a feast. I enjoy the luxury of a world which is no longer mine. In two days our Lufthansa jet flies to Frankfurt.

But before the departure over and over again people ask me the same questions. Why did I climb Everest a second time? Who is paying me for it? Who is backing me? That's what people want to know. I was also asked which flag I had taken with me, for which country I climb. I say that I do it for myself, on my own incentive, with my own means.

'I am my own homeland and my handkerchief is my flag,' I say, quoting a favourite belief. The Chinese do not understand. They think in patterns which only recognize the collective, not the individual. They shake their heads.

Already rumours are circulating in Peking's diplomatic circles that I am not the first solo climber to reach the summit of Mount Everest; in the Guinness Book of Records it says otherwise. That leaves me cold.

On 10 September I land at München–Riem airport. To the question, how did I manage to climb the highest mountain in the world alone, and compelled by my need to communicate I say spontaneously:

'I would have had no chance alone on Everest had I employed the technique which, as an expedition climber, I have used before, because I would have worn myself out. It was only possible with good acclimatization and very light-weight equipment. I had no fixed high camp. I carried a small tent with me like a snail shell, and I proceeded as slowly as a snail. I dismantled my house, carried it on my rucksack, put it up again, carried it as far as just under the summit.'

It's all part of the game but it is not amusing to be taken for some sort of yeti by the journalists waiting at the airport. While I answer the questions I have the feeling of hopeless 'don't-understands'.

'Why did you go completely alone?'

'I am always afraid of being alone.'

'Was it only crazy record seeking?'

'Records arise out of the increase in technical and physical performances in known spheres. My solo climb was a thrust into the unknown. Unknown not only on account of the weather conditions during the monsoon, unknown above all in respect of the boundless possibilities of the human body and spirit.'

'Will you give up mountaineering now?'

'No.'

'And where do you want to be in ten years' time?'

'That I don't know. I only know that I can earn my bread at an advanced age, and that is all. I would like to secure as much liberty as possible at the least possible expense, no more.'

'Will there be a television film of the solo climb?'

'I should have thought it was obvious that I didn't film myself during my solo ascent. A filmed solo ascent would be a contradiction in itself. It was hard enough to take a few photographs. That only worked because I have adapted my ice axe as a tripod. Consequently there are only a few pictures of this trip.'

'What have you brought then?'

'Not much.'

'And what sense has the undertaking?'

'That I can't explain. But I am mad enough to contend that above all else the inexplicable gives meaning to life.'

Even before my exclusive report appears in *Stern, Quick* rushes out with all the prejudices which it has against this expedition and me personally:

'What does it matter if Messner the fanatic climbs Everest or wherever, alone, in record time and without oxygen gear? Is he researching new routes which many later can follow? Does he procure scientific data about the physiology of athletes? No. This tremendously clever utiliser of the human body brings nothing back to the valley other than the enhancement of his own dubious fame, combined with some variable degree of monetary gain.

Messner is the anti-hero whose slip into a crevasse everyone awaits just as avidly as collisions in motor racing. Yet Messner is more a tragic figure than a shining hero . . . he was born too late – all the summits are conquered, almost all routes of ascent mastered. To achieve something new this climbing giant must take chancy risks and set up records which point the way to a terrible future.

The mountains as a beaten path to glory for eccentrics – that is a consequence of Messner's solo climb. Thousands upon thousands of lowlanders who believe climbing to be child's play like any other. The alpine boom, not least triggered by Messner, pants its way up mountains, badly equipped and without the iron lungs of its idol, and pays for slips with its life.

Messner too pays for his success. His wife left him. And he himself becomes – despite all his efficiency – ever more unsociable. Although as a mountaineer at the peak of his career, he is as a person on the way down – eternally on the run from civilisation and the ever-mounting expectations of his fans.'

What am I to say to that? Nothing! Did I expect to be understood? Yes and no.

After three days' work at the office of the *Stern* editor and at the BLV publishing house I drive to Villnöss for a night at home. This valley in South Tyrol is the place to which I must always return, with which I am united and in which I am rooted, because its scenery has decisively formed me. There are in it always peaceful places with views full of the most beautiful harmony. Nevertheless it becomes less so year by year; for housing estates and factories continually spring up. Perhaps one day this valley too will be built up, built to death, and I shall have to take myself off to Nepal or Tibet if I want to experience an inhabited countryside in which man sensibly integrates that which he creates.

I sleep in my house, greet my parents and the dogs, and drive next morning back to Munich. Am I actually running away from myself?

Meanwhile the *Stuttgarter Nachrichten* has also chipped in about my solo trip. On 4 September 1980 it says:

'The exceptional loses for the general

Tibetan woman.

public its sensational character if it takes place often enough. Perhaps it will also happen to Reinhold Messner this time!'

Is it time for me to give up, to follow mountaineering high point now lies behind me.

'What more do you want to do?' The question concerns me because it comes from a friend. One of my best friends gave up climbing years ago, led a

Shigatse with Tashi Lhunpo.

a middle-class profession, like an old friend at the reception in Munich has advised me? What more do I want? As far as the public is concerned, since 1978 my sensational climbs – Everest without oxygen and Nanga Parbat solo – are unsurpassable. In 1965, at the age of 35, after his grandiose winter first solo ascent of the Matterhorn North Face, Walter Bonatti was worn out by the climbing scene. My absolute

'sensible' life, pampered his wife and children, worked industriously and intensively. Last week he died of a heart attack.

Each must go the way which is right for him, and each of these ways is different. I was not born for travelling around cities with my lectures or for a contemplative life at home in South Tyrol. At least, I am not capable of it permanently.

I buy an air ticket to Kathmandu. On 17 September I want to be in Nepal in order to celebrate my 36th birthday. Nena has already flown out there from Karachi. For the post-monsoon period I have a permit for Lhotse, the fourth shining piles of clouds float like cotton swabs in the air.

Now I am off again – flux, change. I often feel a need to be inactive, and from that develops a 'lust for adventure,' the desire to venture something, to expend

Sculptures of Buddha on the way to Lhasa.

highest mountain in the world, also solo.

I leave everything behind. Out of thousands of letters I take only one with me in the aeroplane, that from Walter Bonatti. He speaks therein of 'the value of the human being as an individual'. So there are still climbers who identify with me. I am glad. I lean back in the seat and look through the window. Clouds fly past. Peaceful, myself to the limits of my abilities. A sense of happiness, when ideas and love of life correspond. A mountain, a scenery begin to live.

During the flight from Delhi to Kathmandu I see the snow-covered chain of the Himalaya through the window. Behind the haze lies Tibet, the land I have wandered through, a prisoner of my obsession like some mediaeval dragon killer. Gezar

In Tashi Lhunpo Monastery.

pleases me. Gezar, the Tibetan hero of legend who fought against giants of another sort. When well on in years he returned to Kham to die in loneliness, he left behind to the Tibetans a wish, to me an idea for redemption:

That of mountains some be not sublime and others not lowly;

That amongst people some be not as powerful and others not as powerless;
That as to possessions some have not abundance while others lack;
That the plateau have no valleys or elevations and the plain be not everywhere flat;
That all creatures be happy!

Tibetan with Xi-stone.

Sceptical Tibetan woman.

Pictures of the Dalai Lama such as this are placed on household altars.

090263 -- lone italian mountaineer ascends mount
qomolangma via north col

090263 -- lone italian mountaineer ascends mount
qomolangma via north col

beijing, september 2 (xinhua) -- italian
mountaineer reinhold messner reached the summit of
mount qomolangma in a solo climb on august 20, the
chinese mountaineering association said today after
receiving a cable from the base camp.

thirtyfive-year-old messner started for the 8,848
metres mount qomolangma via the north col in chinas
tibet on august 18 without aide and without using
oxygen. he reached the top at 15:20 hours on august 20.
he stayed on the top of the world for 40 minutes and
returned the same route. on his way up, he crossed
a hitherto unclimbed gorge 8,700 meters above sea
level.

messner previously reached the peak from the south
side in nepal in 1978. he thus became
the second man in the world to reach
the summit of qomolangma both from the south side
in nepal and the north slope in chinas tibet. japanese
mountaineer yasuo kato was the first man to achieve
this feat.

two chinese mountaineering teams had successfully
climbed mount qomolangma, one in 1960 and the other in
1975. end item

Peking press release.

The return to Munich.

Bronze figure of Gezar.

Through Tibet to Mount Everest – after the Cultural Revolution.

Mount Everest, at 8,848m the highest mountain in the world, is no longer a puzzle from the Nepal side, which has been well-explored and often climbed. The Tibetan north side of the mountain – called Chomolungma by the local people – is still full of mystery. All expeditions foundered before Tibet closed its gates. In 1980 Mount Everest was once again accessible to foreign climbers from the north also. Now I have climbed Everest from Tibet too; alone, without oxygen, during the stormy monsoon period. In 1980, after the opening up of Tibet I was one of the first to travel there and climbed Mount Everest up its historically interesting side, the North Face. Here are all the routes to the summit up to 1980:

Changtse

North Col

North Ridge

Rongbuk Gl

– – – –	Normal route (Hillary)
‖‖‖‖‖‖‖‖‖	South Buttress (Poles)
– – – –	South-West Face (Bonington)
―――	West Ridge (Americans)
··········	West Ridge Direct (Yugoslavians)
–x–x–	North-West Face (Japanese)
–·–·–	Chinese route (Mallory)
××××××	Messner variation

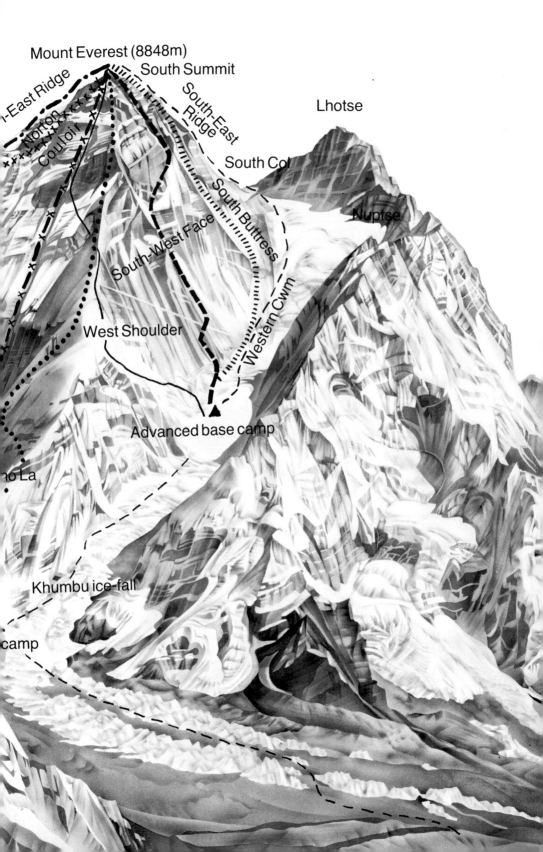

Mount Everest (8848m)

South Summit

Lhotse

-East Ridge

Norton Couloir

South-East Ridge

South Col

Nuptse

South-West Face

South Buttress

West Shoulder

Western Cwm

Advanced base camp

o La

Khumbu ice-fall

camp

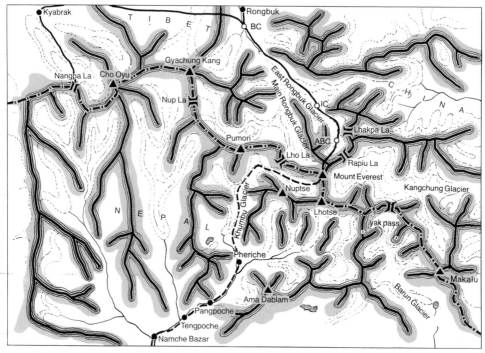

— — — — — March in to Mount Everest from the south (Nepal)
and route of ascent, 1978.

—————— March in from the north (Tibet/China) and route of ascent, 1980.

—··—··— Line of frontier between Nepal and China.

In 1978 and 1980 I got to know Mount Everest from the south and north. I climbed to all four cols (South Col, Rapiu La = east col, North Col, and Lho La = west col). Thus I was able to take a look at the most important glacier basins and faces of the mountain and to get a better grasp of its history. On my first ascent in 1978 from the south I was the first to achieve the summit without oxygen, thus on my second ascent there was the challenge to climb the highest mountain in the world alone, with, above all, Tibet and its people at the forefront of my interest as well as personally getting to know that region which the British expedition climbers had opened up in the 1920s.

At the same spot where the British pioneers set up their base camp, I camped for more than 2 months (BC). From there I put an intermediate camp at 6,000 metres (IC) and 500 metres higher my advanced base camp (ABC) as starting point for the solo climb to the summit. From base camp I made numerous acclimatization and reconaissance sorties to the north, west and south. Thereby I got to know the local peasants and many yak nomads. It became clear to me why the Chinese central government suddenly relaxed many of the decrees restricting liberties in Tibet, and I experienced a people that in spite of 20 years of oppression has remained true to its self-exiled god-king. As in a vision I saw during the ascent the roped pair of Mallory and Irvine, missing since 1924, and since my return know what it must have been like then.

In 1978, together with Peter Habeler, I climbed Mount Everest by the normal route from Nepal. A last look at the highest mountain in the world which rises like a small pyramid above the Nuptse-Lhotse wall, taken during the return from the 1979 Ama Dablam expedition.

Mount Everest from the north with long wind streamers on the historically interesting North-East Ridge. The massif, normally a rock peak, is here covered with monsoon snow.

Although I knew that Mount Everest was also accessible from the north, as a precaution I requested a permit for a solo ascent of Everest via Nepal.

After the Manirindu Festival in Thyangboche I learned in Kathmandu that the Japanese Naomi Uemura intended climbing Everest alone in 1980/81.

Against expectations, I obtained permission in 1980 to climb Mount Everest by way of Tibet. So a second dream was fulfilled. I was able to experience Tibet after the Cultural Revolution. The Potala – formerly the seat of the god-king Dalai Lama – was even being restored. The Tibetans were being allowed to pray once more.

The central Himalayan chain from the north.
Five 8,000-ers at a glance. Far left Makalu, the
two peaks centre left of the picture are Lhotse
and Mount Everest. Cho Oyu forms the western
boundary of the massif in the centre, and Shisha
Pangma is the highest elevation in the broad
mountain range on the right.

A large proportion of the valuable bronze figures in Tibet's monasteries were destroyed or
transported after the conquest by the Chinese, especially during the Cultural Revolution. A few
were concealed by the Tibetans and sunk in rivers for safe keeping.

In a few monasteries, such as the Potala palace in Lhasa and Tashi Lhunpo in Shigatse, almost all the statues and wall paintings were preserved.

Since 1980 the Tibetans have once more been free to practise their religion. Already, thousands make pilgrimage to the holy city. In the monasteries the butter lamps burn.

In the mountain villages the houses are still as they have been for hundreds of years. Children in traditional Tibetan costume play amongst sheep, goats and yaks.

The Mao badge on the cap of a Tibetan child is generally only a meaningless appendage. In their hearts almost all are inspired by the Dalai Lama.

View of modern Shekar from the mountain monastery. Corrugated iron huts and precise streets now characterize the village. The monastery and the fortress, formerly one of the most beautiful constructions in Tibet, were completely destroyed by the Chinese rulers.

Not only at the entrance to the shop do the old and new Tibet meet. Many communist cadres are still stationed in the most important centres in Tibet. They are to be withdrawn gradually. The Tibetans are to be allowed to administer their country themselves.

281

At the same spot at which the English pioneers camped in 1922 and 1924 I set up my tiny base camp in 1980 in the upper Rongbuk valley.

Mount Everest, which shuts off the valley in the background, was already deeply snowed up. It was warm, a bit green and the water froze only occasionally. The memorial cairn to those who lost their lives on the first Everest expeditions disappeared long ago.

Two hundred paces away from my base camp I found the memorials to the Japanese and Chinese climbers who were killed during the reconnaissance and ascent of Mount Everest in 1979/80.

Under an overhanging rock I discovered clay offerings, a reminder of the many hermits who had lived in the Rongbuk valley.

This simple painting by a lama, dating from the turn of the century, shows the flourishing monastery of Rongbuk in which up to 50 years ago 400 monks still lived. Far left the winter seat of the Rongbuk Rimpoche, far right Mount Everest.

Rongbuk Monastery today is a total ruin. Roofs have fallen in, all valuable statues have been looted, paintings are peeling from the walls.

The only things still standing in the Rongbuk Valley are chortens (tombs) in which dried clay figures have been preserved. Latterly these holy places too have been left to run completely wild.

After a few days at base camp Nena and I trekked for a week across the Tibetan plateau to the west in order to acclimatize. In this way we got to know the mountain people.

We were able to observe how Tibetan yak nomads hunt wild ass and blue sheep with primitive muzzle-loaders.

Although most Tibetan villages are now linked by jeep roads many local people still ride their Tibetan ponies from one village to another.

286

The long-haired yak is still the most important domestic animal in the mountains. It gives milk and wool, the flesh is dried, and the dung is still the most used fuel in Tibet, a country which has few trees.

Above all the old folk told me, so far as I could understand them, of the devastation by the Red Guards during the Cultural Revolution, of the countless Tibetans who were driven out, placed in work camps and killed.

Over *After this acclimatization trip Nena and I climbed together with three yaks and two Tibetan drivers to advanced base camp at 6,500 metres above sea-level.*

287

After an ascent to Mount
Everest's North Col I found
myself compelled by the monsoon
to return to base camp. From
there we went by jeep across
endless upland pastures to the
foot of Shisha Pangma.

We reached the highest villages,
observed the yak nomads at their
work and reconnoitred the North
Face of Shisha Pangma.

*We overnighted in the tent or between boulders.
Nena cooked. We had only essentials with us
and thus the freedom to go anywhere.*

291

On 16 August I climbed with Nena for the second time to advanced base camp under the North Col. To the left the evenly graded North Ridge, my planned route of ascent.

After ten days of fine weather – a monsoon break – the conditions on the mountain were excellent. With the increased cold there were no avalanches to fear.

Our tiny tent (below) stood at 6,000 metres, a midway point on the route to advanced base camp at 6,500 metres, which was protected from the wind between two stone walls (right).

Over

On 18 August at 5 a.m. I left advanced base camp. Two hours later I plunged eight metres into a crevasse. From camp, after sunrise, Nena photographed my solitary track to the North Col of Mount Everest with a telephoto lens.

Although I had promised myself in the crevasse to give up, nevertheless I carried on climbing, without concerning myself about the return journey. Here in centre picture is the North Col.

I was already above the North Col as the first of the morning sun touched the summits of Cho Oyu and Gyachung Kang. The beautifully shaped Pumori seemed already to lie beneath me. Although far to the west the first cloud banks were in evidence, I did not concern myself during these hours with the weather. I made fast progress.

With a rucksack weighing 15-18 kilos I dragged myself, leaning on two ski-sticks, towards the summit. I took all photographs along the way with the self-release on my camera, which I had to mount on my ice axe for this purpose. Up to 7,800 metres Nena was able to follow me from camp with the telephoto lens.

After the first bivouac at about 7,800 metres I tied my tent loosely to my rucksack so that it would be able to dry. Each additional gramme of weight costs energy in the death zone. Because a lot of snow lay on the North-East Ridge, I traversed the North Face beneath the 'first' and 'second step', diagonally right as far as the Norton Couloir. The 'first step' stands out as a knob against the sky in the middle of the picture, the 'second step' is the sharp cliff to the right of that.

My tent, which I took down each morning and put up again each evening, was self-supporting – a Gore-tex cover stretched between two crossed semi-circular aluminium poles. I had the tent specially made for this solo climb.

On the morning of 20 August after my second bivouac at about 8,200 metres the weather at last got bad. The valleys filled with mist, and navigation was very difficult. I left almost everything behind in the last bivouac.

300

From the lower base camp Mount Everest was no longer visible on this day. For Nena in advanced base camp it appeared in the morning behind a hazy veil; later in the morning it disappeared completely in the clouds.

From up above I had only momentary glimpses of the glaciers and summits beneath me. Just below the summit I saw once more, through a hole in the mist, the ridges of the North Peak and the East Rongbuk Glacier.

After the last clear view of the winding stream of the Rongbuk Glacier (below) it still took me an eternity to reach the summit of Everest, which is recognizable by the Chinese survey tripod. It rose only about knee-high out of the monsoon snow. Completely exhausted I sat on the top for three-quarters of an hour.

After I had got to know Mount Everest from the north too, its earlier history became clear to me. I was able not only to recognize the individual spots where the pioneers had been, above all I was able to relive various events. It was as if I could see the camp of yesteryear and share the anxiety of those men, like Noel:

'Presently we saw figures come out to the edge of the shelf. They were coming to make a signal to us . . . I saw them place six blankets in the form of a cross . . . This was the signal of death.'

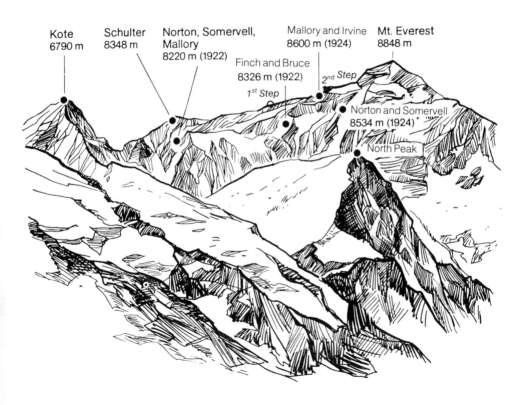

Kote
6790 m

Schulter
8348 m

Norton, Somervell,
Mallory
8220 m (1922)

Finch and Bruce
8326 m (1922)

1st Step

Mallory and Irvine
8600 m (1924)

2nd Step

Mt. Everest
8848 m

Norton and Somervell
8534 m (1924)

North Peak

Daheim, 27. Juni 1980

Lieber Reinhold!

Ich schreibe Dir heute nach Tibet, obwohl ich nicht weiß, ob Dich dieser Brief je erreichen wird.
Du lebst so in einer anderen Welt als Deine Brüder u. damit meine ich nicht nur die Berge.
Ich weiß, Du mußt es, paß auf Dich auf!
Heute vor zehn Jahren warst Du mit Günther auf dem Nanga Parbat.
Damals habe ich gehofft, daß Du jetzt bei uns bleiben wirst.
Du bist wieder aufgebrochen und ich habe Dich trotz allem nicht zurückgehalten. Ich tue es auch jetzt nicht.
Inzwischen hat sich hier in Europa so vieles verändert, der Horizont ist enger u. enger geworden.
Ich habe Deine Art zu leben mehr und mehr begreifen gelernt.
Bleib in Tibet wenn es Krieg od. Revolution bei uns gibt u. bleibe vorsichtig.
Es denkt an Dich!

Deine
Mutter

At Home, 27 June 1980

Dear Reinhold!
I am writing to you today to Tibet, although I do not know whether this letter will ever reach you!
You live in such another world from your brothers and by that I mean not only the mountains.
I know you must do it, look after yourself!
Ten years ago today you were on Nanga Parbat with Günther. At that time I hoped you would stay home with us.

You set out again and in spite of everything I did not hold you back. I do not do it now. Meanwhile so much has changed here in Europe, the horizon has become narrower and narrower.
I have learned to understand your way of living more and more. Stay in Tibet if there is war or revolution here and be careful.
Thinking of you!
Your Mother.

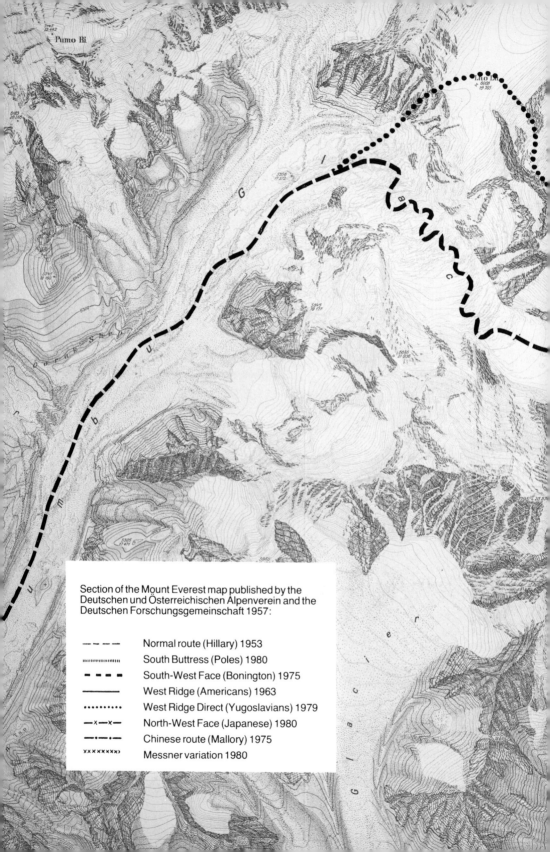

Section of the Mount Everest map published by the
Deutschen und Österreichischen Alpenverein and the
Deutschen Forschungsgemeinschaft 1957:

– – – – Normal route (Hillary) 1953

ᴍᴍᴍᴍᴍ South Buttress (Poles) 1980

▬ ▬ ▬ South-West Face (Bonington) 1975

────── West Ridge (Americans) 1963

••••••••• West Ridge Direct (Yugoslavians) 1979

–×–×– North-West Face (Japanese) 1980

–·–·–·– Chinese route (Mallory) 1975

×××××××× Messner variation 1980

Chang La

Rongbuk Glacier

Mount Everest

H O R N M O L U N G M A

Lhotse

Lhotse Shar

Mount Everest – Chronicle and Reading List

*If in the highlands there are neither
mountains nor valleys the flocks will no
longer find shelter;
If the plain is no longer flat it will be bad for
sowing;
But if people are equal, equal to their
leaders, all bad things will pass;
That happiness may spread throughout
Tibet!*

Gezar's Gattin Dugmo

Mount Everest – Chronicle and Reading List

[All updating after 1980 by the translators]

Mount Everest

Location: Nepal Himalaya (Kosi section) in the Mahalangur Himal, which forms the border between Nepal and Tibet along the northern edge of the Khumbu Himal.

Longitude: 86°55′40″ E
Latitude: 27°59′16″ N
Height: Main Summit 8,848m
South Peak 8,765m
North-East Shoulder 8,393m

Early designation number: XV
Nepalese name: Sagarmatha
Tibetan name: Chomolungma (or Qomolungma); approximate meaning 'Goddess Mother of the Snow'. According to official documents of this time and reputedly much earlier, the district around Cho-mo-lung-ma was called Lho-Chamo-long, 'Bird Land to the South'; it very probably lies, therefore, in the Everest–Makalu Group. Chomolungma is today understood as encompassing the whole Everest massif or the Everest–Makalu Group in the Khumbu Himal. C.K. Howard-Bury, leader of the first Mount Everest expedition, heard the name Chomo Uri, 'Goddess of the Turquoise Peaks', for Mount Everest.
Maps: Sketch maps can be found in the Everest books of 1921, 1922, 1924 as well as Ruttledge 1933. The following modern maps are readily obtainable and are recommended: 1:506,880 Sheet Nepal East, 3. Edition – GSGS, 1969. DMS (MoD), London. 1:126,720 Trekking Map: Lamasangu to Mount Everest 1975. Mandala Maps, Kathmandu. 1:100,000 Mount Everest Region. 2nd edition 1975 RGS, London.
1:500,000 Khumbu Himal. The so-called 'Schneider Map'. 1965. FNH, Munich.
1:25,000 Chomolungma–Mount Everest–Mahalangur. 1957 AV(DAV-ÖAV), Munich & Innsbruck.
1:50,000 Mount Everest. National Geographic Magazine, November 1988.

Mount Everest, the highest mountain in the world, has attracted more attention from geographers, mountaineers and journalists than any other mountain in the Himalaya. It was seen for the first time by a non-native in 1849; the first attempt to climb it followed seventy-two years later; a further thirty-two years later the summit was reached. All expeditions prior to 1949 went through Tibet as Nepal was inaccessible to foreigners. Expeditions from the Nepalese side took place between the years 1950 and 1979; since 1979 Tibet has again been accessible to non-Chinese. The successful British expedition of 1953 was the ninth attempt on the mountain – leaving aside three solo attempts and an officially unrecognized Russian venture. Up to the present day more than 200 people, including six women, have reached the summit, several of them now without the aid of bottled oxygen.

Whether Irvine and Mallory could

already have been to the top in 1924 is a point of controversy. There remains, however, a strong possibility that M. Burke, the cameraman with the British South-West Face Expedition 1975, did reach the summit. At least fifteen climbers have been to the top more than once, the Sherpa Sundare a record five times. The peak has been climbed by eleven major routes and was first traversed in 1963. In 1988 Marc Batard (French) climbed the South Col route in less than twenty-four hours, but the route had been previously prepared. The fastest ascent for an unprepared line was that made by E. Loretan and J. Troillet in 1986 when they took forty hours to climb the Hornbein Couloir on the North Face. The height difference to be overcome from the Western Cwm up the South-West Face amounts to about 2,225 metres; from the Upper East Rongbuk Glacier, 2,350 metres; from the Lho La up the West Ridge, about 2,850 metres; from below the ice-fall via the South Col, about 3,500 metres.

Attempts and Ascents up to 1988

The Briton Julius Behrens (1827–1888) planned, according to family legend, an Everest expedition. Probably inspired by an ascent of Mont Blanc, it remained at the idea stage.

1892 With the title 'Can Mount Everest be Climbed?' an article by Clinton Dent appeared in the October 1892 edition of *Nineteenth Century* in which he said that it should be possible to climb Everest.

1893 Lieutenant C.G. Bruce and Captain F.E. Younghusband discussed the idea of climbing Mount Everest while in Chitral.

1899 Lord Curzon, Viceroy of India, wrote to D.W Freshfield that he would try to obtain a permit in Nepal for an attempt on Everest.

1904 Captain C.G. Rawling, who accompanied Younghusband to Lhasa (1904), subsequently led a group from there to Gartok and on to Simla. During this journey they observed Everest from the north.

1905 The Alpine Club considered a systematic attempt on Kangchenjunga, or Mount Everest. Major Bruce and his Gurkhas were to have been chosen for that.

1907 The Secretary for India vetoed the idea of an Everest ascent.

1907 *The Times* discussed the plan and veto of the expedition, conceived by Lord Curzon and probably to have been led by Major C.G. Bruce, and including Dr. T.G. Longstaff, A.L. Mumm, three Alpine guides and half a dozen Gurkhas.

1908 Bruce worked out a new plan. By way of Nepal they would approach the mountain via the valley of the Dudh Kosi.

1909 A Sherpa told General Bruce the name for Mount Everest was Chomo Lungmo.

1911 Curzon asked the Maharajah of Nepal about permission to climb Everest.

1913 Dressed as a Mohammedan, with native companions from Darjeeling, Captain J.B.Noel penetrated into north-west Sikkim as far as the Langu Pass in Tibet. Only 65 kilometres from the mountain they were held up by Tibetan soldiers and forced to return.

1918 The Royal Geographical Society opened new negotiations for an Everest permit.

1920 Lieutenant-Colonel C.K. Howard-Bury negotiated for a permit in India with Sir Charles Bell, Political Officer in Sikkim and representative of Great Britain in Lhasa, and with the Viceroy.

1921 First reconnaissance expedition with nine members and Lieutenant-Colonel C.K. Howard-Bury as leader. Dr. A.M. Kellas died during the approach march. Possible routes from the east and north were investigated. G.L. Mallory and G.H. Bullock reconnoitred the Rongbuk and West Rongbuk glaciers from which they wanted to try to reach the Western Cwm, which they had seen from a col north-east of Pumori. They judged the ice-fall to be steep. The chances of reaching the col between Everest and the south peak (Lhotse) from the west were practically nil. On 24 September Bullock, Mallory and Major E.O. Wheeler gained the Chang La (North Col, 6,990m) from the Kharta and East Rongbuk glaciers after Mallory had failed to find a way from Rongbuk.

1922 Second expedition with thirteen members and five Gurkhas under the leadership of Brigadier General C.G. Bruce. This time the North Col was reached from the East Rongbuk glacier. Mallory, Major E.F. Norton and Dr. H. Somervell reached a height of 8,225 metres without oxygen apparatus. Captain G. Bruce, the leader's nephew, and Captain G.I. Finch, using oxygen, reached a height of 8,320 metres. During the third attempt the whole party was swept away by an avalanche just under the North Col. Seven porters died as a result.

1924 Third expedition with ten members and four Gurkhas and again under the leadership of General Bruce. During the approach march he became ill with malaria, fell out, and Norton took over the leadership. Norton and Somervell got as high as 8,540 metres; without oxygen apparatus Norton went on alone to a height of 8,750 metres (the height record without oxygen until 1978). A.C. Irvine and G.L. Mallory were observed briefly by N.E. Odell making for the summit but did not return.

1933 A further expedition with fourteen members, two Signals Officers and five Gurkhas under the leadership of H. Ruttledge ascended by way of the North Col; P. Wyn Harris, J. Longland, L.R. Wager and eight porters went as far as 8,350 metres. On the first summit attempt Harris and Wager found, some twenty metres below the ridge and about 230 metres east of the 'first step', an ice axe which could only have belonged to Irvine or Mallory. Like the previous party F.S. Smythe reached 8,570 metres after E.E. Shipton had turned back. In the same year the Houston Mount Everest Expedition succeeded in the first flight over Everest, using two Westland biplanes. The rewards were a valuable series of survey films, and many photographs of the mountain massif.

1934 Solo attempt on the North Col route by M. Wilson, who had crossed Tibet disguised as a deaf and dumb Tibetan monk. He died of exhaustion in his tent under the North Col.

1935 A small reconnaissance group with eight members, plus Tenzing Norgay, carried loads to the North Col under the leadership of E.E. Shipton. The Western Cwm was studied by

Shipton and the southern route judged possible. H.W. Tilman and E.H.L. Wigram judged the West Ridge from the Lho La to be impassable in its lower section. Wilson's corpse was found on the East Rongbuk Glacier.

1936 The second Ruttledge expedition foundered in early monsoon snows.

1938 The small expedition led by H.W. Tilman got to a little over 8,000 metres.

1945 Shipton planned an expedition. Tibet did not permit a party in either 1946 or 1947.

1947 The Canadian E. Denman made a solo attempt. With Tenzing and Ang Dawa he travelled secretly through Tibet to Rongbuk. At the third try they climbed to the North Col, but were obliged to turn back shortly afterwards.

1950 A small group of five members, organised by American Charles Houston, walked from Kathmandu into the Solo-Khumbu region. Houston and Tilman went up the Khumbu glacier and studied the great ice-fall. Tilman was of the opinion that October could be a favourable month for future attempts.

1951 A third solo attempt, again without permission, was risked by the Dane K.B. Larsen. From Darjeeling he travelled through the Dudh Kosi valley to Namche Bazar. From Namche Bazar he crossed the Nangpa La west of Cho Oyu into Tibet and reached Rongbuk via Kyetrak. On the North Col his Sherpas refused to set up a camp. They immediately descended.

1951 On a British reconnaissance expedition, inspired by M.P. Ward and led by E.E. Shipton, the New Zealand-ers E.P. Hillary and H.E. Riddiford pushed further into Nepal. The biggest part of the ice-fall was traversed and a possible route to the South Col noted.

1952 The first Swiss expedition to Mount Everest, led by Dr. E. Wyss-Dunant. They reached the South Col (7,986m). R. Lambert and Tenzing reached a height of 8,600 metres before turning back.

1952 A second Swiss expedition reached a height of 8,100 metres in the post-monsoon period.

1952 Of a large Russian expedition, which attempted Mount Everest at the same time from the north, there was no official report. The summit team started from about 8,200 metres and went missing. As J. Tamm, the leader of the planned Russian Everest expedition of 1982, has intimated, this wrecked attempt is 'unknown' in Russian mountaineering circles, and the Russian Mountaineering Federation has publicly denied that a Russian attempt on Everest ever took place.

1953 First Ascent: British expedition with fourteen members, among them a physiologist, a cameraman, Sirdar Tenzing Norgay, and as leader Col. John Hunt. It was Tenzing's seventh expedition to Mount Everest. The South Col was reached via the Lhotse Glacier and Lhotse face. R.C. Evans and T.D. Bourdillon reached the South Peak (8,765m). The second summit team, E.P. Hillary and Tenzing, reached the summit on 29 May.

1956 The third Swiss expedition under the leadership of A. Eggler followed the route through the Western Cwm to the South Col. Two groups, J. Marmet and E. Schmied, H. von Gunten and A. Reist, reached the summit.

1958 A Chinese reconnaissance expedition with three Russians climbed from Rongbuk to the North Col.

1959 Chinese expedition travelled as far as Lhasa. On account of the uprising they diverted to the Mustagata in Sinkiang (Kun Lun).

1960 First successful expedition via the North Col. The expedition consisted of 214 men and women, Chinese and Tibetans. Three members took more than a day to climb the last 350 metres (i.e. the 'Second Step'). They reached the summit in darkness. They produced no proof of the ascent. On the summit were: Wang Fou-Chou, Chan Ying Hua, Liu-Lien-man.

1960 An Indian expedition was forced to turn back just below the South Peak by violent storms and driving snow.

1962 After deceiving the Nepalese authorities, three Americans and a Swiss went via the Nup La to the West Rongbuk Glacier – without permission – and climbed via the East Rongbuk Glacier to the North Col. They got to 7,600 metres.

1962 The second Indian expedition reached a height of 8,450 metres.

1963 A mammoth American expedition with N.G. Dyrenfurth as leader divided itself for an attack from two directions. The first South Col party reached the summit on 1 May. The West Ridge team reached the shoulder, where two tents with their six occupants were blown thirty metres down the mountain in a storm. In a detour across the North Face W.F. Unsoeld and T.F. Hornbein climbed the West Ridge to the summit a few hours after the second South Col group and descended to the South Col. This was the first and until 1988 the only traverse of Mount Everest.

1965 The third Indian expedition led by Lieut-Com. M.S. Kohli got nine men to the top.

1965 The Nepalese government prohibited any mountaineering activity in their country. The ban remained in force until 1969.

1965 Chinese reconnaissance of the north side (up to 7,500m) and on the East Ridge. They became stuck in the snow.

1966 Second Chinese Everest expedition via the North Col. This expedition, in the spirit of the 'Chinese Cultural Revolution', ought to have ended in catastrophe (Maoist visionaries without sufficient equipment).

1967 Chinese scientific expedition in the northern Everest region. Scientific survey station on the North Col (*c.* 7,000m) and in the foothills.

1968 The third Chinese Everest expedition via the North Col route did not succeed.

1969 Japanese reconnaissance expedition to the South-West Face.

1970 A Japanese expedition camped on the mountain and divided into two groups – eight for the South-West Face, sixteen for the South-East Ridge. Only two teams, from the South Col group, reached the summit.

1970 The Japanese ski expedition with thirty-four members and 800 porters managed a ski descent by Miura from the South Col – a loss of height of about 2,000 metres to the Western Cwm in less than two minutes – but six Sherpas were killed in a glacier avalanche.

1971 An international expedition with thirty members from thirteen countries, lead by N.G. Dyrenfurth, wanted to work in two groups: one on the South-West Face and one on the West Ridge. The death of Major H.V. Bahaguna, plus illness and disease, and arguments caused by a lot of publicity, left the expedition divided against each other.

1971 An Argentinian expedition in the post-monsoon period had to turn back on the South Col route.

1972 Two further attempts on the South-West Face by European and British teams failed.

1973 Guido Monzino's large Italian expedition with 100 Sherpas and 2,000 local porters as well as three helicopters got two teams to the top via the normal route.

1973 A Japanese expedition, divided into two groups, got to about 8,400 metres on the South-West Face. One party succeeded in reaching the summit from the South Col without an intermediate camp.

1974 A Spanish expedition gave up in the pre-monsoon period.

1974 During the attempt by a French expedition on the West Ridge Camps I and II were completely destroyed by an avalanche, and the leader and five Sherpas killed.

1974 An expedition from China climbed from Rongbuk to the North Col for training.

1975 The Japanese women's expedition put the first woman, Junko Tabei (with Sherpa Ang Tsering) on the summit via the normal route.

1975 A large Chinese expedition (400 members), led by Shih Chan-chun, climbed the peak from the north for the second time. Nine members (eight Tibetans and a Chinese), among them the Tibetan woman Phantog, reached the summit.

1975 The second British South-West Face expedition, led by C.J.S. Bonington, had enormous success. Haston and Scott were the first pair to reach the summit – P.D.Boardman and Sirdar Pertemba the second. During their descent and only a few hundred metres from the top, they unexpectedly met M. Burke who wanted to go to the summit and then catch up with them on descent. Burke was never seen again.

1976 On the British–Nepalese expedition two climbers got to the top on the South Col route.

1976 An American expedition started up the mountain on the South Col route and were successful.

1977 A New Zealand expedition, who planned to climb the mountain via the South Col without Sherpas, reached the South Col but not the summit.

1977 A South Korean expedition made a very fast ascent of the South Col route in the autumn.

1978 A major Iranian–Chinese expedition got to 7,500 metres on the North Ridge.

1978 First ascent of Mount Everest totally without the use of artificial oxygen by R. Messner and P. Habeler. They were attached to the first Austrian Everest expedition led by W. Nairz. These two and five other members reached the summit.

1978 A German (leader K.M. Herrligkoffer) and a French (leader P. Mazeaud) expedition co-operated well to get seven Germans, three Frenchmen, a Polish woman, a Swiss and an Austrian as well as three Sherpas up the normal route (South Col) to the top in the autumn. Second ascent of Everest without oxygen on 10 October by H. Engl. Third ascent without oxygen by the Sherpas Ang Dorje and Mingma on 17 October. Third ascent of the mountain by a woman by the Pole, W. Rutkiewicz. H. Engl, as well as Sherpas Ang Dorje and Mingma, ascended together with climbers who used oxygen apparatus and broke trail.

1979 A very strong, dynamic Yugoslavian expedition succeeded in making the complete passage of the entire West Ridge.

1979 During a Japanese reconnaissance expedition on the north side of the peak three Chinese died in an avalanche under the North Col.

1979 A German team, favoured by good conditions, put several groups on the summit. On the descent from the summit two members died of exhaustion.

1980 A Polish group risked, for the first time, an attempt at a winter ascent. In February, in severe storm and cold, one rope made it to the top. A marvellous achievement, even if in Nepal it is not officially recognised as a winter ascent unless carried out in December or January.

1980 A strong expedition from Japan split into two groups in Rongbuk. One made the first complete ascent of the North Face, a second repeated the classic route up the North and North-East Ridge. Yasuo Kato became the first non-Sherpa to climb Mount Everest twice.

1980 The Basque expedition which made the ascent in May was the first Spanish expedition to succeed on the highest mountain in the world.

1980 A Polish expedition made the first ascent of the South Buttress, a route between the South-West Face and the South-East Ridge.

1980 In August, from an advanced base camp on the East Rongbuk Glacier, R. Messner climbed alone to the summit via the North Col and in part a new route on the North Face.

1980 An enormous trekking-type Italian-Nepalese expedition only got as far as the South Peak despite great use of material and Sherpas.

1981 A British winter expedition did not get far via the Lho La.

1981 N. Uemura failed in a solo winter attempt (Sherpa support as far as the South Col) on the normal route.

1981 A French military expedition failed below the 'second step' on the classic northern route from Tibet.

1981 Japanese mountaineers had to give up just short of the summit after they had climbed the West Ridge.

1981 In the autumn an American medical research expedition went up the Western Cwm and the South-East Buttress, keeping on the right-hand side of the Buttress and left of the Geneva Spur until just below the South Col, where they erected their highest camp at 8,075 metres. From there they climbed along the South-East Ridge to the summit. On 21 October C. Kopczynski and Sundare Sherpa reached the highest point, on 24 October. C. Pizzo and Tenzing Jr. reached the peak, as well as P. Hackett solo, after the Sherpa accompanying him had turned back.

1981 In the autumn a two-man New Zealand expedition climbed alpine-style up the Khumbu glacier and Western Cwm to the West Shoulder and up the Hornbein Couloir. The team had to give up at a height of 7,700 metres due to storms and exhaustion.

1981 Also in the autumn, an American group reached a height of about 6,600 metres on the East Face, before they abandoned the route on account of avalanches and snow-slab danger.

Afterthought by the Author, 1982

In February 1982 Captain Noel, Professor Odell and Reinhold Messner met in London. For hours they discussed the disappearance of Mallory and Irvine in 1924 on the north side of Everest. This conversation, and above all the arrival of sensational news from China, gave rise to new material for 'the mystery of Mallory and Irvine'.

On 8 June 1924 Mallory and Irvine were seen for the last time on the North-East Ridge of Mount Everest. Odell, a highly experienced mountaineer, who accompanied the expedition as geologist, saw Mallory and Irvine for the last time through a hole in the mist. They were engaged in climbing one of the steps on the North-East Ridge at more than 8,400 metres. Ever since Mallory and Irvine went missing, people have puzzled over the questions, did the pair reach the summit and where did they die?

Odell (who was to die in 1987) recalled all the details, and surmised like many historians that Mallory and Irvine perished while descending from the summit. Other historians, and Reinhold Messner, are of the opinion that Mallory and Irvine would not have been able to climb the 'second step', the second rock step on the summit ridge. Odell agreed with Messner that he probably sighted the two climbers on the 'first step' and not on the 'second step'; but considered that Mallory and Irvine would have been able to turn the second step on the snow-covered East Face. Reinhold Messner tries in this book to prove that despite this possibility, on the grounds of time and difficulties, a summit success without a bivouac would have been unthinkable. And a bivouac during the ascent would have weakened the climbers too much. In 1933 members of a new British Everest expedition found one of the two ice axes taken by Mallory and Irvine. It lay to the right below the 'first step'. In 1982 it became known that Chinese mountaineers in 1960, on the occasion of the first and long-disputed Chinese ascent of Everest from the north by Mallory and Irvine's route, found a stick, a piece of rope and two oxygen flasks. These are said to have lain above the 'second step'. As between 1924 and 1960 nobody but Mallory and Irvine can have climbed the 'second step' it was proved by this find that Mallory and Irvine, or perhaps only one of them had overcome or by-passed this difficult step. Thereby they had had the key to the ascent. Reinhold Messner, who in this Everest book still holds that, even after all the documentary evidence available to date, Mallory and Irvine were not the true first ascensionists of Everest, is ready to revise his statement if traces of Mallory and Irvine really have been sighted above the 'second step'. After his remark about the relatively easy terrain above the 'second step', Mallory, that fiery spirit, would not have returned from the final slopes of Mount Everest without having first been to the top. By the Chinese discovery, therefore, the mystery of Mallory and Irvine could largely be solved. So far we lack photographs of the finds themselves. The saga of Everest has, however, been furnished with new material thereby. Why the Chinese only 'went public' twenty years after this historically important find is something of a riddle.

1982 A British lightweight expedition to the unclimbed North-East Ridge came to a tragic conclusion in May with the loss of P. Boardman and J. Tasker somewhere above 8,200m.

Reinhold Messner, John Noel and Noël Odell in London, 1982.

1982 A strong Russian expedition climbed a new route on the South-West Face (eleven men reached the summit).

1982 The Japanese mountaineer Yasuo Kato was lost after reaching the summit of Everest on December 27 (his third ascent); another member supporting him also failed to return.

1983 American mountaineers made the first ascent of the impressive East (Kangshung) Face when on 8/9 October six men reached the summit. Two Japanese teams reached the summit at almost the same time as the first successful group, climbing via the South Buttress and South-East Ridge respectively.

1984 Phil Ershler (USA) reached the summit alone on 20 October, having climbed the North Col and North Face by way of the Great (Norton) Couloir. (An earlier American attempt in 1982 was halted by the death of Marty Hoey.)

1984 Two Australians, T. McCartney-Snape and G. Mortimer, forged a new direct route up the North Face in October, finishing in the Great Couloir. It was a lightweight ascent, using no artificial oxygen.

1985 A Norwegian expedition put a record seventeen people on the summit during a pre-monsoon climb of the South Col route. Summiters included C. Bonington and the American millionaire D. Bass who, at fifty-five, became the oldest man to have climbed Everest.

1985 A Spanish (Catalan) expedition undertaken during the monsoon period put six men on the summit following the classic (Mallory) North Col/North-East Ridge line. They climbed without artificial oxygen.

1986 Sharon Wood (Canada) became the sixth woman to climb Everest when she reached the summit with D. Congden via the West Ridge (from the North) during May.

1986 E. Loretan of Switzerland and J.Troillet of France made a swift ascent in August (monsoon period) of the Hornbein Couloir on the North Face without artificial oxygen.

1988 S. Venables (G.B.) with a small pre-monsoon Anglo-American expedition reached the summit via a new route up the East Face to join the South-East Ridge at the South Col. No artificial oxygen was used.

1988 A large pre-monsoon 'Friendship' expedition, comprising Japanese, Chinese and Nepalese climbers assaulted the mountain simultaneously from North and South, stage-managing twelve people to the top at almost the same time. Two more members reached the summit later, including Sherpa Sundare; this was his fifth ascent of the mountain.

1988 A British expedition successfully climbed the dangerous 'Pinnacles' section of the North-East Ridge to the North-East Shoulder during the post-monsoon period. They were unable to continue to the summit and descended by the North Col route.

1988 A large media-backed French expedition to the South Col/South-East Ridge put several people on top, including Marc Batard, who climbed the (prepared) route in an astonishing twenty-two hours.

1988 Stacy Allison became the first American woman to the summit of Everest, climbing with the Seattle-based expedition, led by Jim Frush. Later, Peggy Luce also made the climb.

Reading List

A

AHLUWALIA, Higher than Everest (1973)

B

BARNES, After Everest ('autobiography' of Tenzing) (1977)

BLAKENEY, 'A.R.Hinks and the First Everest Expedition 1921'. G.J. 136, p. 333 ff.

BONINGTON, Everest – South-West Face (1973)

BONINGTON, Everest – The Hard Way (1976)

BONINGTON/CLARKE, Everest, the Unclimbed Ridge (1983)

BOUSTEAD, The Wind of Morning (1971, relating expedition of 1933)

BRIGONE, 'Il Expedición en los Himalayas–Everest 1971' La Montaña 15 (1971), p. 32–36

BRUCE, The Assault on Everest 1922 (1923)

BULLETIN DER IND. BOTSCHAFT, Vol. 15, No.7 Everest Expeditionen, p.5ff.

C

CARR, The Irvine Diaries (1979, relating to 1924)

CHARTWELL PRESS, Everest – a Guide to the Climb (folding map, 1953)

[CHINA], Photographic Record of the Mount Jolmo Lungma Scientific Expedition 1966-68 (1977)

[CHINA], Another Ascent of the World's Highest Peak – Qomolangma (1975)

CHOMOLONGMA, 'Everest-Karte des ÖAV', Jahrbuch (1957), p.12

CLARK, Six Great Mountaineers (includes Hunt, Mallory) (1956)

CORBETT, Great True Mountain Stories (1957)

D

DENMAN, Alone to Everest (1954)

DIAS, Everest Adventure. Story of the second Indian Expedition 1962 (1965)

DITTERT et al, Forerunners to Everest (1954, relating to 1952)

DONOUGHUE, Everest (Jackdaw folder, 1975)

DYRENFURTH, To the Third Pole (1955)

E

EGGLER, Everest-Lhotse Adventure (1957)

ENZINCK, Der große Berg. G.L. Mallory und der Mount Everest (1966)

EVANS, Eye on Everest (1955, relating to 1953)

EVEREST- Ein Bildband

F

FELLOWES et al, First over Everest (1933)

FINCH, Climbing Mount Everest (1930)

FLAIG/ZORELL, Im Kampf um Tschomo-lungma, den Gipfel der Erde (1923)

G

GOSWAMI, Everest – is it Conquered? (1954)

GREGORY, Picture of Everest (1954, relating to 1953)

GRUDA, Mount Everest: auf Tod und Leben

H

HABELER, Everest Impossible Victory (1979)

HAFNER, Everest – ein Schauspiel in fünf Akten

HASTON, In High Places (1972)

HAYES, Trekking to Mount Everest and Solu-Khumbu (guidebook) (1975)

HEDIN, Mount Everest (1922)

HERRLIGKOFFER, Mount Everest, 'Thron der Götter' (1973)

HERRLIGKOFFER, 'Mount Everest 1972'. HJ.33, p.14-17

HERRLIGKOFFER, Mount Everest. Ohne Sauerstoff (1979)

ROBERTSON, George Mallory (1969)
ROCH, Everest 1952 (1953)
RUTTLEDGE, Everest 1933 (1934)
RUTTLEDGE, Everest the Unfinished Avenue (1937, relating to 1936)
RUDOLPH, Chomolungma und ihre Kinder (1978)

S
SAYRE, Four Against Everest (1964)
SCOTT, God is my Co-Pilot (1943)
SEAVER, Francis Younghusband. p.303 ff. (1952)
SHIPTON, 'Mount Everest Reconnaissance 1935', AJ.48, p.1-14
SHIPTON, Mount Everest Reconnaissance Expedition 1951 (1952)
SHIPTON, Upon That Mountain (1943, relating to 1933, 1935, 1936, 1938)
SHIPTON, True Book about Everest, Men Against Everest (1955)
SHIPTON, Mountain Conquest (1967)
SHIPTON, That Untravelled World (1969)
SINGH, Lure of Everest – the story of the First Indian Expedition (1961, relating to 1959/60)
SMITH, True Stories of Modern Explorers (one chapter) (1930)
SMYTHE, Adventures of a Mountaineer (1940, one chapter relating to 1933)
SMYTHE, Camp Six (1937, relating to 1933)
SOMERVELL, After Everest (1936, relating to 1922, 1924)
STEELE, Doctor on Everest (1972, relating to 1971)
STOKES, Soldiers and Sherpas (1988)
STYLES, Mallory of Everest (1967)

STYLES, First on the Summits (1970)
STYLES, On Top of the World (1967)
SWISS FOUNDATION FOR ALPINE RESEARCH, Everest-the Swiss Expeditions 1952 (1954)

T
THÜR/HANKE, Sieg über den Everest (1953)
TILMAN, Everest 1938 (1948)

U
ULLMAN, Americans on Everest (1964, relating to 1963)
ULLMAN, Kingdom of Adventure Everest (1947)
ULLMAN, Tiger of the Snows/Man of Everest (1955, relating to 1935, 1936, 1938, 1947, 1952, 1953)
UNSWORTH, Because it is There (includes Bruce, Mallory, Smythe) (1968)
UNSWORTH, Everest (1981)

W
WIBBERLEY, Epics of Everest (1954, history to 1953)
WILSON & PEARSON, 'Everest – Post Mortem of an International Expedition', Mountain 17

Y
YOUNGHUSBAND, Epic of Mount Everest (1926, relating to 1921, 1922, 1924)
YOUNGHUSBAND, Everest the Challenge (1936. 1st ed. to 1935; 2nd ed. to 1936)

Picture Credits

Title Page: Mount Everest from northern base camp (Rongbuk) (Messner archives)

Front endpaper: The ruined Rongbuk Monastery and Mount Everest in 1980 (Messner archives)

Back endpaper: Rongbuk Monastery and Mount Everest – hand-coloured black-white slide from 1922 (Capt. John Noel)

Page 1: Reinhold Messner on Rongbuk Glacier (Nena Holguin)

Page 2/3: Mount Everest from the north (Messner archives)

Page 18/19: Mount Everest from the south above the Nuptse–Lhotse wall (Messner archives)

Page 54/55: Mount Everest from the east with the Kangchung flank (Doug Scott)

Page 98/99: Nomads with yak caravans on the Tibetan plateau (Messner archives)

Page 142/143: The ice face leading to the North Col (Nena Holguin)

Page 170/171: Shisha Pangma from the Tibetan plateau (Nena Holguin)

Page 188/189: View from 8,000 metres to the north (Messner archives)

Page 306/307: Section from the Mount Everest map published by the Deutschen und Österreichischen Alpenverein and the Deutschen Forschungsgemeinschaft, 1957 (by kind permission of the ÖAV)

BLV Archives: Page 58, 59, 61, 62
CMA/Beijing: Page 107, 108, 109
Uschi Demeter: Page 17, 178, 265
Andrew C. Harvard: Page 153 (bottom), 154
Nena Holguin: Page 294/295, 296/297 (top), 301 (top)
Capt. John Noel: Page 9, 10, 11, 12/13, 14, 15, 16, 43, 44 (bottom), 303
Royal Geographical Society: page 7, 31, 48 (bottom), 49, 75, 87, 88, 126(bottom), 155

Pictures also used by kind permission of the Publishers: C.K.Howard-Bury, *Mount Everest – die Erkundung 1921*, Verlag Benno Schwabe & Co., Basel 1922 (Page 6/7, 24, 28). C.G.Bruce, *Mount Everest – der Angriff 1922*, Verlag Benno Schwabe & Co., Basel 1924 (Page 33, 34, 35 (bottom), 36, 37, 38, 74, 76, 83, 96.) E.F. Norton, *Bis zur Spitze des Mount Everest – die Besteigung 1924*, Verlag Benno Schwabe & Co., Basel 1926 (Page 32 (bottom), 39, 40 (top), 41, 44 (top), 45, 46.) R.Faux, '*Everest – Goddess of the Wind*,' W. & R. Chambers Ltd, Edinburgh 1978 (Page 42, 48(top)). Dennis Roberts, *I'll climb Mount Everest Alone – the Story of Maurice Wilson*, Robert Hale Ltd, London 1975 (page 70,

73, 80). F.S.Smythe, *Camp Six – An Account of the 1933 Mount Everest Expedition*, Hodder & Stoughton, London 1941 (Black Jacket ed) (Page 47)

All remaining pictures were provided by the author from his own archives.

N.B.: The pictures on Pages 9 to 16 are hand-coloured black/white slides from 1922/1924

Reference Sources

L. BAUME, *Sivalaya – Explorations of the 8000-metre Peaks of the Himalaya* Gastons-West Col., Reading; Mountaineers, Seattle 1978

I. CAMERON, *To the Farthest Ends of the Earth* Macdonald, London 1980

H. CARR, *The Irvine Diaries* Gastons-West Col, Reading 1979

E. DENMAN, *Alone to Everest* Collins, London 1954

R. FAUX, *Everest-Goddess of the Wind* W.&.R. Chambers, Edinburgh 1978

K.GRUDA, *Mount Everest: Auf Tod und Leben* W. Fischer Verlag, Göttingen 1980

E. HILLARY/D. DOIG, *High in the Thin Cold Air* Hodder Stoughton, London 1963

H.S. LANDOR, *In the Forbidden Land* Heinemann, London 1898

W.H. MURRAY, *The story of Everest* J.M. Dent & Sons Ltd, London 1953

H. RUTTLEDGE, *Everest 1933* Hodder & Stoughton, London 1934

F.S. SMYTHE, *Camp Six – An Account of the 1933 Mount Everest Expedition* Hoddder & Stoughton, London 1937

The quotations printed in the first main chapter were taken for the most part from the following books, by kind permission of Verlag Benno Schwabe, Basel: C.K. Howard-Bury, *Mount Everest – die Erkundung 1921;* C.G. Bruce, *Mount Everest – der Angriff 1922;* E.F. Norton, *Bis zur Spitze des Mount Everest-die Besteigung 1924*

The section 'Maurice Wilson' (pages 69–79) is a resumé of the book by Dennis Roberts, *I'll Climb Mount Everest Alone – The Story of Maurice Wilson* Robert Hale Ltd, London 1957.